TURNING STONES

Marc Parent

with a Foreword by **Anna Quindlen**

TURNING STONES

My Days and Nights with Children at Risk

Harcourt Brace & Company

New York   San Diego   London

Library of Congress Cataloging-in-Publication Data
Parent, Marc.
    Turning stones: my days and nights with children at risk/
Marc Parent.
      p. cm.
    ISBN 0-15-100204-5
    1. Parent, Marc. 2. Child welfare workers—New York
(State)—New York—Biography. 3. Abused children—
New York (State)—New York—Case studies. 4. Child
welfare—New York (State)—New York—Case studies.
5. New York (N.Y.) Bureau of Child Welfare. Emergency
Children's Services. I. Title.
HV743.N49B876 1996
362.7'68'092—dc20 [B] 96-15074

Designed by Lydia D'moch
Printed in the United States of America
First U.S. edition
  B C D E

10/06

CONTENTS

This book is an account of the author's experience of circumstances involving at-risk children during the four-year period of his service in the New York City's Emergency Children's Services. The names, locations, and characteristics of persons and events described in the book have been altered and are not intended to identify actual places or individuals. Some aspects of the narrative have been dramatized in order to effectively recreate the actuality of the author's experience of certain events.

Foreword

DURING NEARLY A QUARTER CENTURY as a reporter I wrestled with twin demons. Sometimes the demons won, and when they did, one diminished me as a professional, the other as a human being.

The first was the struggle, often unsuccessful, always difficult, to make the people in my stories human, not stock characters or stick figures. I wanted them three-dimensional, living, warm, so that the readers understood their problems and their pain. The second was the sense of disgust I felt after I had done my stories and then walked away, notebook in hand, to someone else, someplace else. The feeling was most vivid when the story mattered most, when I left the apartment of a battered woman with the strong suspicion that she would have fresh bruises before the ink was dry on my copy, or said good-bye to a couple with a missing child, going on with my life while they were frozen in a glacial grief of their own.

I never had these feelings more strongly than when I was writing about the children caught in the bottlenecks of New York City's child welfare system. They had to live on the page because to so many they were merely ciphers, or statistics, or even children beyond ordinary caring, tainted somehow by their own abandonment or abuse. And it haunted me when I left one of them at what I had been told was the fifth foster home, wondering about the sixth or the seventh, wondering if a decade hence I would recognize the little boy with the liquid eyes in the photograph of an adolescent criminal on page five of the tabloids.

In my own small way, I abandoned these children. In the stories and columns I wrote, I tried not to fail them as well. No matter how stirring my prose, it never, ever felt like enough. The kid who'd been beaten to a bloody pulp by his own mother. The toddler raped by her uncle, so that they had to sew her up in the emergency room. You work with words all your life and then find out there are times when they just can't do the job.

As someone accustomed to getting the facts, I found the city's child welfare agency, which went by several different names during the time I occasionally covered its so-called clients, an infuriating hall of mirrors. Its myriad shortcomings, its frequent malpractices, were hidden behind a cloak of state-mandated secrecy; there was one employee whose essential function seemed to be to tell us that she could tell us nothing about any child under its care. Even when children were so brutalized that they died and were buried in tiny particle-board coffins, even when foster parents were accused by police of sexual abuse worse than what had led the children into care in the first place, the response was always the same: no response. It was like beating your head against a wall.

So the information came from others: nonprofit groups dedicated to reforms, group homes for troubled kids, the many good foster parents disgusted with the system, the families themselves. But it felt a little secondhand; you could rarely watch the system as it worked—or more important, didn't work—rarely see the children examined, the parents questioned, the foster placements made. I felt an odd kind of sympathy for the people who could have opened that window for me, the rank-and-file caseworkers who were sent day to day into some of the city's roughest neighborhoods to examine kids who had allegedly been neglected, abused, or abandoned. There were not enough of them to get the job done; the number of cases they carried made inevitable the failure that surrounded their work like a stench. Some of them did confide in me anonymously over the years. But it was worth their jobs to talk to reporters openly, much less take us on their rounds or tell us how they felt.

So when Marc Parent took me to breakfast one morning and told me he had been one of those people and that he wanted to write about what it had been like, I knew he had a book. I just didn't know he had this one. I didn't know he would be able to do what I had never done: simultaneously make the children live on paper and do them some lasting good at the same time—protect them in a palpable way. He had burned out, walked away, and then decided to come back to help again with his memories, his stories, his cases, his kids. I didn't know that he intuitively understood what it took me years to learn: that the person you keep running into, when you see the bruises and the cigarette burns and hear the wails, is yourself.

He spoke to me that morning about Sean, the boy he kept on the phone for a long, long time while the kid threatened to cut his little brother's throat. But when I read Sean's story set down on paper, for maybe the first time in my life I wasn't looking at one of these kids as I would a fetal pig on the dissecting table in high school, making him a subject, an object, a noun, a verb. I was inside his little chest, heart pounding with his terror. And on the other end of the phone was Marc, terrified himself. He didn't have the skills for the job, he only had the will to do it right. Mostly, he did.

There aren't any heroes here, which is what I always suspected I'd discover if I managed to pry some bricks from the wall the city had built around the child welfare system. And blame is harder to lay than you might imagine. The mother who threw her kids out the window did it out of burning love, to save them from hellfire and damnation; the woman with the attitude who said she hadn't hurt anyone was telling the truth. The caseworkers bitch and moan and make jokes and often try their best, which is rarely good enough. Their training is inadequate, and the number of workers is far too small for the number of families in trouble. Some of the cases would require a battalion of cops, doctors, and social workers to handle; instead there are two kids fresh out of college with good intentions and a handful of forms.

Anyone who has covered New York knows that investigations of the child welfare system and plans to improve/ upgrade/reform it are as predictable and perennial as the hottest day of the summer, and about as enduring. There are new commissioners, blue-ribbon panels, boards. But as I knew as a reporter and know even better today, the people who could make any real change in the system are people like this one wide-eyed boy from Wisconsin keeping a homicidal eight-year-old on the phone until the cops bust in the apartment door. The blue-ribbon panels can go home and read this book. The politicians, too. If they are good people they should be ashamed of themselves.

I was ashamed, listening to Marc tell his tales in a luncheonette across the street from the pretty little private school where my own three kids—never hit, never starved, never left alone, monitored, mentored, cossetted, loved—were in social studies class or outside at recess. I was a good reporter, but a story, no matter its effect, is never really a worthy substitute for action. Here he was prepared to do both.

If I were writing this in one of my novels I would never name him Parent; the wordplay would seem too obvious. But the truth is that for an instant, when it mattered, that was the role he played. These were his children, in precinct houses, in hospital beds, in morgue drawers, bleeding, crying, insisting that nobody did nothing, they were fine, it was an accident, they only wanted to go home. They are our children, too. This is the story of those who failed them, told by one man who did not. Read it and weep.

Anna Quindlen
April 1996

TURNING STONES

Prologue

BACK HOME THE AIR SMELLS like clover, from the first spring mosquito to the last fall deerfly. The early harvest of baby corn is ready for blanching and canning by the time barefoot calluses are just about right for full-speed sprints across the blacktop. Raspberries are ready to fall into your palm at about the same time and you have to be quick to get them before the blackbirds. Throughout the summer the rain visits like a favorite relative, refreshing hot swimming holes and backyard kiddie pools in a white boil. Growing up in central Wisconsin was a little like living in the middle of a big mud puddle. I lived in a town called Marshfield and the name fit the place. It's the second lowest point in the state. A town called Pittsville is a few feet lower and a couple miles north. I grew up slowly, carefully almost; caressed by the gentle tassels of September corn—milk fed and butter bred. White squeaky lumps of cheese curds were turned out of the Wenzel Dairy, a short bike ride up the road. A quarter got you a bagful, enough to last the whole day and get you halfway to a stomachache. My pals were fat and happy. Country boys; river soaked and honey-toast fed—harmonica whistlers all of them. We'd toot every variation of "Oh! Susanna" until the sky turned dusk gray, and after polishing off a hot can of cherry pie filling over slices of Wonder bread, we'd doze off in front of a dying fire on the banks of a small river that scrolled its way under stars and through back fields with the abandon of a curious roving hound. Everything runs on a schedule in the flat fields of home. Things go the way things have always gone from rain to worms, and once you learn the rhythm, you can tell the trees up the river by the color of the water.

People don't leave, back home. No reason to. There's enough milk and bread, enough road and houses, there's enough warm breeze and wide open perfect sky in one acre of fertile Wisconsin for every adult and all their children as well as their children's children and all the dogs and cats and hamsters and horses that come with them. For the most part, the people that do wander out never stray too far. You have to drive a long way to get to any place that doesn't feel like Marshfield. The important things that make Wisconsin one giant sameness don't really change much from town to town, so the people who move out of Marshfield aren't really remodeling the house as much as they're rearranging the furniture.

I did leave, and when my plane left town, it actually left Wisconsin. More than that, it left the Midwest, and even more significantly, it landed in New York City. The backwoods cadence I'd learned to follow seemed of little use to me when six months later at twenty-three years old, I was hired by Emergency Children's Services, a small branch of the city's

Child Protective Services. It was an office of about seventeen people in charge of keeping the city's children safe nightly, from four in the afternoon until eight the next morning, and all day on weekends and holidays. Keeping the children safe generally involved making unannounced midnight home visits to wake everybody up, strip everybody down, and look for bruises, among other things. When we found kids in trouble, we took them with us. All of this caused no small amount of screaming and blood-soaking threats, as I'm sure you can imagine. Taking someone's child is just a little easier than ripping their arms off. If you think mother bears get mad when you mess with their cubs, you won't believe the levels of freak we humans can get to.

This story is set in New York, but it's really about America. This is how children are mutilated and sometimes killed by their parents and this is what we do about it. This is how I succeeded and how I failed these children, but more than that—this is how I kept on trying, using the tools of my upbringing to work through situations they were never meant to handle. This is what I was allowed to do and what I was held back from doing. These are the tasks I could handle and the tasks I fell short of. My four years at Emergency Children's Services took me on a trip through the darkest basement of human behavior, to a place where parents become perpetrators and children lie still on the floor.

Along the way I was forced to tromp through some dark hallways in my own basement, each broken child escorting me downstairs night after night to show me the beams that were strong and the ones cut with worms and about to collapse. Five nights a week the little guides hauled me down to shape my foundation, revealing to me which truths to strengthen and which ones to grind up and haul away. Throughout the four years, the sound of hammers and saws downstairs was the sound of growing up. Back home, people work like fiends on the house, but they leave the basement dark. Although I didn't know it at the time, I think that's why I had to leave.

I know in my heart that I've saved the lives of many children. It's hard to describe the way I feel when I think about that. As soon as I'm about to say anything, the complexity of it overwhelms me. Satisfaction begins to tap it—there's more, but I just can't find words for it. At the very bottom of me, a place I don't go to very often, there's satisfaction, and I think it has something to do with the kids who are walking the planet because of the efforts I made at crucial points in their lives. I never feel proud about the good things I managed to do at Emergency Children's Services. I don't spend much time patting my back about it all. It was my job. Everyone in the office saved lives. It was what we were supposed to do—saving a life wasn't above and beyond the call of duty. It was expected. When the job was done well, I felt satisfaction—a much more expensive drink than pride. A trumpet blast of pride comes easier than the glowing ember of satisfaction. People working in the business of life and death know this and are grateful for satisfaction alone and above everything else.

There are teenagers falling in love and learning to drive, eating chocolate and listening to the rain on this day, because of me—because I was there at the right time and did the right thing. There's one, however, who will never feel the sun too hot on his face, never fly too high on a swing, or feel a rush of joy at the first snowfall—and that's because of me, also. I saved children from death, but I let one go. Many lived because of my actions, but one was killed. Not with a gun or a fist or a knife or a rope, nothing so tangible as a ball of fire or a drop of poison. Not because of what I did, but because of what I didn't do. Doesn't make a difference, dead is just as dead, all the same. All the talk and agonizing doesn't make a difference to a boy in the ground, but it might make a difference to the rest.

You hear about children falling through the cracks when they die in the care of the system. Let me tell you something: there is no system, there are only people—children don't fall through cracks, they fall through fingers. I know because a little boy fell through mine. The person who says "fell through the cracks in the system" is really saying that someone blew it, and that blame is going to be spread so broadly that accountability will fall to no one. I was part of a long chain of people who could've saved the boy, but that doesn't make me less guilty, it only makes more people less innocent.

This is a confession.

There's a sound that whispers through the room as I write about the events told here—scars that have healed over being torn open to bleed one last time. There's no way to prepare for this stuff, just like there's no way to prepare for a punch in the face. I wasn't prepared at twenty-three to handle the things I saw at ECS. I never got comfortable in the field. There's something about the inner city after the sun goes down that makes anyone with a heart beating red blood feel like an alien. Even though I was able to return to earth with a punch of the clock, I got jittery every time I went out. I didn't belong there, but neither did the families I visited. It wasn't right, but there it was and there we were. Writing from these memories brings up the sights and smells of the place with a startling freshness that sometimes catches me off guard. I've begun many evenings with uneasy trepidation as I sat in front of a blinking cursor waiting for events to steep in my mind and pour out of bouncing index fingers like the sloppy spout of a teakettle. In the course of completing some of the more graphic sections of text, I was visited by the same nausea that came knocking when the events actually happened.

While I was on the job, I kept a file on many of my cases and I've referred back to it to keep my memory correct and true to the facts. The people here are real, but because I never carried a tape recorder with me, I've had to re-create their voices from my memory of what they said. In many instances I remember exact conversation; but even when I haven't remembered exchanges word for word, I remember vividly how people acted and what they were *like*. In all instances I've tried to write dialogue that serves them truthfully. Some individuals have been obscured to protect their identity and I've changed all names and specific locations, but tried in every way to choose replacements that are compatible with their originals.

I want to say one more thing to a very specific group of people—the people who watch the needle go in when they get a shot, who look under the tables in greasy all-night truck stops, the people who've allowed themselves to drift in a lifeless exhale to the bottom of a shallow river and lie still, contemplating a watery corpse—you know who you are. I've written this for you, too—for you curious ones who haven't limited yourselves exclusively to the intellectual concerns of human suffering as it relates to child abuse but instead have asked me on so many occasions with a twinge of voyeuristic guilt, "How bad does it get—what's the goriest night you've had?" I've obliged the question, so many times, with a grim flash of red that's left everyone in the room stammering to change the subject. I don't know why we want to go to this place, but I know we do. I've been asked about the nights of gore more than about the nights of grace—so here you are and here we go. *This is as bad as it got. These are the goriest nights I had.* Buckle up for a rough ride and don't be surprised if by the end, you find you've broken off a bigger piece than you can neatly handle, and you wind up visiting some dark hallways in your own basement to do a little remodeling.

Finally, this is told for the children who walk daily with careful steps through a maze of unthinkable pain and fear. Because they live it, we must examine it, and we must do so without blinking. If we blink, if we flinch or lose interest, if we get overwhelmed or become weary, *if we turn away*, they are doomed. For their sake we must perch in the corners of their bedrooms in relentless vigil of unblinking light, and we must watch. If we succeed, maybe we find out why these things happen. Maybe we figure out what to do about it. Specifically, this is for Sean, Ben, Cousin Tony, Little Davey, Raphael, Dearest Shaniece, Paul, Tisha, Keisha, Blein, Robby, Rick, Chucky, Melissa, and Baby Doe, whose deaths and injuries are laid out here and have left their permanent welts across my being, hurling me from arrogant youth to humbled adulthood. I tell your stories with an enormous hope that if we keep you in the front of our minds, your brothers and sisters in fear and pain might one day have it better.

You are not forgotten.

1

Begging a Knife

MY ROOMMATES WERE JUST ROLLING out of bed on a crisp September Sunday when I left for work just before noon. As I walked out of my apartment and looked into the cloudless blue sky, the morning seemed drenched with peace, but I was going to work and I knew better. I'd only been with the agency for two months but was already wise to the kind of wreckage a beautiful weekend might hold. Bumping around on the downtown train, I wondered if I would spend the day reading the paper or talking to a doctor about the extent and indications of lacerations found on the back of some seven-year-old's thighs. Maybe I'd have to make a quick exit on some man waving a rusty kitchen knife. It was the uncertainty of the coming day that was the hardest thing to deal with because there was no time to prepare, no time to shield your eyes or hold your breath. Sometimes it was—BAM—"Good morning, did you get to look at the paper today yet? Anyway, you gotta go to the field right away, here's the case—it's in the *Post*; they're outside now. Don't talk to them. We got a car for you. Get going." Or else it was "Good morning, how's it doin'—listen, it's really slow and I know you just got in but could you take your lunch break?"

Thunk-whump.

Just as I pulled my time card from the slot, a supervisor craned her neck around the partition of her cubicle. "Is that Marc?" she yelled as she looked over. "Marc—it's you. There's a case on your desk right now, you have to look at it right away. It might be serious—right on your desk there." My stomach bristled at the unknown of something that might be serious. "On your desk, Marc." I jerked my head around the office. I didn't have a desk. "On your desk over there, hurry up—," the supervisor yelled again. She was behind the partition. I couldn't see her.

"What desk?" I asked.

"Your desk—," she said.

"I don't have a desk."

She popped her head back out. *"Over there, Marc—over there,"* she said, indicating the back. "Hurry up—read it over and call the home. On the desk in the back there—I thought it was your desk."

"Okay," I said heading back. "I don't have a desk though."

I sat down to begin my third month at Emergency Children's Services, and picked up the case. Reports that came into ECS categorized the abuse covered in the case. There was a place for a check mark next to every unthinkable thing that might be inflicted on a child. This menu of abuse sat under the heading "Suspicion Codes." They were: DOA/Fatality; Fractures; Subdural Hematoma, Internal Injuries; Lacerations,

Bruises, Welts; Burns, Scalding; Excessive Corporal Punishment; Child's Drug/Alcohol Use; Drug Withdrawal; Lack of Medical Care; Malnutrition, Failure to Thrive; Sexual Abuse; Educational Neglect; Emotional Neglect; Lack of Food, Clothing, Shelter; Lack of Supervision; Abandonment; and finally, the catch-all phrase checked on just about every report and usually the understatement of the year—Inadequate Guardianship.

The report in my hand had checks next to "Lack of Supervision" and "Inadequate Guardianship." The vitals read like any of the others I'd come across over the past several weeks: Three people—a mother and two sons. The case address was in Queens, called in by a psychiatrist. The boys were two and eight years old. Then a flare shot through my veins—someone had written "possible 911" across the top.

> Both children are alone now. The eight-year-old in the past has attempted to kill his younger brother. Eight-year-old is now afraid of being in the apartment alone with his brother. He is afraid of what he might do. He is afraid he is going to hurt his brother.
> ADD. INFO: Mother has a history of cocaine use.

The case read like the sound of a bell—the gates flew open and it was ride 'em cowboy on every level from there on out. *"Call the source of the report first?"* I called out with a waver of adrenaline in my throat.

"Just call the home," came the reply. *"See if anybody needs an ambulance."* I rolled my chair across the carpet to a phone shared by the other desk and hopped my fingers over the keypad. Waiting for the connection on the other side, I was just barely aware of similar urgent situations unfolding across the rest of the office. A busy afternoon. Of course when you've got about seventeen people covering a city of over seven million,

you're gonna get busy afternoons. The phone rang once and was picked up immediately.

"Hi." The voice of a boy.

"Is this..." I flipped back to the first page of the report. "Hi—is this Sean?"

"Who is it?"

"This is...my name's Marc." I'd called before figuring out what to say exactly. "You don't know me, Sean. Is this Sean?"

"It's loud over there," he said.

"...oh...I'm calling from an office—"

"What kind of an office is that?"

"Is your mom home?"

"This is Sean—"

"—all right, good. Sean, is your moth—"

"What kind of an office is that?"

"Can I speak to your mother, Sean?" He didn't answer for a moment. His breath purred at my ear. "Sean?...can I speak to your mom?"

"Well...what do you think?" he asked in a slow voice.

"Is she there, Sean?..." More breathing.

"...no..."

"Is there anyone with you?"

"My brother."

"Your little brother, Ben?"

"...yeah..."

"It's just you and Ben at home?"

"What kind of an office is that?"

"This is the office where I work. It's an office that helps out kids. I'm calling you because someone told us that you and Ben were left alone. They said you were afraid—"

"I'm afraid?"

"Yeah...are you afraid right now, Sean?"

"Yes, actually, you could say that."

"What are you afraid of?"

"Well"—he drew in a breath and let it out—"I'm afraid of

a few things that might seem strange." His speech was exact and careful. Like he was reading difficult assembly instructions on a new toy.

"Wha'dya got, Marc?" the supervisor hollered from her cubicle.

"—on the phone with him," I shouted back.

"Who was that?" Sean asked.

"That was my boss. What are you afraid of, Sean?"

"What does your boss want, Marc?"

"She wants to know if you and your brother are okay."

"I'm afraid of a fire . . ."

"Is there a fire in the apartment?"

"No, but I'm afraid that the building will burn down anyways."

"Where's your mom at, Sean?"

"I'm afraid of a gas leak in the building."

"Do you smell gas right now?"

"No."

"Do you know where your mom is?"

"I don't know where she is," he said. "And there's guys in the hall."

"Where's Ben?"

"He's in his crib."

"Is he okay?"

"Ben is fine. As long as the guys in the hallway don't come in here and get us. I got the door locked, but I'm trying to keep him quiet so they won't come in here."

"Who are the guys?"

"I don't know. Drug dealers. Our apartment is on the corner of the hallway where they always are."

"How long has your mom been gone?"

"She left at ten-thirty." It was twelve-thirty already. Two hours.

Sean warmed up to me quickly and began to reveal the fears that took shape the moment she left them. I would encounter children left alone countless times in the coming years, but never again would I experience a little boy like Sean—deeply intelligent but also, unfortunately, the possessor of an imagination just as profound, that called forth demons like bolts of lightning to set the house on fire.

"Okay, baby, I'm leaving now," Jenny Duma called out as she gathered up her things. Sean was curled up in a corner of the kitchen. He'd used up every argument he could think of to stop her from leaving him and his brother alone. She made no indication of changing her mind despite his most dramatic admonitions. There was nothing left for him to do but withdraw into a corner and prepare for her absence and the onslaught of fears that would follow. "The baby's sound asleep," she said, hiking the purse over her shoulder. "If you keep quiet, he might even stay out until I get back. Be good, Sean." The door slammed behind her; he listened to her footsteps fade down the hallway, turn the corner, and begin the clip-clop down the stairs. Then there was silence. Then he was alone.

He sat on the floor where she left him and stared at the door. She said she'd be back in a little while but a little while was an imprecise measure of time as he saw it and he was keeping track. A little while, from the mouth of his mother, was anything from a crack in the plaster to the whole roof caving in. He looked at the clock on the stove. Ten-thirty. His grandmother came for her weekend visit just before two o'clock. Three and a half hours. Who knows when Mom would roll back in, but you could set a watch to Grandma. He only had to make it for three and a half hours.

Sean was a boy who knew himself and knew his fears. They were coming for sure, dark thoughts that were as familiar and well traveled as the lines of an old baseball glove. Sometimes they were rational scenarios that could actually happen— floods, tornadoes, explosions, criminals, that sort of thing. But there were other times when the fears were just plain outrageous—a sudden gush of blood down his face, wolves chewing madly through the wall, hands igniting with flames. It didn't matter if the fears were exotic or domestic, they were as real in the moment as the nails on his fingers.

Sean was as good a boy as any, his heart as pure and intentions as clear as baby brother asleep in the crib. Not a mean bone in his body, as they say, but there was something else. Sean had exhibited troubling signs of mental illness for the past year, and had recently revealed the kind of behavior he was capable of—the leaping conclusions he could make about his fears and how to stop them, about how to protect himself from the boogeyman at all costs. Mental health professionals had pleaded with his mother to have him treated for his own safety as much as for the safety of others he encountered. They told her that Sean is capable of *violence,* at least, and that he should be monitored closely in the presence of other children. Just that month, Sean had demonstrated his abilities on little brother Ben when they were left alone. Ms. Duma came home to find handprint bruises around brother Ben's tiny neck, and cried as she listened to Sean explain the convolution of thoughts that led him to bring Ben within inches of his life. She responded well initially—having Sean seen by psychiatrists and medicating him as they prescribed—but she quickly slacked off, becoming inconsistent with follow-up visits and forgetting which pills were for what. It had finally reached the point where it was as if nothing were being done at all for a problem that was substantial to begin with and becoming more so as time went on.

Sean looked about the quiet apartment. He thought about watching TV for the distraction but then decided against it for fear of waking brother Ben. It began almost immediately. Irrationality snuck into him like a stench. Gas. *It's gas,* he thought. Another breath and he was certain it was true—he sensed the distinct smell of gas. His body filled with panic at the thought of the whole building flying apart in a ball of fire. It happens. He'd seen it on the news every once in a while—a slow leak from the boiler and the whole building blooms with flame. Anything could spell disaster once the stage was set—a spark of static electricity between the nose of a cat and a little boy's hand. He rocked with the thought of every rafter and support flying into the sky on trails of smoke like a thousand oddly shaped rockets. He saw it all as he sat there. Another breath and the smell of gas made his belly ache. Another breath and why did she have to do it? Why did she have to leave? *People inside don't stand a chance,* he thought. He'd seen it on the six o'clock—the crush of brick and metal taking care of whatever life the blast leaves behind. Then you lie as the meat in a sandwich of drywall and sheet metal where the third floor used to be, screaming out to would-be rescuers who either get there too late or pull out the wrong Pick-up-Stix and send the second half of the building slamming through your forehead. It happens. He'd seen it on TV—buildings just like his, people just like him. Each breath rolled into his chest like mercury.

He stood slowly—the air was dry, one spark would end it all. As he rose, he looked out the window. A red cloud. Turning red, actually—the only thing in the sky. The color seemed to be generating out of the cloud's middle and slowly spreading to its sides. He walked to the window on careful steps for a better look—*One spark is all it takes,* he thought again. By the time he made it to the window, the cloud had turned into a face—deep red and swirling with turbulence. People in the street were going about their business just as if everything was fine, just as if there wasn't a big red cloud with a toothy gri-macing face hanging above their heads. Suddenly the face looked directly at him. He raised his hands across his eyes and almost tumbled backward.

Voices in the hallway made him jerk. An argument. *The dealers,* he thought as he ran quietly to the door to listen. The guys in the hall were shouting. Sean grabbed a chair from the kitchen and dragged it to the door so he could look out the peephole. There were four of them. He couldn't make out what they were saying but he could tell it wasn't friendly. They gestured wildly. The smell of gas was intense now, it made Sean dizzy. *Drug dealers and junkies fighting about money—has to be,* he thought. Suddenly two of the men looked over at Sean. He pulled back from the peep and held his breath. He knew they couldn't see him, but the way they looked over—straight into him, just about. His breath skipped in his throat. He looked over his shoulder. The red cloud leaned closer toward the window. Its face glared at him. He covered his head for a moment and then turned back to the door, rising again to the peep. This time, as he looked out it was almost as if the men were standing on his eyeball. They were directly in front of the door. Sean could practically feel them breathing. He jerked back and ran quietly to the opposite wall. The cloud covered the entire window. He felt it caving in on top of him—the gas, an explosion, a red whirling face, dealers, junkies—all of it within the first seconds of being alone. It made him angry, but more than anything, it made him ache for his mother's return.

As it happened, Sean was due for a visit to the psychiatric clinic that day. An hour after the appointment was to take place, the psychiatrist called to beg Ms. Duma to bring Sean to his follow-up. She found a very frightened and very alone young boy, and because she knew Sean's history, she asked him if he thought he might hurt his brother. Yes, he said, he was afraid he might have to kill him. After doing some quick work to stabilize the situation, she rushed in the report. Twenty minutes later I was on the phone with him. After I established that the brothers were safe for the moment, I allowed Sean to go into the details of his fears—the gas, the red-face cloud, the men lurking at the front door. The more he talked, the calmer he became. He was like no other kid I'd ever encountered. Smart way beyond his years. Animated, articulate, and a mind on turboboosters with the kill switch busted off. He'd jump from cereal-box prizes to plate tectonics within a matter of seconds.

My supervisor eventually came to my desk with her eyebrows arched in a "What's up?" look. I wrote "kid's a genius" on a paper in front of me. She picked it up, gave it a look, and threw it back in front of me.

"Wha'dya mean the kid's a genius?—I don't care if he's a genius, Marc—" she said. "Tell me whether or not he's gonna pull his brother's head off." I nodded and she walked back to her desk.

"—end of the world is coming today," Sean said into the phone.

"What was that, Sean?—I missed that."

"What I said was that I'm afraid the end of the world is coming today."

"...Why would you think something like that, Sean?"

"Oh, I can predict this sort of thing," he said.

"You can tell that the world's gonna end today."

"Listen," he said carefully. "I already saw the cloud, which I just told you about—the red face? There's gonna be more of those, I guarantee. And when you see those, of course, everybody knows that tornadoes come next. Only they're not like regular tornadoes—they're actually very small, but they're strong, and I mean *strong*. They come from all around for as far as you can see—literally thousands of them, perhaps more. They sweep over the earth and wipe it clean—all the buildings and people, the trees and everybody's—the pets, dogs and birds and cats and you know that the cat is the devil's favorite animal but that does not matter. They go just like everybody else. Then everything explodes. The entire planet. Huge chunks of the earth's core shoot into the sky. And the sky is on fire—everything burns." He paused a moment and then his voice went up in a warning, "I'm afraid that's gonna happen pretty soon now."

"Well, whatever happens, Sean, let's just stay on the phone together, no matter what," I said. "All right?"

"Oh, I'm not going anywhere—believe me. I'm pretty glad you called."

"So did your mom leave you the phone number of a friend or a neighbor in case you get scared like this while she's gone?"

"...no."

"You don't know any of your neighbors?"

"No way—nobody talks to anybody in this building."

"All right, well it's a good thing I called then—"

"I'm studying about flag signals almost every day now. You know how to do flag signals?" he asked.

The turn was a little sharp for me; I was at a temporary loss for words.

"Flag signals—" Sean said again. "When you're out at sea and you have to communicate with another ship but the radio's broke or in case the enemy might be listening—you know—you have to use flag signals."

"Sure, I know about those," I said, racing to keep up.

"You know flag signals?" he asked, amazed.

"No, no, I just know about them. I don't know how to do them but I know about them."

"Because I was gonna say—if you knew flag signals then boy would I ever want to meet you. My favorite flag, my favorite one of all has a parallelogram over the square of the cloth. What I like about it is the fact that it forms four equal triangles—if the geometry is perfect then the triangles are symmetrical. It's why I like it. I can draw one pretty good, but that's no surprise—I draw them all the time! I can't get the triangles perfect yet, but I'm getting pretty good at it, anyways.

"The best flag I ever made is on one of my T-shirts. My mom let me use the T-shirt because it was old and Granny was gonna get me and my brother new ones. Otherwise there is *no way* she would've let me use it. I cut it perfectly square and I used Magic Markers from my school to make the design and did it ever turn out good—and I mean *really* good. I was surprised myself, even. I got it hanging on my wall. It's the distress signal. When a ship is in trouble, or like if it's under attack or something?—then the flagman goes to the bridge and makes a signal with this flag. They only use this flag if it's really serious—I mean *really* serious, like a sub attack, maybe . . . then they would use it. It's actually the most important signal of all because if you do it, the whole fleet comes to the rescue, and I mean on the double. That's why I practice it. Out of all of the signals, I think it's the best one to know how to do. I practice out the window of our building every night before I have to go to bed."

When we began it was flaming chunks of the earth's core. Now it was flag signals. Sean just needed someone to talk to—someone to keep his head from telling him horror stories. It was clear from the moment we said hello that his skull housed a thought factory on a twenty-four-hour shift, producing flaming chunks when upset and doing flag signals when calm. As he went on about the flags, the relief he felt from talking to a concerned adult became clear. I let him continue until he was a good distance from panic and then dove to the heart of things.

"Sean?" I asked, "Do you ever feel like hurting your little brother?"

"Oh sure," he replied easily. "Sometimes it's very hard to resist my urge to kill him. About two weeks ago I almost choked him to death. I was about to kill him but then I decided not to."

No joke. Sean was the kind of kid who meant what he said. The weight of the situation hit me like a medicine ball. Suddenly I was snipping wires to defuse a bomb. Nobody said anything in the training about it getting this deep this quickly. I tried to conceal the jump in my throat as I went on. "What about right now, Sean? Do you feel like you want to kill him right now?"

"Before I was almost going to, but not right now. I was just about to cut him in his throat and Dr. Miller called just in time." Dr. Miller was the psychiatrist who initiated the report in front of me.

"But right now you don't want to kill him?" I asked.

"Well . . . right now I don't think I have to kill him—he's being quiet. He was crying before and that's when I almost did it. 'Cause of those guys in the hall—we gotta keep it down so they don't know we're in here. If they hear Ben crying then they'll bust in the door and get us. He was screaming before and I was trying to get him to stop crying but he wouldn't so I went to the kitchen and got the butcher knife and I was gonna cut him in the throat but then Dr. Miller called *just in time.* Then he fell back asleep."

"So then you just let him sleep."

"Yup. I didn't have to kill him which is good because I really didn't want to but those guys outside—I gotta keep it quiet in here otherwise it's a definite thing that they *will* come in here and get us."

"Where's the knife right now, Sean?"

"On the floor over by the crib."

"Are the guys at the door now?" I asked.

"I'm not sure. Hold on, I'll check—don't hang up."

"I won't, don't worry."

He put the phone down and I heard him move the chair back to the peep for a look. In a moment, he was back to tell me "the coast is clear." I got him to put the knife away and we talked a little longer until the situation was stable and Sean was at ease. He said he was relieved to be in touch with me, that he was glad Dr. Miller made the report. I had him write down my name and phone number. I told him I was going to speak with my boss to see how we could help him. He was pleased to hear it. I told him I wouldn't let him down. He was pleased to hear that, too.

"Whatever happens, we're gonna work something out so

that the two of you will be okay," I said. "You can count on me."

"You can count on me, too," he said back.

Then I made a huge mistake—I hung up.

2

THE OFFICE WAS HUMMING pretty steadily. As soon as I put the receiver in its cradle, the person on the next desk picked it up and began dialing. Folks were pairing up to do field visits. Many were eating. There was a line of three people waiting to do computer clearances on their cases at one of the two terminals in the office. A supervisor came to where I sat—a huge blond woman putting in her last year before retirement. She put two more cases in front of me and told me not to take all day on one case—that they were flying into the office like locusts and so I'd better pick up the pace.

"What's happening with that one?" she asked, flexing the permanent scowl across her mouth. I began to tell her, but she cut me off and told me to come into her office. I got up and followed her to her desk. She was the kind of person who just loved training new people; the conversation immediately took an academic tone. She took long pauses to sip coffee as she went over standard agency doctrines. My case was a perfect illustration of the problem of children at home unsupervised, she said. A problem I would encounter many times on the job. Had I done the computer clearances on the case, she wanted to know. Not yet, I told her. What about the source of the report—had I contacted the source yet, she asked. No, not yet, I said. She looked up to the ceiling and shook her head like I'd tracked mud all over the carpet.

"*Marc*," she groaned, "*we always contact the source of the report before anything else.*"

"Right, I know, but—"

"Oh, you know," she said, cutting me off. "You know, but you didn't do it, did you? We call the source first and then we do the clearances, *then* we call the home."

"Okay, but—"

"Marc. Marc"—she put up a hand and pinched the bridge of her nose like she had the world's only headache—"don't give me an argument, there are no buts here. That's the way we do it and that's the way you'll do it too—call the source, check the computer, call the home."

"You told me to call the home first—"

She laughed and rolled her eyes in a mock of outrage. "Oh boy, I had an ex-husband like you—"

"Well, that's what you told me—"

"I did no such thing, mister," she said in a high voice. "Don't even try it."

"—to check and see if the kid was gonna hurt his baby brother..." Her face went slack. "Which is a real possibility, I think." She pulled the case from my hands and gave it a quick look.

"Oh good lord—this is the possible 911," she said. "I thought it was a different—I forgot I gave you th— this is the one with the kid who's gonna—this is that crazy kid case."

"You wanted me to call the house first to see if—"

"Yes, yes of course I wanted you to call the house first— this is a possible 911. This is a serious case—my God, Marc, a case like this and you let me go on about computer clearances?!! C'mon now, let's get with the—"

My phone rang. These phones didn't ring unless you gave someone the number. I knew it was Sean and I knew it was trouble. I dove at the receiver and put it to my ear.

"Is this Marc?" It was Sean. He was panting like a sprinter. Ben was screaming in the background.

"Sean—it's me, what is it, what's going on—"

He spoke with a restrained calm over the wailing of his brother. *"Well, I called you because I have to do it now—"*

"—Wait, wait—*Hang on. Sean. Sean?*—"

"*I gotta do it right now—I gotta kill him*—"

"—HANG ON—SEAN, SEAN—"

"—*The guys are gonna hear him, they're gonna get us*—"

I jumped up and crashed my chair into the desks behind me a couple times to get the attention of someone who could call the police as I spoke as quickly and calmly into the phone as possible. "*Wait, wait, wait, wait, wait, wait*—just hang on one second and tell me what's going on, okay?" I slammed my hand on the desk and waved my arms over my head.

"*The guys are right at the door*—" His voice shook as brother Ben unleashed the full force of his lungs against the piercing whistle of his throat.

I kicked like a crazy person against a file cabinet while speaking softly into the phone—"*Sean. What about Ben? What are you doing with Ben?*" My supervisor came running over. The office hushed. I hit the speakerphone and the tiny panicked voice rang across the office.

"*I'm gonna cut him in his throat so he quits making so much noise.*" The supervisor arched her head to the ceiling and pounced on a phone to call police.

"Sean—Sean, listen to me, can you wait for one second? Sean—" He begged his brother to stop screaming as I spoke.

"*It's no use,*" he said coming back to the phone.

"Sean—just tell me what you're gonna do before you do it. Okay? Stop for one second and tell me what you're gonna do."

"*I gotta cut him in the throat*—"

"All right—all right, but before you do it—listen—Sean?"

"*Yeah*—"

"Tell me where the knife is . . ."

"*I gotta do it right now—those guys*—"

"SEAN—SEAN, SEAN—LISTEN. *Sean, listen—you gotta tell me where you're holding the knife.*"

"Well, I got his wagon on him—I put his wagon on top of him to hold him down—"

"Where's the knife? Sean—"

Suddenly he dropped the phone. He screamed over Ben's squall, begging him again to be quiet. The phone distorted with the volume of his outburst. I screamed into the phone but I was no match for the clamor between the two of them. A picture flashed through my head of Sean pushing a butcher knife through his two-year-old brother's neck to the scratchy sound of me hollering through the receiver on the floor. You could hear a pin drop in the office—everyone standing around me listening to the mayhem as it played out on the phone's small speaker. Sean yelled at his brother, but it was impossible to understand what he was saying. With him away from the phone, I was utterly useless—instantly transformed from a player to a spectator. The more Sean pleaded for Ben to be quiet, the clearer it became that he really didn't want to kill his brother. If he'd wanted to kill Ben, it would've been done already. He wouldn't have called back. The call was a last-ditch attempt to calm his mania. I was ready to do the job but first he had to pick the phone off the floor. *He's gonna do it,* I suddenly thought, and waited helplessly for the sickening sound of young Ben's decapitation—the piercing scream suddenly muddied, a voiceless struggle, a gargling rasp, and then silence followed by the sound of Sean's slow footsteps back to the phone. My stomach lurched to the edge of my throat as the screaming continued.

The supervisor concluded the 911 with a request for an ambulance in addition to police. Everyone in the office stared at one another, listening to the snarling chaos and waiting for the worst. Several ran off, not wanting to hear the sound of a messy execution. I called into the phone between the brothers' shouts and then gave up, sinking to my seat. The frenzy between them sounded like animals at slaughter. A gory climax seemed inevitable.

Suddenly he was back.

"—*you still there?*"

I jumped to my feet. "SEAN, LISTEN TO ME—*you gotta stay on the phone. Don't leave the phone again. I'm gonna help you, I promise. But we gotta make a deal—Sean?*"

"*Yeah—*"

"*You gotta make a deal with me that you won't leave the phone again—*"

"*All right—*"

"*No matter what happens, you stay on the phone. I promise I'll help you.*"

"*Okay.*"

I had him for the moment. He gave me an inch so I went for a mile. A little help from Ben would've been nice but that didn't seem likely. He kept the volume on high, bawling like he'd never stop.

"Did you do anything to Ben just now?"

"Not yet—"

"He's okay?"

"Yeah."

"We gotta make one more deal, Sean—all right? About the knife. We gotta make a deal about the knife. *Sean?*"

"Yeah."

"*You gotta always tell me where the knife is and—*"

"By his throat," he said.

"*You have the knife on his throat?—*"

"Yeah."

"Is the knife *touching* his throat?"

"Yeah."

"Sean. Listen to me now: you gotta back that knife up about five inches and then I'm gonna help you. *You do not want to kill your brother*—I know you don't want to do it. You pull the knife back five inches and I'm gonna tell you how to get your brother to stop crying." Ben was tiring to a whimper.

"Okay."

"You got the knife away from his throat?"

"Okay."

"Do you?"

"Yeah," Sean said. Ben calmed down a bit more.

"Sean. I want you to promise to tell me if the knife gets any closer to your brother than those five inches."

"Okay."

"You promise?"

"Okay."

"SAY IT."

"I promise to tell you."

"If the knife gets any closer than five inches—"

"Yeah."

"He's getting quiet now," I noted. Someone gave me a pat on the back.

"Yeah," Sean said, still out of breath, "but I gotta keep the knife so if he—I gotta kill him so he doesn't—*if he starts to cry again I gotta do it or those guys—"*

"Okay, okay. Sean—okay, but right now he's only crying a little bit and you got that knife pulled way back—"

"Yeah."

"Now listen, Sean, listen. I'm gonna tell you something"— Several in the office were nodding their heads at me and giving a thumbs-up. I didn't know what to say next but I kept talking just the same—"You don't hear the guys at the door anymore, right? Now listen. I know you heard them before, but you don't hear them now. Do you? You don't hear them because you're talking to me and they *know* you're talking to me. They're not even gonna think about doing anything to you while we're on the phone 'cause they're scared of guys like me. You don't hear them anymore, do you?"

"Maybe they're just being quiet—"

"Sure they're being quiet—they know I'm on the phone. They know what I'm gonna do to them if they get anywhere

near you and Ben. Go ahead and take a look if you want. They might still be out there, but no way are they gonna try to get in—not while I'm listening, they're not stupid. Hey, listen," I continued, "they don't wanna get me goin' on them, that's for sure. I twist guys like that into knots and I'll do it to them if I have to—I'm not kidding."

I kept it up until Sean was convinced there was a giant on his side. I told him I was big and that I was known to go after people who bothered my friends. I had Sean describe the guys so I'd know who to look for if I needed to crack their heads. That was good, he told me and went into a detailed description.

The sequence bought us a few precious minutes until Ben began to rev his engine again. Several moments later, he was back to top speed and begging his big brother for a serious flesh wound. Sean said he had to bring the knife back to his brother's throat. I talked him out of touching blade to skin but knew that it was only an inch or so away and that if the cops didn't get there soon I'd be out of tricks and the boys would be out of luck. Ben's whine went high. Sean screamed at him, but stayed on the phone. He told me the blade was still off his brother's neck, but that he had to bring it closer. I jabbered a blue streak on impulse alone, not knowing where I was going but content with any direction south of a blood-soaked carpet. We went back and forth with each other at a blinding pace— Sean setting the fires and me putting them out. After a good bit of convincing, I got him to lift the wagon off his brother. Might be the thing to stop the crying, I reasoned.

No sooner had Sean lifted it off than there was a torrent of pounding at the door. Sean screamed like it was the end. The banging was furious. For a split second, I thought, *Well, what the hell, the guys in the hall* were *out to get him.* Sean was true to his word about staying on the phone as I tried to tell him it was police, not junkies, at the door. He yelled right over me, terrified that his worst fears were being realized. After

begging through the breaks in Sean's panic, I was able to convince him he was safe. Just as the cops were about to break
through the door, Sean walked over and let them in.

The office cheered as the cop's voice informed us the boys
were safe, and I let out a giant exhale. The case marked the
end of being handled with kid gloves. From that point on I
would be shoulder to shoulder with the most senior caseworkers in the office—fair game for the grimmest of tragedies and
most shocking of outcomes, the kind of stuff that curls your
eardrums whether you're a person who's seen it all, or a person
who only thinks they have.

Thirty minutes later, I was driving to the precinct to get
brother Ben and bring him back to the office. The ambulance
had taken Sean directly to a psych emergency room, where he
was promptly admitted. I would never meet him face-to-face. I
had told the cops to make sure Sean had his flag before he was
taken from the home. He would have plenty of opportunity to
do distress signals in the coming weeks. The cops said they
would make sure he had it.

3

Ms. Duma called the precinct as I was getting ready to
take Ben. She had just read the note on her kitchen table from
the cops, informing her that Sean and Ben were presently in
the custody of the City of New York. The desk sergeant put
me on the phone and she hand-delivered a first-class ranting
before I could even say hello. The attacks flew out of her mouth
like rusty nails—Who the fuck do I think I crack, crack, crack,
and I should take my fucking report and shove it up my bang,
bang, bang, and no one has the right to take her fucking whack,
whack, whack, and I can just go to etc., and etc., and etc. I sat

quietly and listened, having no desire to get tangled in the barbed wire she was laying.

After a while, she tired out and began to cry. Neither of us spoke for a long time. Finally, I reached out, telling her that Ben was with me and that he was okay—that Sean was in the hospital and that he was okay, too. I told her how Sean almost killed Ben a few hours ago. She didn't believe it. Sean can get panicky, she said—he's an anxious boy, it's happened in the past, but he would never kill Ben. I told her she was wrong, that it would've certainly happened tonight. No way, she said. I told her about the knife and about little Ben pinned under the wagon. No way, she said again, it's impossible, and who am I to tell her what her children are gonna do. What about the medicines, I asked, if Sean is just "panicky" then why does he have to take pills? But it was no use—she wasn't gonna go there. Sean would never kill Ben and that was that.

"Where did you go today, Ms. Duma?"

"Oh..." She paused. "I went to see some friends of mine."

"What for?" I asked.

"Oh, I had to ask one of my friends for some money so I could go back to college."

"Do you use drugs?"

"No, sir," she answered quickly.

"You don't use any drugs, and you definitely weren't using any drugs today."

"That's right."

"Have you ever used drugs?"

"No, sir. Not anymore."

"No, you've never used drugs—not anymore..."

"That's right," she said.

"So did you get the loan?"

"What?"

"The money. The loan for your higher education."

"Oh...I don't see what that has to do with all of this. I don't think I have to tell you that," she said.

"You're probably right," I said. "You probably don't have to tell me that."

I told her I'd mail the 701-b—a removal form that explained under what legal process the children had been taken and what she might do to have them returned. We had hundreds of 701-b's xeroxed and left in sloppy piles throughout the office. Everyone who went into the field carried a pack of them. They were filled with fancy words and declarations but were really nothing more than glorified listings of daytime office numbers and Family Court addresses. Parents of children removed by the city were instructed to call the appropriate phone number for the office covering their address and say hello to the caseworker, whose butt would need to be shined repeatedly in the coming weeks.

I answered a few more of Ms. Duma's questions—no, I couldn't tell her the hospital Sean was at, and no, I couldn't give her the address of Ben's foster home. No, I wouldn't be on the case tomorrow, it would go directly to the field office where it would be assigned to someone else, and no, I didn't know who that person would be. She asked for my name and number, which I gave her. I told her my last name several times until she asked me to spell it.

"*P-a-r-e-n-t.*"

"Oh, Parent? Like somebody's—like a parent? Your last name's *Parent?*"

"Yup."

"You gotta be kidding me—taking people's kids away with a last name like Parent?"

"Yeah."

"Well I guess you got the right job, then."

"I guess I do," I said. "Good luck in college."

"I *am* going to college," she said.

"Well don't forget to spend some of that loan on a good hot-air popcorn machine," I said, "—used mine a lot more than I thought I would." We hung up shortly after that and never spoke again.

I exchanged technical case information with various cops and the desk sergeant to satisfy my agency's enormous appetite for numbers. This was State Register #A34293, on DS-2221, REPORT OF SUSPECTED CHILD ABUSE OR MALTREATMENT, Local District/Agency 73, recorded in Albany by P12-25, ECS Local Case #325447, Local Register #486-1. With that done, we traded a full complement of handshakes and well-dones. I turned to leave and strode down the steps of the precinct with Ben heavy and strange in my arms. The sun was going down, setting everything on fire and bringing an end to the perfect Sunday. By the time I crawled into Manhattan, the sun was still fading but the child was out. The case was done for me. I unbuckled the youngest Duma and took him into the office like a father bringing a sleeping child to bed, but without any of the coordination. He woke for only a moment as I set him down on the plastic chair in a corner of the office where children waited for placement into emergency foster care. I watched him sleep, with his head tipped to the side. The pristine beauty of his little neck sent a chill across my back; the soft pale skin that had worn a carving knife as a scarf. It felt awful to leave him on the chair but the day could've ended much worse. I tried to keep that in mind as I walked away.

I handled three more cases before clocking out on the end of the shift. The long subway ride home was a noisy meditation on the day. The train picked me up at Canal Street and dropped me off on 110th at Central Park West. As I rode, an image played in my head of eight-year-old Sean doing distress signals with a homemade flag out his tenement window. I wondered if anyone ever caught a glimpse of him, high above, arcing the flag through crisp movements of communication. What scenes played in his head as he practiced, what naval fleets cruised the horizon of the city? And what was he thinking now?—cut off from his home, his mother, his brother, in a white hospital room with nothing to call his own except the best flag he ever drew on an old T-shirt.

Sean may have had his problems, but he was a smart kid—the day's lesson was not lost on him, I'm certain. It wasn't lost on me: It doesn't matter how good you are at flag signals if no one is watching—the distress call is only as good as the person looking out for it.

When the train reached my stop, I emerged from the station holding my breath and dodging various unidentifiable dark piles on the stairway. Much later on, when I finally decided to hit the hay, I had trouble falling asleep. Staring at the ceiling, I wondered what the hell kind of ride I'd managed to sneak onto. I had been warned in training that the job would have its rough moments, but nobody ever told me I'd be begging a knife off of a two-year-old's throat. Lying there, I wondered if I had what it took to handle similar situations of the same or greater magnitude.

I grew up quietly and had it good; nothing unusual—a great childhood. I loved my parents then and I do now. I grew up with two younger sisters. I never hit them and they never hit me. I never saw my parents have an argument, but I did see them mad at each other once or twice. We were never really poor. I always had my own room and I never went to bed without a nice snack. We went on vacation every summer. I was never spanked or hit or left home alone or screwed by a weird uncle or baby-sitter. I have no skeletons in the closet or emotional scars or feelings of inadequacy stemming from my upbringing. I was never cut with a kitchen knife or cracked with a belt buckle or burned with a cigarette or whipped with an electrical cord. I was never locked in a closet. I was not born with a positive toxicology for cocaine. My parents were not alcoholic and didn't use drugs. As far as I could tell, neither did their friends. So who was I, the kid from the sticks, to pass judgment on the people I would visit over the next four years, saying, *You keep your kid, and you don't?* It seemed crazy. I wrestled to find a scrap of logic in the whole thing until my eyelids finally filled with cement. In the final seconds before nodding off I gave myself a break and accepted the fact that however ill-equipped, I was able to prevent a carving knife from plunging into a two-year-old's neck. So along with being a long and harrowing day, it had also been a good day—good enough for Ben and good enough for me. The rest didn't really make a difference.

4

I GOT FROM THE COZY MIDWEST to the lumpy bed on 108th Street after finishing college when a friend told me at a party that if I came to New York, I could stay with him for a month. At the time I had a degree, my car, a girlfriend, my family, lots of pals, and a pretty good stereo. I was feeling a little too comfortable and secure for my age and needed to go to a place where none of this mattered. New York seemed like a good place to strip naked, so I took my friend up on his offer and landed in Manhattan two weeks later to begin the one-month skinny-dip. Riding the bus into the city from the airport, I felt a squeeze in my throat as I began to realize how poorly equipped I was for the excursion—suffice to say I had brought too many white sweaters and not enough cool shoes.

My friend had a one-room studio on East Sixth Street between First and Second Avenues that he shared with a moody French modern dancer who could never shut up about the calluses on her feet. Unfortunately, my dear friend hadn't let his roommate know about my one-month stay and when he swung the door open and introduced me to her, she looked at him flatly and said with a thick French accent, "Why does this guy have two suitcases for?" I lived for that month in their studio, which was smaller than my old bedroom. Both of them were very busy modern dancing here and there so I was left alone every day from about ten to six. For the first two weeks it rained straight and I sat on the floor eating popcorn watching old *Dating Game* and *Hogan's Heroes* reruns on a tiny black-and-white television the dancer found on the street. Dark days and darker nights. I slept on the floor with the dancer's bike pedal on my shoulder and a banging radiator at my ear. Once as I walked out of the bathroom before going to sleep I saw a large rat cram itself into a hole in the wall next to my pillow. Because the place was so small, there was no way for me to completely lie down without my head becoming a welcome mat for Mr. Big and Stinky. So that I wouldn't suddenly wake up one evening with my lips chewed off, every night from then on I covered myself with crumpled Doritos bags, hoping I'd wake up if it rustled toward me.

I was terrified by the clamor of the city. The first day I went out, I walked about forty blocks before turning around exhausted. I waited at bus stops on the way back, but each time a bus arrived, it was so full of city faces that I'd turn away in a panic just before stepping on.

Tensions were running high between me and the dancer by the end of the month. Between my two big suitcases and my dirty popcorn pans, her bike pedal and her nightly sexual marathons with the men in her dance class, there wasn't much room for civility. There's nothing quite like pretending to be asleep with a bike pedal pressed against your neck while a frustrated French modern dancer has sex ten feet from your head.

By the time my one-month wild ride was over I couldn't stand New York. Still, I knew I hadn't yet tapped the city and I couldn't leave without getting at least a sip of it. Besides, the gag of fear was just beginning to loosen and I had already thrown out all my white sweaters. This was no time to leave.

By the end of my first year in New York, I had lived in nine different apartments.

5

MY FIRST JOB IN THE CITY was with a lavish home for re-tarded adults who had rich relatives with a lot of guilt. I was hired as a "counselor" whose duties also included toothbrush-ing, shaving, changing fouled sheets, and masturbation control. One of the first things I was told on my first day by my big orange-lipsticked supervisor was, "They all love to masturbate! If somebody starts up in the TV room, you just tap them on the shoulder and tell them to go to their room for a private time." After each forty-hour week, I took home two hundred dollars.

Six months after landing the job I was fired. The supervi-sory staff much preferred the "counselors" to brush teeth and shut up rather than discuss raising the level of care given. When I started to bring up novel ideas like "Let's change the menu once in a while" or "How about we stop using the television as an 'activity group,' " I was released from my duties. The supervisors who came to the residence twice a week were more interested in spending their two hours talking about "behav-ioral constructs" and "group conflict paradigms" than getting new mattresses or fixing toilets. I always felt that working lights and painted walls did a lot more for the folks than chocolate-chip tokens for not wetting the bed. After making these few observations, I was deemed "not good with supervision" and canned. I'm sure they'd have a different story.

I spent the first day after being fired in Washington Square Park feeling devastated and trying to figure out what was next. It was a glorious June day in the Village and I would turn twenty-three before the month was over. Six months ago I had landed in Manhattan for the first time. As I sat on a bench reflecting on that, it seemed like maybe it was time to chalk it all up and buy a plane ticket back to Wisconsin. When I think about that day, I can only really remember a single snapshot, as if the entire day held a singular event.

I'm sitting on a park bench looking at a fountain that has just been turned on for the summer. One mighty jet shoots skyward from the cement as children and their mothers play peek-a-boo in cascading fists of water. I sit alone until I'm joined by a barefooted, bare-chested man in overalls who sits on the other side of the bench. His eyes are glazed and he stares at me from some netherworld as his palms whap out a chaotic beat. I am trying to ignore the thumping drum solo telegraphing through the bench and up my back, when the man springs up in a full heavy metal jam. His hair makes dull whumps against his head as he jumps and shimmies from drum to invisible drum. Suddenly, he stops running and his dirty toes grip the cement. He bears down to a furious soundless beat. His arms flail, arcing madly in the spring day. People walk around him calmly. The fury is too much for his arms to bear alone and, slowly, his entire body begins to jump in skyward bursts.

On the fifth jump, a large knife pops out of his overalls and lands on the cement. The man continues to jump, beating sluggishly at the air. Two jumps later his right foot slams squarely on the blade, pushing the steel firmly into the center of his arch. He jumps two more times. The back of the blade sticking from his heel clinks on the concrete and he stops instantly with a little groan. With his shoulders humped forward, he stands for about twenty seconds as a pool of blood grows around his foot and spills away in tiny red rivers. He looks around, lost, and begins to walk aimlessly, bellowing with the anger of a badly shot animal. He doesn't limp. His right foot falls firmly with each step, sounding a dull clink and leaving a greasy red footprint behind. The blood is candy red against the cement in the bright sunshine. I stand up to approach the man but stop cold at the red puddle. Each greasy footprint is splashed in a sloppy trail leading to the man, who has finally slumped to his knees, fists clenched and shaking.

That was the day. I remember those red footprints. The only other thing I remember about the day was receiving a call from a friend about a job opening with the Bureau of Child Welfare in their Emergency Children's Services division. I didn't know what "Child Welfare" or "Children's Emergency whatever" meant, but I thanked her for thinking about me and told her I might check it out.

6

COUGHING AND SNIFFING, Henry Goodman looked at me across the tiny green metal desk. "I'm sorry. I have a terrible cold," he said. "I can't shake your hand." He wore a short-sleeved blue-and-green plaid shirt with a purple knit tie. He was in his late forties. He looked slightly overweight but he did have a cold, and a cold makes everyone look slightly overweight.

"This is a field job," he began. "You know that, right? Especially with Emergency Children's Services. If you're hired for this job, you're gonna do a lot of fieldwork. There's heavy client contact, all right?"

"All right," I said. "Sounds good." I didn't have any idea what he was talking about and I didn't ask. I was twenty-three.

"Well, just as long as you understand that." He was looking through my application. "Is Wisconsin nice?" he asked.

"Wisconsin is a great state," I answered.

"Yeah, we've got a lot of kids from Wisconsin in the office and we really like them," he said. "It must be a good place."

"There's other people from Wisconsin working here?"

"Yeah," he said. "I think about five. Really good kids."

That explains it, I thought. When I called about the job,

the woman who answered said there really weren't any openings. Disappointed, I asked if I could drop off a résumé for future consideration.

"Sure," the woman said. "You know you have to have a college degree to be considered for this job, you have a degree?"

"Yeah," I said. "A fresh one from Wisconsin."

"*Wisconsin?*" she said, surprised. "Well then, we'd better have a look at you."

I thought she was joking but she set up an appointment for me to meet Henry Goodman the next week. Up to this point, I hadn't met anyone in the city from dear Wisconsin. The thought of working with five other cheddar heads was just too much.

Henry Goodman blew his nose and swabbed it clean. "Sorry," he mumbled. "I hate a spring cold. I always get a cold in the spring, it's the worst, you know what I mean? The weather is just getting nice and everyone's going to the shore. Anyways..." He clumped up his hanky and stuffed it into his shirt pocket.

"All right," he said, handing me a blank sheet of paper, "I want you to describe me, and this room, and write it down on this paper."

"What do you mean?" I asked.

"I mean just describe my appearance—what I look like, and do the same thing with the room. Don't worry about details—don't go crazy or get wild or anything," he said, chuckling. "Just make simple accurate descriptions, nothing fancy."

He leaned back in his little chair like it was a big sofa and tried to look casual. I stared at the white paper and felt my palms start to sweat. I looked at Henry Goodman. He was staring silently at the empty white wall to his left. I was thinking, *What—do I say you're a stud and then I get the job?* I looked back to the paper. I wanted to write *Well it sure is quiet right now, and I think it's getting hotter.*

He took his eyes from the wall and looked at me. "Some people really go crazy with this. Just keep it simple. Describe me and the room." He returned his eyes to the wall. Keeping descriptions simple was always difficult for me, but I did my best.

I am sitting in a white room approximately ten by fifteen feet with a drop ceiling and one neon light. There is a window on the south wall. My interviewer is a white male in his forties, about 5'8", 190 lbs. with short brown hair, glasses, and a mustache. He has a terrible cold.

I handed him the paper. He pushed his glasses up his nose, snuffling and coughing as he read. He burst out with a short laugh. " 'Window on the south wall,' you Wisconsin people kill me—moss on the wall so it's south, right?" He laughed again. "My grandfather always knew north, south, east, west —wherever he went. I could never do that. South wall, that's great."

"It's the north side that has the moss," I said.

"Right, right, no shade—no moss, right? That's the way it goes, right?" he said still laughing.

"No shade—no moss," I said.

"That's great," he said, shaking his head and wiping his nose. "I hate the woods. Okay, so anyways the training for this first batch of hiring starts next week. We've already submitted our hires but I think I could get you in if you could make it. It's two weeks of nine to five and then you're here four to midnight with the standard two days off. It's twenty-four thousand a year with benefits."

"What do I exactly do from four to midnight?"

"Well, sometimes not much," he said. "Other times you'll be running. We're mandated by the state to investigate allegations of child abuse in the five boroughs during the hours the daytime field offices are closed. We get cases called in by doctors, neighbors, teachers, police, relatives, even the kids themselves—just about anybody. They're prioritized in the office and the emergencies are handled by our caseworkers who usually go to the field to basically make sure the reported children are okay...oh, and if they're not okay, you remove them. They'll explain all this in the training."

"People let you into their homes?"

"They have to let you in," he said. "And once you're in, you do whatever you need to do. The people let you—they have to."

"But how come they let you?" I asked.

"Look," he said. "They just let you, okay? They have to. It's not Wisconsin here. People are used to the intrusion; agencies are walking on these people all day, you just do the same thing in the middle of the night. Don't worry, they'll tell you all about it in training. So, you think you're up to it?"

"I think so."

"You ever been investigated for child abuse in any state?"

"Nope."

"Have you ever been arrested?"

"Nope."

"Can you make next week's training?"

"...Uh, yes, I can," I said.

"Then we'll see you in two weeks."

We stood up and he walked me to the door. We stepped out of his office and he shouted to some people toward the back, "Hey look, another one from Wisconsin!—tellin' me I got a window on the 'south wall'—can you believe it?!" He looked back to me as I was leaving with a wide grin. "Welcome to Child Welfare."

And he shook my hand.

7

EVERY JOB HAS ITS TRAINING PERIOD and, more often than not, that period lacks any resemblance to what you actually end up doing. The training for ECS was no different. I don't fault the city for what its training covered but for what it failed to cover. There were two weeks of solemn discussions on child protective issues, but little on getting a drug dealer to let you into an abandoned building or talking a restless police officer into sticking around until you get through with a case and back to your car.

If I had two weeks to prepare a group of folks to enter the world of child protection (no easy task), I'd start by telling them that mastering the art of good casework is a little like staring into the shuttering eyes of a rabid canine and saying "nice doggie" until you find a shotgun. Then I'd leave them with a favorite office tenet—If ya ain't scared, ya ain't workin'.

Sitting around a large table at the training center, fifteen of us exchanged jolly first-day-on-the-job good mornings with wide eyes and wider smiles. Twelve black, three white, eleven women, four men. The head trainer, Zoey Nichols, introduced herself and we went around the table sharing our expectations about the job and which office we were assigned to. Zoey smiled with eyebrows raised and nodded around the whole table. It was an enthusiastic group. The smiles would start to droop around the second day with discussions about things like doughnut burns (indicates child's buttocks were forcibly held down in a tub of hot liquid) and gum lacerations (indicates force feedings). Two weeks later, there would be only eleven to say good morning to.

Zoey gave us our introduction: "Child protective workers carry a charge from society to ensure the life and safety of children who have been reported as abused or neglected by their parents or caretakers. When life-endangering circumstances are suspected, the child protective worker often encounters very complex and troubled family environments which require great sensitivity to the elements of crisis and the torn fabric of relationships that may at any time turn to desperation and violence. The job of the worker is characterized by contradictions of role: the task requires an investigator as practiced as a policeman, and a social worker as skilled as a crisis therapist. The goal of the worker is split between assessing the current risk to the child and the longer-term threats of the final destruction of the family."

And so it went.

She forgot to add the fact that we'd all be threatened with our lives at some point, one of us would probably be punched in the first year, and most of us would gain between five and fifteen pounds.

During the introduction, Zoey walked among us distributing slips of paper. When she finished she returned to the front of the room.

"I've given you these slips of paper and I want you to jot down some of the basic questions and concerns you have about becoming a child protective worker. On the back of the paper, I'd like you to write one thing you're excited about."

After a moment of silence, we all began scratching busily on our paper. For my concern about becoming a child protective worker I wrote about wondering how to get people to let you into their homes. I still hadn't figured that one out and so far no one was telling me. I turned the paper over and tried to think of something I was excited about. I was being paid. That was exciting. I was being paid as I sat there. Before the job with the retarded folks, I'd worked since sophomore year in high school—all manual labor, all minimum wage. Here I hadn't lifted a thing and my hands weren't dirty. I had finished two cups of coffee, talked all morning, and was being *paid*. That was exciting. I didn't write that down. Instead I wrote

some save-the-world thing about being excited to direct hu-
manity toward a constructive course to blahblahblah-rid-
society-of-a-poison-blahblahblah—something I could jabber on
about with conviction and a thump on the table. I was good
at conviction when I was twenty-three. My time with Child
Welfare was a rocket ride into a world of grays. Before I was
hired, I had seen nothing and knew it all, by the time I quit, I
felt like I had seen it all and knew nothing.

After gallons of coffee and smiles with Zoey, we were given
small certificates on thick paper "suitable to hang in your office," according to the man who came to bestow them upon
us. *What is this guy's real job?* I thought as he handed the
papers out proudly. Whatever his function was, it hadn't taken
him into a Child Welfare office for quite some time. He gave
himself away with the "hang this in your office" bit. There
were no offices at ECS, there were desks—they belonged to you
during the shift and to someone else when you clocked out.
Following his suggestion would've meant thumbtacking the
forehead of the nearest coworker. With the training ended, we
exchanged congratulations and shared cake and more coffee.
Zoey lathered us with good-byes and good-lucks and scattered
us like dandelion fluff to land where we may.

Armed with the two-week training, I was off to spend the
next four years playing the rescuer to scared kids in the middle
of the night—the ones who revealed their cuts and bruises and
whispered about the adult in the next room—the ones in emergency rooms who pushed back tears while pointing to the penis
of an anatomically correct doll and nodding. I walked out of
the training center with my certificate folded in my back
pocket, still wondering how on earth I'd get people to let me
into their homes. In a little over two months I'd be begging a
knife off a two-year-old's throat and feeling the first gusts of
panic over what I'd gotten myself into. I still wouldn't really
know how I'd gotten people to let me into their homes, but
after the encounter with Sean and Ben as well as other hammer

blows of the same magnitude, the question would become less important.

Shortly after being hired by ECS, I had found my first real home in New York City. It was on 108th Street and Amsterdam Avenue, just south of Spanish Harlem on the Upper West Side of Manhattan. The apartment was on the fifth floor of a sometimes elevator building on a street that had been left to drug addicts, welfare moms, and young white kids looking to get experienced. My buddy James got the apartment a year before my arrival in the city and promptly filled it with Wisconsin orphans who needed a roof over their heads and a phone to call home. The apartment was cheap because it was rent-controlled and the last tenant had lived there for ages. After a long life the tenant died, his apartment was put on the block, and James moved in. Before renting the apartment, the landlord had the goodness in his heart to have the body removed, but that was about all. The man had few possessions but left behind a clothes closet that could've belonged to William S. Burroughs: rich black and brown wool suits and old derbies which were worn gratefully by all of us and were always referred to as the "dead guy clothes." I lived on 108th through most of my time at ECS. There were six of us for the most part, although at various times, up to ten shared its four rooms and kitchen connected by a long hallway.

The room I shared with James was moderately sized and uncluttered—one dresser, two futons, two fake zebra suitcases, and a huge old television with the tube missing. The walls were painted marine blue and covered with crudely drawn smiling piranhas which circled the room. The back wall was almost entirely covered with a large drawing of a man being eaten alive. Piranhas surrounded him in a feeding frenzy of tiny jaws and big teeth. The man's eyes were wild and panicked. His muscular arms and torso were jagged with bite marks and his legs were decorated with a few piranhas that hadn't yet let go.

Each night before I went to sleep, the sight of him mixed with the sounds of drug deals and turf wars churning up from the street below. I'd stare at the man, listen to a fight or two, and drift into sleep.

Mornings at 108th Street started around ten-thirty and lasted into the early afternoon. About two blocks from our building was a Hungarian coffee shop where, for the price of one cup of coffee, you could drink an entire pot. It was a marvelously casual place with full-length windows opening onto the sidewalk and sometimes decent, but always interesting, art on the walls. Across the street was the majestic but eternally unfinished Cathedral Church of St. John the Divine. Sooner or later, after tossing on some dead guy clothes, we'd all end up there, spread out among several tables, sharing sections of the *Times* or trying through a hangover to put together the events of the previous night until our knees were all bouncing with caffeine. Occasionally someone would speak up about something in the paper and we'd all hammer on about it with reverent yammering until all opinions were hung out to dry at least twice.

I was the only one with a steady income. The others got by on various odd jobs, money from home, and occasional waiter shifts or acting jobs. This didn't pose any real problem as our building was on a rent strike and had been for the past year. Two other buildings on the block were doing the same. Large white sheets were hung permanently from fire escapes declaring in red spray paint, RENT STRIKE—UNIFY AND SMASH OPPRESSION as well as other various good feelings like RAT INFESTED and NO HOT WATER, BUILDING SUCKS, LANDLORD SUCKS. Our building was of the "rat infested" and "landlord sucks" persuasion.

I think a lot of folks don't actually believe the fact that people live with colonies of rats in their walls, that it's not uncommon to see the fat little titans trundling casually from bathrooms to kitchens to bedrooms, that for some, day-to-day living is peppered with the sound of *gnawing*. Well I'm here to tell you, rats aren't just for gutters anymore. The rats at 108th crawled on our counters and died in our laundry piles; they lived in our shoes and drowned in our toilet. Hearing them in the walls was not so comforting, either. Mice seem to fit so nicely in the small spaces between apartment walls and floors, but rats are a whole different animal. Before going to bed on many nights I could hear them falling and bumping across wall supports like small herds of migrating caribou. At first the rats at 108th weren't any big hairy deal, so to speak. It got bad over time, however. Really bad, as a matter of fact. Nothing short of god-awful, to be exact.

Late October now. Light flakes of snow have already twirled like ashes through the tall buildings of lower Manhattan and I'm excited to begin my first winter in New York. The job still feels crazy but it's slowly becoming somehow familiar. I'm not comfortable yet, but I do know everyone's name and I've got a desk drawer to lock a pen in. I've joined in the camaraderie and have learned for the most part to roll with the rhythm of conversations that would've tripped me up a few months earlier. I've eaten my first fried pork rind.

So this is Emergency Children's Services. A pale gray film covers everything in the office—people included. It's hard to tell if the dinge is caused by the bath of inadequate neon lighting or the fallout from secretly smoked cigarettes smoldering in every other closed desk drawer. The four-to-twelve shift is ready to hand the guns to the next tour. I've spent the night in-house on phone cases. Everything's finished up and the shift is winding down. I've called my friends at a nearby bar to tell them I'll be there shortly, and not to tire out the bartender before I get there. People are returning from an evening in the field. The ones with smiles are carrying bags of soul food from favorite Brooklyn restaurants, the ones without are carrying bundles of dirty children. One of my favorite people in the office, William Samuels, is just punching in. He's had a wild night in the field and he's a little out of his tree about it. Not one to suffer in silence, Willie fills us in on the demon he danced with in a dark Brooklyn hallway. All is crazy and all is calm, and it's just another night on the job.

2

The Zombie Place

It's very nice to feel you're nothing.
You're just nothing when you're near a volcano.

—Katia Krafft

WILLIAM SAMUELS PUNCHED IN from his field visit jacked out
of his mind on adrenaline. His fingers jammed the time card
into the clock which thunk-whumped in a sort of high five as
William yipped and reached for a second card. He always
punched in and out twice even though this was one of the few
cardinal sins in the agency that could land your rear promptly
on the sidewalk without a two-week notice. William Samuels
didn't much care about that, it seemed. He said his card was
lost once in the timekeeper's office and he didn't get paid until
he gave up his left nut. The second card was his "backup," as
he called it. Willie was one of the first people in the office to
introduce himself to me, and our desks ended up being side by
side. He described himself as the office's one and only Hispanic-

American, half-blooded Cherokee and Seminole ordained preacher of the one and true Lord Jesus Christ. He was wiry as all hell with big hair, black weasel eyes, a goatee, and sweaty fingers. I'd guess he was either a fifty-five-year-old who looked thirty-five or vice versa. I couldn't tell. For Willie, working at ECS was just paying the landlord. What he really did, what he *really* was, was a doo-wop singer. Tenor. He said he had his own AM radio show out of the South Bronx called "Jesus Is." He'd hand out fliers with information on show dates. I'd frequently tune in, but I could never find the station. I always wondered if "Jesus Is" ever really made it out of Will's mind and onto the airwaves. I always wondered, but never to his face. This was a man who could get intense, if you know what I mean. Not the kind of gas can you wanted to light matches around.

Thunk-whump. The second card slammed into the clock and William howled. No more than a few people glanced up from their desks as it wasn't unusual for Willie Samuels to howl.

"I papped that sucker with the buck. Jabbed that poppy in the shoulder—pam pam," he said as he whipped out a buck knife from the back pocket of his tan slacks, opened its rust-spotted seven inches, and turned the handle around so the blade pointed down from his palm.

"Gotta back up on a pit—them suckers, gotta back-a-lack my brother—then PAM—jab that sucker in the shoulder—shanked that poppy. You gotta shank a pit." Willie looked straight at me with crazed glee in his eyes.

His field partner, Yvette, was just punching in behind him. Calm as could be, she announced, "Willie stabbed a pit bull."

A supervisor popped out from one of the cubicles surrounding the perimeter of the office. "Did you visit the case?!"

"Are you crazy?" Yvette cocked her head back. "We got the fuck out of there."

Outraged, the supervisor shouted across the office, *"You didn't visit the case??"*

Yvette proceeded to her desk without pausing. "You go visit that fucking case. He stabbed that man's dog. I'm not crazy."

Willie Samuels was making careful steps backward, glancing over his right shoulder, the knife sticking from his right hand. "We got to the address. It was on the fifth floor, all the way down the hall—and that shit *stunk*, man, that was one smelly motherfucker." He stopped moving and continued, "I saw this white pit at the end of the hall—told Yvette to step down 'cause them shits don't bark. It was lookin' right at me, man, and I knew it was comin' for me. I shouted to the man behind the door, 'Call off your dog, man.' I told that brother, told him to call his shit. I told him twice I ain't gonna deal with this pony, but that brother didn't say shit. I pulled out my buck slow behind my back and the dog started trotting down the hall for me. Fucker wasn't even growling but them shits don't say nothing when they're coming for you. I crouched down—can't run from a pit—I just turned my back to him and hunched down, he was comin' straight for me. When he got to me I stepped back into him and gave him a backhand with Mr. Buck. *Pam.* Jabbed my man square in the shoulder and that fucker jumped up and started yellin' "—Willie whooped like a stuck dog, laughed and high-fived a few of the boys in the back—"I sent that white pony back to my man with a red fuckin' badge. That shit was bleeding."

"You can't just turn around and not visit the case without calling me—I don't care what happened," the supervisor screamed at Yvette. "I don't care *what* happened. You better hope nothing happened to the kids on that case."

"You better hope nothing happens to the next people who go out there," Yvette said plainly. "That man with the dog was pissed."

Willie continued slapping hands with his pals in the back of the office as he put the knife away. "Doing the fuckin' *can-can* back to my man drippin' shit the whole way. I don't mess around with no pit bull. I don't play that. Right?—I *dignified* the fucker. The shit was stupid."

"*I want you to call 911 on the case* NOW *and come into my office* NOW," the supervisor shouted to Yvette.

William continued to recount his story to the group in the back who gave sporadic cheers of "you got it, brother" through mouthfuls of fried pork rinds and orange soda.

Ten o'clock.

Yvette quietly called 911. I heard her telling the operator about dog blood in the hallway. Another night at ECS.

About the same time on East Tremont in the Bronx, young Raphael stood in his small bedroom stoned with fear. His younger Cousin Tony had stopped moving about a minute ago, but blood continued to drip from his nose and ears. His youngest cousin, Little Davey, was in the corner lying on his side crying, the kind of soft rasping cry that comes after a whole lot of screaming. Raphael's mind was hazing over. The events of the last hour were dimming, but the fear remained like a spotlight. And there was that blood. There was just so much blood coming out of Cousin Tony—*coming out of his ears.* Fat lips and black eyes were nothing new, but bloody *ears,* good Christ. Raphael's body stiffened as fear poured over his shoulders and down the backs of his arms. Little Davey in the corner was puffing up badly. Two purple lines were drawing themselves down the sides of his nose. Dark blue streaks zigzagged across his back and chest. Raphael felt a tightness in his throat that he choked back with a loud *hup,* startling Little Davey into quick silence. Then, with clenched shoulders, clenched stomach, with his clenched fists, with everything clenched, Raphael walked to the phone and dialed 911.

2

AT TEN-THIRTY OUR ELDEST CASEWORKER, the white-haired spitfire Wilda Hidalgo, was on the phone two desks down shouting at the perpetrator on her case. The guy was at the Twenty-eighth Precinct and about to be incarcerated for screwing his twelve-year-old daughter. Wilda Hidalgo was a veteran relic of Child Welfare, usually flying around the office with three reports in her hand and trailing a small hurricane. Tonight she sat on the phone with Chee·tos-colored fingers waving in the air, giving all hell. "Jou are a *scum* guy . . . listen to me fella . . . no—*jou* listen to *me* fella . . . jou are not fooling nobody, I am taking de chi—. . . jou are a sick—. . . jou call yourself e man?? . . . Eh?? You sick guy? . . . I'm taking de child . . . I AM TAKING DE CHILD."

She put the receiver on her desk. "I don *baleeve* dis people." She put the guy on the speakerphone and his tinny voice distorted as he screamed his defense. Wilda looked blankly around the office as the shouting little voice in her phone grew in its fervor. Heated phone exchanges were not unusual at ECS, but Wilda always felt a need to hit the speaker and broadcast the shouting across the office. It was like she needed a witness to back her up before she started ripping a head off. There were times when the office was empty that I'd hear a screaming barrage out of the blue and stand up looking over partitions to see Wilda just staring at the phone.

"Dis fella is a cherk," she said, gazing at the phone for a moment while an entire Family Court hearing ran through her mind at light speed. She'd heard the arguments (or as many as she cared to), and after a nanosecond of deliberation, reached a guilty verdict. Guilty that night, anyways; guilty enough to take a child. Guilty enough to hang a family.

She turned off the speaker and picked up the receiver. "I am taking dis child from jou because jou are a scum guy." She slammed the receiver down and shouted into the air, "Dis guy is a real scum. Somebody get me a car; I am going to take de child."

I had spent the entire evening as one of six people comprising the in-house crew. We handled all cases not requiring a field visit. It'd been a slow night. I handled three positive tox cases. They were almost always called in by hospital social workers when toxicology tests done on newborns came back positive for drugs—usually cocaine. The office got five to eight of these a night, and handling them was a little like pulling weeds: a call to mom to ask how come she'd given birth to a little junkie, followed by a notification that the newborn would be held in the hospital pending follow-up by the field office. Moms would generally say, "I used drugs, I was stupid, I'll never do it again" or "I don't use drugs—someone must've slipped it in my cigarette" (lots of those) or "I use drugs. Take my damn kid, you've got all my others." We'd document the response to the allegations, sign off on the case, and send it out to a field office for follow-up.

I'd chosen to be the in-house person because it was my supervisor's birthday and I wanted to enjoy the party the unit was throwing for her. I received my last case of the night as I finished a reheated square of killer homemade mac 'n' cheese. The party had been so-so but the food was great. Everyone had chipped in five dollars toward a blue porcelain unicorn, which was received by the supervisor with a few too many "it's wonderful"'s and "you shouldn't have"'s. I think she hated it. We ate lavishly and by the time the night was out, all the phones smelled of collard greens and baby-back-rib sauce. The birthday cake was a giant pink penis from an erotic bakery, which the supervisor devoured with a small plastic knife. She snickered a little too intensely as she cut the testicle portion off, and I suddenly felt like I knew a lot more about her than I cared to. It was your average tacky workplace party, the only difference being the peripheral phone conversations about the blood and bones of New York City's latest tiny victims.

At 10:45 the supervisor plopped a case in front of my mac 'n' cheese. "Sorry, Marc, you gotta go out on this case with Jerry. It's his case so it'll be easy. You'll just be going for the ride. Thanks again for the unicorn—it's wonderful, you really shouldn't have."

I grabbed a coat and put my things along with what was left of my mac 'n' cheese in my locker. I went to get a car, passing Jerry as I did. Jerry was a thirty-something Caribbean man, always quick with a wise-guy smile and a bit of patois. Whenever we'd go to the field together, he'd wait until we were thirty miles out in some godforsaken street and start to speak to me in complete patois, or "Island French" as he called it. Jerry's patois always sounded like the most joyful language on earth. I couldn't understand a word of it, but Jerry would carry on until I joined in with my best patois inflections. We'd carry on for a few blocks like a couple of fools until we were both in tears. Sometimes, when I'd find myself speaking fake patois in the middle of the night tooling through the burned-out East Bronx, Wisconsin seemed far away and life's course seemed strange.

I told Jerry I'd get the car. He slammed his fist on his desk and stood up shouting to his supervisor, "I gotta go out with *Parent??!!* Oh no. *No,* man. I am not going out with this guy. He is a real nut, this guy." His eyes were serious but the curl on the edge of his lip was giving him away. He hit his desk again, shouting at the cubicle his supervisor was in, "No, man . . . no way, man. Have you ever been to the field with this guy?"—he gave me a quick wink—"You take your life in your hands, man, you take your damn life in your hands. This is no joking. You don't know till you go out with him—he's crazy, man." When we were sent out together, Jerry threw the mock tirade with a conviction that made it funny every time.

"I'm supposed to get off in an hour, Jerry," I said, joking. "You'll have me back in an hour, right?"

"I'll get you back by the weekend," he said, still very "pissed off." "Now get the car before I quit this damn job."

It was coming to the end of the shift and almost all of the cars were in. I was able to sign out the coveted car #495, the nice one, the one that didn't stink like a dusty thrift store. I walked back past Jerry.

"What car you get, boss?" he shouted up.

"495, big man," I said, flashing the keys. He looked at me for a moment overly amazed, stood up, and shouted to the office again, banging his desk very seriously, "I *only* go out with this guy, he is *the boss*. This guy knows the right *people*, man. I *only* go out with him, now on. That's it, man."

He turned with a smile and headed for the computers to run clearances. There were two computers at ECS; both very plain with green stick letters on a black screen. These things were on perpetually, dusty screens glowing green in a manner so unwavering it bordered on tenacity. The very ones I used are probably on right now. They worked like soldiers, but they weren't pretty. The keyboards were splashed with stains from every food group. Letters used most often were clean and worn smooth, their keys yielded to imperceptible pressure. The ones used less frequently—the x, the tab, the symbols—were almost completely obscured with the grime of the office and they pressed like the keys of a poorly maintained antique. We all had a personal password to log in to the mainframe. It was the agency's way of keeping track of each worker's computer activity. New passwords were assigned every few months, but there was usually a working one scrawled somewhere on the keyboard that everyone would use instead of their own.

I went back to my desk and waited for Jerry to finish up.

I sat down to look at a copy of the case and was punched in the face. I began to read the contents but all that really mattered were the words "probable fatality."

"This is gonna be a fatality." I ran the case to my supervisor. "Hey, this is a probable fatality. You're sending me out on a case like this at eleven o'clock?!! This is gonna take all night."

"Sorry, Marc," my supervisor said through a mouthful of penis cake. "Everyone else in the unit went out tonight, you were the in-house per—"

"I know, I know I was the in-house person, but it's eleven. This is going to take *all night*. A midnight person will be walking in any second—I've been out till four A.M. two nights this week already. I'm gonna have more overtime than straight time on this check."

"We can't wait for a midnight person, Marc," she said. "And you're next for a field visit."

"You don't wanna go out with me, Marc?" Jerry was feigning sorrowful rejection across the office from his desk. "What've you got against me, boss? What'd I do to you?"

"No c'mon, really, Jerry," I shouted back, "I've been out late too many times the past couple weeks. Some people around here punch out at midnight every night."

"But *you* get the satisfaction of knowing you do such a *good job,* man." The curl in his lip wasn't so charming at the moment.

"C'mon, Jerry," I said. "You know what I'm saying. Knock it off."

"I'm hurt, man. I am really hurt. You can really hurt a guy, man. Okay, listen—you go with me, I buy you a...I buy you a jumbo ice cream, man."

"C'mon, Jerry—knock it off." I looked down at my supervisor, who was starting in again on the cake.

"You get a car yet?" she asked, looking up.

"I got a car," I said, turning and walking back to my desk.

"See if you can get 495," she shouted. "I bet it's in!"

"I got 495," I said.

I sat down to read the case and could hear Jerry in the front shouting to me, "A super jumbo ice cream, man. This is no joke—any damn flavor!"

> Tony Melendez 5 yrs old on line 03 is in a coma at Jacobi Hospital and is expected to be a probable fatality. Child was covered with bruises and numerous fractures. His 4 yr old brother David on line 04 is also covered with bruises but does not require hospitalization. It appears both children were beaten. The mother, the 4 yr old child, the aunt, and her 9 yr old child Raphael are at the 125th Pct. with Bronx Detectives. Raphael was not injured.

3

JERRY AND I STEPPED OUT OF THE OFFICE, it was medium-coat weather, slowly changing to heavy-jacket. The wind was kicking up, turning the night's trash into a *Fantasia* animation. Newspapers and plastic bags roamed down the street, occasionally launching up to second-story height for a peek. An aluminum take-out container rolled past us on its side, clicking against the cobblestones as it raced up the street. It made me think of the way animals rush for the safety of cover as a storm rolls in.

Back in Wisconsin, Duaney Schultz and Randy Weigel would always grab a gun and a dog and head for the woods as a storm came on. They said the meat of a raccoon was sweeter if it was shot running from a storm. I remember following them once when they got one. The rain started as they were gutting it, and by the time the hot downpour hit, the carcass was hanging from sticks in the front yard with its tail lopped off and already forgotten in Duaney's dresser drawer. After a lazy few hours of laughs and Jolly-Good soda, I left for home, passing the hanging coon as I did. The heavy clouds had turned the afternoon into a twilight at the far end of Duaney's very large, very unkempt lawn. I stood before the raccoon with warm rain running down my cheeks. The body was propped up and stretched wide open with sticks, its arms contorted skyward hallelujah. Rain dripped from the sides of the slashed belly as I leaned forward for a closer look. I was alone so I could gaze without the fear of giving myself away to Duaney and Randy who'd laugh long and loud at a boy who hadn't seen at least a hundred split-open raccoons. Inches from my face, the body opened before me like a darkly inviting flesh tent. With the intense unthinking drive of curious childhood, I crouched down and leaned forward until my head was completely surrounded by the insides of the carcass. My knees pushed into the muddy ground, and as I straightened up into the body, a dull sweet smell pulled through my nose like an old flannel sheet. My breath echoed around my head, turning the air hot and damp. Muffled rolling of thunder crept through my ears as I drew in my deepest breath and let out a long meaningless scream. It resonated up the animal's shoulders and back to my ears with a hollow wet sound. A soaking scream. Head wrapped in a coon and woozy with rain, the sound of my voice sunk into the carcass and hummed through the wet fur in a meat scream. Caught in an intoxicating web of irrational momentum, I bit down into the greasy flesh walls. With my jaws locked tight, a memory flickered in my head of a time when I bit a boy who held my face in a puddle. My dad found out and was as mad as I ever saw him get. He took the kid to the hospital for a tetanus shot. That kid never bothered me again. I relaxed my jaws, spitting red foam down my chin as I slowly backed out of the animal with a bland gut taste on my teeth. Through the soaking rain, I looked up at the raccoon, whose dripping head was craned skyward. One eye was open and looking a little too far sideways. The other eye was a slit peering straight into the dark sky, begging for a hot Wisconsin twister to turn it loose from its tangle of sticks to soar with spinning barn doors. I walked home and soon forgot about the day, but I never did forget that meat scream.

"You driving or riding?" Jerry asked as we approached the car.

"Riding, if you don't mind."

"Sure thing, boss—no problem," he said, and I flipped him the keys. We got in the car and headed uptown, stopping at a deli first to get two large coffees. Double-parked on Sixth Avenue (you could double-park in the mayor's bathroom in these cars), I ripped sipping holes in the lids while Jerry looked for a good station on the radio. Car #495 had a radio.

"K-Rock okay with you, boss?" Jerry asked fidgeting the dial.

"Yeah, K-Rock's good."

"You're a rock-and-roller kind of guy. I can see you are a rocker, man," he said. "Me? I'll take the jazz. Just give me the smooth jazz and I'm all right—"

"Jazz is good, too—old jazz."

"That's okay, man," Jerry said. "Tonight we rock on. Rock and roll, man."

"Really, Jerry, jazz is fine—find a jazz station."

"No, no, I insist. We rock and roll all the way up. Maybe on the way down, if you are a nice guy, I find you the good stuff. When it's late, you can really find the good stuff. The old jazz, man."

He snapped the car in gear and we barreled up the FDR with the Velvet Underground droning on about what Lisa says. Crossing the Willis Avenue Bridge into the Bronx, Bob Seger was telling how the night moves. Tell it Bob. Tell me how the night moves. It was already one o'clock. Jerry and I hadn't said much on the ride up. It often went that way especially when going into a really terrible case. You never get used to a bruised and broken five-year-old corpse no matter how many you've seen. The drive to a case like this was a silent meditation. A time to put on the hip boots for the smelly black mud ahead.

The car rattled over the metal grid of the bridge as we entered the prime-time underworld. I wish I could say the Bronx is just a delightful place, I wish I could say the Bronx has gotten a bad rap—I love it when things aren't as they seem. Unfortunately, most everything you've probably ever heard about that dreary acreage is true. There are undoubtedly some wonderful places in the Bronx. I've never been to them.

The stoplight just over the bridge serves as an unofficial customs station where the local unofficial directors of cultural affairs can make unofficial searches of foreign vehicles, if you know what I mean. A group of men inspected our car from the corner as we slowed to a stop. I used to feel a little like a hotshot in a city car, especially in car #495, especially with Bob Seger blaring out of the windows, but now that I think back on it, the boys on the corner probably figured we were with sanitation. Sanitation drove the same cars as ECS and they *all* looked as good as #495. At any rate, the car afforded us safe passage through customs that night—the light turned green and we rolled through with nothing more than suspicious glances.

4

THE 125TH PRECINCT sat like a green-eyed beast, its mouth open to the street, pouring out men in blue twenty-four hours, seven days. Jerry and I walked inside and to the front desk. They were expecting us. Before we could utter a word, the desk sergeant looked at us and said, "Upstairs, guys. Second door right. They're expecting you." We hadn't even said who we were. A black guy and a white guy in the middle of the night without guns driving a sanitation vehicle—gotta be Child Welfare. Maybe the clipboards gave us away.

We walked upstairs and into the Detective Unit where we were met by a police assistant and escorted to another door that led into the offices where the guys were with the two mothers and the children. The room was just big enough to hold the eight cluttered desks that took up most of the space. The walls were covered with an office plaid of mug shots and district maps. Fluorescent light bathed the air a jittery pale green. Ms. Carr and her sister Ms. Melendez sat on small wood chairs near the door. Ms. Melendez's child David sat next to her staring at the ceiling. He was wearing some baggy light-green underwear. His face was badly bruised. Raphael sat by himself a few seats down. They all looked like they had been there a long time. Five detectives relaxed in various positions at their desks. They all had colds and they were all eating hard-boiled eggs. Detective Borrero sat toward the back with his feet up on the desk. He was a large man in his forties with a full head of salt-and-pepper and a small mustache. When we stepped in, he sat up, wiped the egg off his hands, and walked over to meet us. We exchanged hellos with the guys and were then introduced to the family. Borrero walked past each one, pointing to them as they were identified. "Ms. Carr, mother of Raphael. Ms. Melendez, speaks Spanish only, mother of Tony and David. Tony, of course, is in the coma at Jacobi. David here looks like he caught a piece of the same arm but he's all right. He was checked out and cleared at the hospital. His mom says he can talk a little, but we haven't heard a peep out of him, won't say a word—course, someone *did* beat the shit out of him. That down there is Raphael. He wasn't beaten, probably got away. Good little guy but pretty quiet, too."

He looked over to Ms. Carr and pointed to me and Jerry. "You see these two guys? They're with the city. Child Welfare. They came here because they're gonna take your kids if we don't figure out what happened tonight. They're gonna *take* your kids, and you won't see them for a *long time*. Maybe never." He looked over to us. "Right?" There was a pause as

Jerry and I stared back. He turned to the mothers. "And there's not a thing I can do about it. You think about that while I speak with these gentlemen. *Try to jog your memory.*" He looked at me and Jerry with his hands out in mock disbelief. "Nobody knows what happened here tonight. One kid in a coma and this one here like a punching bag"—he looked straight at the mothers—"*AND NOBODY KNOWS WHAT HAPPENED.*"

We hadn't even taken off our coats yet.

Detective Borrero took us to the back of the office to fill us in on what they knew so far while the other guys made phone calls and peeled eggs. He sat at his desk and we pulled seats around him.

"Hard-boiled egg?" Borrero asked.

"I'm okay, thanks," Jerry said.

"Well," Borrero said, indicating his top drawer, "you know where they are if you get hungry later." Shuffling through the papers on his desk, he continued, "This shit kills me," he said. "I don't know how you guys do it. With kids, I mean. It's like, I see guys busted up every day—these guys they come in here and they look like shit. Really, but *kids*... that's tough to take. I don't know how you guys do it. I mean, did you look at that David kid's face? And his little body? It's like... *I* got kids, right, *I* got a little guy and I look at that kid there, and I just wanna break someone in half. I don't care if it *is* the mother—I just want to nail whoever did that to that kid... Anyways. You guys gotta hear that all the time, right? But it's true. I don't know how you do it... You guys don't have kids, do you? Maybe that's it. You got kids?" he asked me.

"Nope, not today," I said.

"I got two kids," Jerry said cheerfully, and he took out his wallet and handed a picture to Borrero, who smiled and turned a frame sitting on his desk to face us. It was a picture of him with his two girls and his "little guy."

"Hey," Jerry said with a big grin, "you don't look so bad in the daytime."

"Well, I have been called handsome by a few," Borrero said, handing Jerry's picture back.

"By a very few," one of the guys on the phone chimed in.

Borrero looked up. "Well, why don't you just hang up and join us as long as you're so busy over there."

"I'm on hold," the guy shouted back.

"Micky's on the phone with the hospital. See, if this kid slips out of his coma and dies, we got a whole different cup of noodles here. If he dies," Borrero said, taking a gulp of coffee, "—cold—If he *dies,* see, then he wasn't just beat up. If he dies, then somebody killed him. And if somebody killed him, if one of these ladies killed him, or if they're protecting the person or persons who *murdered* this kid— . . . see? Right now we're not investigating a murder. If somebody killed this kid, it's gonna get hot in here."

There were already too many greasy foreheads and beaded upper lips for my taste.

"Okay, here's the deal," he said as Jerry pulled out a legal pad to start his notes. "We spoke to Ms. Carr and—Melendez is Spanish only, did I tell you guys that?—All right, according to Carr, the apartment belongs to her and her son, Raphael. They've lived there alone for the past three years after she was separated from the kid's father whom she was never married to. Raphael is her only child. She says she is completely cut off from the father although she has heard from friends he's in Puerto Rico.

"Okay. A year ago, her sister, Ms. Melendez there, comes to America as an illegal with her two children and lives with Carr and Raphael in their apartment. Carr gets Melendez a job off the books at the restaurant she works at and everything is just great."

Borrero picked up his mug and slogged back another gulp of cold coffee. His face puckered and he looked around. "Hey someone make up a pot of coffee, I'm killing myself with this."

He set the mug down, reached into his drawer, and pulled out a round white egg. "At any rate," he said, tapping it against the desk, "it all comes down to this: I ask these ladies very simply, 'What happened to Tony and Little Davey?' and every time they say they don't know. *They don't know.* Their own kids. *Beat to shit.* They were out, they say. They were out working. No sign of forced entry. Mom doesn't have any bad debts or enemies. The kids were alone and someone just waltzed in and beat the shit out of them for no reason. 'What did the kids say?' I ask the mothers. These are your kids and their blood is all over the house—what do you do? Talk to them, right? 'Who did the kids say beat them?' I ask. They say they don't know. The kids don't know. They don't know. Nobody knows. Right? So, it's like now I'm looking for someone who's invisible."

"Have you talked to Raphael yet?" Jerry asked.

"We did a little but the poor kid was petrified. I didn't really press it yet. He knows what's going on and I think he's protecting his mom. We were hoping to get one of the mothers to confess but we may have to lean a little harder on the kid, poor guy. Like on top of all he's been through tonight, he's gotta turn in his mother, right? It's sick. I think I'll get him to talk if I need to, but right now he's real shut up. We're gonna heat up the women a lot more before we go back to the kid."

"And what about the other kid, Davey?" Jerry asked.

Borrero plopped the last bit of egg into his mouth and picked up the coffee mug again. "He's only four years old. He hasn't made a squeak. I haven't seen him even talk to his mother. It's weird." He looked in the mug. "Micky, you still on hold?" Micky slowly turned his chair to face us and nodded.

"Well you've been forgotten, my friend," Borrero said. "Now be a dear and go make us a fresh pot, will ya? Call them later."

Micky hung up and walked toward the door. "You make the next one," he said as he left the room.

Borrero looked back to Jerry. "Did you guys run a clearance on these ladies for a past record of child abuse?"

"Oh yes," Jerry said. "Ms. Carr was reported three times for beating Raphael two years ago. The cases were investigated and the disposition was indicated. He was removed from his home but Family Court sent him back five months later."

"She was reported for beating the kid three times?" Borrero asked almost gleefully. Jerry nodded showing him a copy of the computer clearance. Borrero looked it over, smiling. "Well... this is very, very interesting. I didn't know about this. Wow." As he read through the reports, his forehead pulled back and his lips got thin. "See, we asked her if she'd ever been reported for child abuse and she said she hadn't. Oh boy. This makes things a little easier."

He called the other guys over and as they surrounded the desk, he leaned back with a grin that bordered on a grimace. "She lied," he said. "She lied and we caught her."

5

As entertaining as Borrero and the boys were, I was continually distracted by young Raphael sitting almost frozen in the far corner of the office. Since this wasn't my case, I had the luxury of taking a backseat while Jerry navigated the potholes. Raphael looked so alone and so out of place. He belonged in a movie theater, laughing with a Coke in one hand, a box of chocolate Sno Caps in the other, and a gut ache to show for it. He belonged on his hands and knees on his living-room floor playing the bucking bronco with a cousin or two on his back. He belonged asleep on his mother's arm in front of the late movie. It was 2:00 A.M. He belonged in his bed. Instead he sat like a tiny stone on the dark walnut chair at Bronx Detectives while men with guns under their arms and eggs in their mouths hashed around decisions that would affect the rest of his life. I decided to walk over and say hello. I felt a little like the doctor that tries to be a buddy while prepping a needle to jam in your butt, but Raphael needed somebody to touch his shoulder. In this most terrible night of his life, he didn't seem to have a friend in the room.

I sat on the chair next to him and he glanced over with dark empty eyes. He was a skinny kid, maybe a little tall for his age, in brown jeans and a blue T-shirt.

"Hi, Raphael. I'm Marc. You hangin' in there?"

He stared forward and didn't make a sound.

"Do you want a Coke or anything?" I asked. "I think I'm gonna go downstairs to get one."

He didn't blink. His hands gripped the sides of his chair.

"I think I'll be going down later, so if you want one let me know."

It was like I was talking to someone else, maybe someone next to him. Raphael had been scared into a zombie. I had seen kids on other cases escape into the zombie place when the black fell around them. It's a place just after screams and right beyond tears. Raphael stared safely from the zombie place at images of the fists that turned his cousins from screaming bloody boys into very quiet ones. Suddenly he turned to me.

"I got school tomorrow," he said.

"Yeah?" I said, "What grade are you in?"

"Do I get to go to school tomorrow?"

"Well," I said after a pause, "I'm not sure. Maybe." But the pause gave me away. I knew Raphael saw through it. "I don't know," I said. "Probably not tomorrow."

Raphael turned forward for a moment, then turned back. "I got baseball tomorrow."

There was nothing I could say. He looked at me with questioning eyes for a moment, and seeing the stalemate, turned forward and returned to the zombie place. I squeezed his shoulder as I got up, and walked over to Little Davey who was sitting next to his mother, Ms. Melendez. I crouched down to say hello but stopped as soon as I looked him in the face. Little Davey made Raphael look like a day at the fair. His hazy gray eyes were a sharp contrast to the vivid scrapes and purple ridges lashed across his face.

Ms. Carr gazed at me blankly. "He's sleepy."

Oh, that's why his face is striped with bruises, I thought. *"He's sleepy."* Yeah, *he's sleepy. Getting beat to shit really is exhausting. Especially when you're a kid. A few full swings with a closed fist and a couple of kicks when they're on the floor and they just tucker right out.*

"Can't you see you're keeping him awake in here?" she continued. "He should be at home in his bed sleeping. This is not good for him. When will you people be finished?"

"I guess we'd all sleep in our beds a lot sooner," I said, "if somebody here could just remember what happened about three hours ago."

"*I don't know what happened three hours ago,*" she shouted. "I told these damn guys that for the last damn hours." Ms. Carr began a chatter of Spanish with her sister and I went back to Jerry and the boys, who were planning the next moves. Given the prior "indicated" dispositions of our reports (as opposed to "unfounded," which would imply unsubstantiated allegations) it seemed obvious Ms. Carr had struck again, this time maybe a little harder than she intended. She had been abrasive and defensive throughout the night and definitely seemed as though she had something to hide. When Borrero confronted her with the proof of the prior beatings, however, it didn't have the effect he had hoped it would. Instead of breaking in half and spilling the liquid gold of a confession, Ms. Carr admitted she had lied and said she had done so simply because she was scared. She was completely unruffled at being caught in the lie and maintained her innocence.

The night dragged on. An hour and a few eggs later, the boys hadn't made much headway. Raphael and I, however, were slowly becoming pals. I had bought him two Cokes that he put down handily, and we had managed to strike up a good distraction of small talk: school (didn't like), girls (didn't like—yet), favorite animals (eagle, polar bear, all snakes), collections (old pennies, rocks). But mostly we talked about baseball. I don't know baseball so I mostly listened—to favorite players, favorite teams, favorite stadiums, best averages, and on and on. He was a really neat kid like most kids after you talk with them awhile—beautiful crystal bowls of innocence and hope, even in the middle of the night, even in Bronx Detectives.

6

AT 3:00 A.M., A CLUTCH FORMED around Papa Borrero's desk to plan an all-out assault on the mothers. We'd all become certain they knew exactly what had happened earlier, and that if they hadn't beaten the kids themselves, they were protecting whoever had. More than anything, it started to seem like they were playing games with us and though no one would've admitted it, I think that's what was really getting everyone crazy. The animosity in the room heated up with the passing wee hours and was fanned by Ms. Carr's flip attitude toward the whole investigation. Rant and rave or cry your eyes hysterical, but don't be flip with the boys in Bronx Detectives. "I think the ladies over here think this is just some kinda big joke," Borrero kept saying. The rest of the guys agreed and collectively decided to turn up the heat. It was a "you go here and I'll fake back" kind of huddle. There was Minnieola—a smartly dressed balding man in his late thirties; Reznick—ageless, either thirty-one or fifty-one, a spook with sunken cheeks and wolverine eyes. He had the biggest gun. And Corderra—an early thirties new-guy-on-the-block; nice tie and crisp haircut. Around the desk, we all listened to Papa Borrero forecast the upcoming emotional breaks of the mothers and what might precipitate them. Micky was back on hold with Jacobi Hospital checking on Tony's condition. Throughout the night after each call he'd shout, "Still hanging in there," and then return to files piled high on his desk.

After devising the plan of attack, Borrero and the boys broke the huddle, walked over to the mothers, and whupped up a thoroughly vicious hellhound. Borrero knew which chairs to bang on the floor without breaking them, and where to hit the bulletin board so it'd make a loud snap against the wall. Minnieola had old soda cans to slam into the trash to drive points home. Corderra leaned in close, shouting a furious translation to Ms. Melendez. Reznick took up the rear with a penetrating wolverine stare that could melt an igloo. Ties were ripped off and tossed across the office, belts were loosened, jackets were thrown, sleeves rolled up and down, and the whole place hummed with the wrath of man.

Through it all Ms. Melendez and Ms. Carr screamed through tears that they were out of the house working when the children were beaten. They claimed Raphael had been caring for cousins Tony and Little Davey while they were out. That when they'd asked him what happened, he didn't know. Raphael said he was in another room when it happened. They were asking us to believe that some sort of mystery wind came seeping through a crack in the floor and pummeled the cousins into silly rag dolls. None of us were close to buying it. There really didn't seem to be any mystery here, especially given Ms. Carr's prior record of child abuse. A removal meant that Raphael had probably had more than a few cuts and bruises. Over time, he had probably figured out how to avoid pressing Mom's kill button, but maybe the cousins hadn't.

Minutes sweated past with no break. I didn't know whether

to marvel at Ms. Carr's stamina or her stupidity as she held up her story of ignorance like an umbrella against a flood of boiling rain. Borrero huffed and puffed, but the piggies were in a red brick house that would not blow down.

Just as the tirade was entering its second wind, Micky's legs dropped from the edge of his desk. He leaned forward with both hands on the phone. *"Guys, guys,"* he shouted with the receiver clutched to his ear. "Doctor who?" he asked into the phone. He looked up. "Bad news, guys." The room froze.

"Spell it...V-A-Z-A-G-O-R-T...Vatzgert?...Dr. Vaza-gort? All right, thank you...no that's all right...that's all right, we'll call you back." He hung up the phone.

"Tony's dead," he said. The words flew out of his mouth like sparks and set the room on fire. "Pronounced dead at 3:38 A.M. by a Dr. Vatzgert or something or other."

Ms. Melendez, who had been quiet all night, let out a shattering wail that filled the very edges of every ear in the room. The purely awful sound caught Borrero, Minnieola, Corderra, and Micky off guard. Something in that roar was more horrible than anything they'd ever felt—the long howl soaring past the bloody atrocities of seventy accumulated years on the force. As the walls echoed with Ms. Melendez's wailing, the men swayed and gaped with horror.

Reznick, however, was not amused. Reznick with the sneaky wolverine eyes. Reznick with the big black gun under his arm, banging on his ribs like black rotted meat. As we stood dazed, Reznick got irritated. He stood up, suddenly seeming much larger than before, and with his forceful rise complete, towered above his desk, looming even larger than Borrero.

He stared with a blank face at the shuddering Ms. Melendez and then turned to Ms. Carr. "GODDAMN IT—WILL YOU TELL HER TO SHUT UP—THIS IS A GODDAMN OFFICE." Ms. Carr's lips turned white. Reznick continued, "IT'S GETTING PRETTY GODDAMN LATE AROUND HERE

AND NOW THIS THING JUST REALLY GOT OUT OF HAND AND I WANT SOME GODDAMN ANSWERS STARTING RIGHT FUCKING NOW—"

Ms. Carr broke. *"We don't know what happened to Tony —I don't know what happened to him—we were working— my nephew is dead and you are going to tell me—*MY SISTER'S SON IS DEAD!"—she turned to Little Davey, screaming through a flood of tears, *"What happened to you, Davey— who did this to you—you gotta talk—*WHO DID THIS TO YOU?—*You have to say—"*

"This is getting sick." Reznick's wolverine eyes were setting back in his head.

"—TELL US, DAVEY—*You gotta talk to these men and tell them what happened to you—who did this to you?—"*

"This is getting fucking sick," Reznick mumbled to Borrero. Everyone was just a bit lost. It was getting sick. It had been sick for a while. It was sick to see Raphael staring urgently forward, grinding his teeth while his own mother begged him to cut her noose.

"Raphael." She leaned toward him, cooing, "You have to talk now, Raphael . . . you gotta talk to these men and tell them who hurt Tony and Davey—"

"Should we just stop this?" Reznick asked Borrero. "The kid's not gonna turn in his own mother and this here is just sick." Borrero didn't say a word as he slowly stroked his mustache and looked at Raphael.

"It's okay, Raphael," Ms. Carr continued with a trembling voice. *"You gotta say it . . .* please . . . who did this . . . who hurt Tony and Davey? . . ."

The room fell silent. Raphael's big black eyes stared intensely forward. He sat as motionless as a rabbit in a sad attempt to blend in with the office walls and the dark walnut chair. He was trying to disappear.

Reznick broke the silence. "Well I've had enough of this—"

"Hang on, hang on," Borrero said quietly. Things were getting confused. We'd been certain the mothers had been involved with the beating, at least indirectly, and we'd been going on that all night, but the river of grief spilling from them was starting to smell like innocence. Before our eyes, they were turning from perpetrators to victims. Quietly, in the disheveled office, we spread out and looked away as Ms. Carr continued with her son.

"Don't be scared, honey, tell me who did this so we can go home...it's late and we should go home now...You don't have to be afraid of the person who did this. You can tell us...You gotta tell us, Raphael."

We all stood motionless staring at Raphael from the corner of our eyes. There was a long silence and suddenly he looked straight at me. I turned and faced him. His eyes pleaded for me. I walked over and sat next to him. I touched his head softly and brought my hand down to his shoulder. I sat with him for a moment until I felt his shoulder soften.

"Raphael, do you know what happened to Tony and Davey tonight?" I asked.

Staring rigidly forward, he gave a slow quivering nod.

"Do you know who did it?"

His eyes dropped tears, but he didn't look sad. He looked petrified.

"I'm not gonna let anyone get you, Raphael. Don't be scared, okay?"

He nodded.

"Do you know who hurt Tony and Davey tonight?"

His head bobbed again as tears ran down his cheeks.

"Will you tell me?"

He turned and looked straight at me with trusting eyes, and nodded. Borrero gently stopped us and took us downstairs to be videotaped.

Raphael saw what happened, he knew who did it, and he told me.

7

Blocks of sunlight fell into Raphael's bedroom as five-year-old Tony and four-year-old Little Davey played with the closed curtains. It was 7:00 A.M. Raphael watched them through half-asleep eyes thinking only momentarily of the days when his room was his own. He hardly ever thought about that anymore now that they'd been with him and his mother for so long, but that morning, for just a moment, he *did* think about it.

His mother had explained to him how her sister and her two boys would be coming to live with them, but only for a month. That was ten months ago. They were from Puerto Rico, a mystical place that would make longing tears drop from his mother's eyes. All he knew of that place were the pictures of his mother in younger, happier, thinner days, holding a swaddling of cloth with a tiny dark head in the middle that he was told was his. He was born in Puerto Rico but came to America before he was a year old and now he was from the Bronx. His mom would always say, "You and me—we're a team, honey," but it was different now that her sister and nephews were around. He thought about how quiet and calm the apartment used to be.

The cousins were unlike any of his friends in school or any kid he'd ever met, for that matter. Rougher somehow. Sometimes, he'd watch them tease and poke at each other until it got out of hand. He'd get startled as they'd turn almost animallike—suddenly grabbing at each other's eyes and kicking each other's groins. Their bodies were small, but they were strong, stronger than Raphael, and even though he was older than them, he would get frightened when they started playing too rough. When the romps got really intense, he'd get just the slightest whiffs of panic at their feral rasps of laughter squashed

between Spanish yelps. Raphael's mother spoke Spanish sometimes on the phone and when she spoke to neighbors, but the
sound of her voice made the tumble of words almost familiar.
There was nothing familiar in Tony and Little Davey's mouth.
They spoke Spanish with the jarring authority of a one-
language tongue. There was a rhythm between the cousins that
he hadn't ever heard, at once mysteriously exotic yet hauntingly
familiar. They were his family, but their blood mixed with an
agrarian lineage that made them feel alien.

And they were in his bedroom.

That morning, as light fell like blocks on his head and the
cousins played savagely on, he gave it only a moment's thought.
Nothing mattered to Raphael. Nothing could tear him from
the anticipation of the coming evening. It was the night of the
slumber party. His friends had talked about it for days, and
tonight was the night. Raphael's mom had said yes last week
and a borrowed sleeping bag sat happily on the chair by his
bed along with his pajamas, toothbrush, and a rubber-banded
packet of his favorite baseball cards. A few quick hours at
school, back home and an early supper, and it would be off to
the buddies for the entire night of laughs over pizza and all the
Cokes you can drink. Raphael couldn't wait.

Rolling to his side, he gazed at his cat lying in a fluffy white
ball at his feet. She stretched luxuriously, and with a wide
yawn, laid her paws lightly on his ankles, completely oblivious
to the cousins and their intrusion on the morning. He pulled
her up to his face and gave her nose a tiny kiss. The cat was
named Nyack and it was the one thing left in the apartment
that was still completely his. The cousins had tried to grab at
Nyack like they had at everything else in his small bedroom,
but Nyack would have no part of it. She promptly returned
their rudeness with a nasty swipe of her claws. After a few tests
of Nyack's resolve, the cousins concluded Raphael had less
painful things to play with. The second time Nyack scratched
Little Davey, Raphael's mom threatened to get rid of her.

Raphael threw a two-year-old's tantrum and got the execution stayed, but the cat was on shaky ground from then on. Another incident of self-defense and dear Nyack would be forced to take the deep sleep. The cat was starting to feel like family to Raphael, more than his own mother, and as he looked into her placid yellow eyes that morning, he made a silent promise to watch her back.

During breakfast the cousins got carried away in a charley horse contest. Little Davey's fist missed Tony's upper arm and slammed a carton of milk into Raphael's face. The cold liquid trickled down his neck and back and soaked into the waistband of his underwear. His mother gave him a paper towel to dry his face but told him he'd be late for school if he changed his clothes. By 11:00, his shirt had dried but his underwear was still sticky. As the day dragged on, a dull sour smell pulled through Raphael's nose, giving him a real gut ache by the time school let out. It had been a long stinky day for him but his spirits remained high. Nothing could stop the mountain of pizza and laughter slowly inching nearer. Before leaving school, the buddies gathered for a final confirmation of the night. On the steps of the school they did a group high five and broke into uncontrollable laughter out of pure excitement. Raphael's queasy sour-milk stomach filled with ecstatic butterflies as he ran home and burst through the apartment door.

He threw his books on the kitchen table and had the stinky shirt off by the time he got to his bedroom. Loosening his pants, he opened the door and was greeted by Little Davey, smiling, with a ripped-up fistful of baseball cards in each hand. Raphael's cards. His favorite baseball cards. Forever ruined. The hours spent in quiet admiration of their shining smooth faces and crisp corners—forever gone. The proud feeling of sharing the well-kept collection with his friends, forever lost. Davey threw the pieces into the air and fled the room, hooting. As the colorful bits fell, they took Raphael with them, and he collapsed to the floor. With his shirt off and his pants at his ankles, he lay surrounded by pieces of his precious collection, choking back a tight lump of steel.

After a few moments, Nyack came to Raphael like cool soothing water and brushed her chin gently against his forehead. Her soft white fur loosened the folds of his furrowed brow and a comforting purr lulled in his ears. She was his angel. He buried his face in her belly and she let him. He was sure she knew what had happened but more than that, he was sure she understood. The cousins had invaded their home, taken their mother, ruined their things, and worn out their welcome. He rolled onto his back and held Nyack to his chest. With their faces almost touching, he gazed into her eyes and she let him. Raphael and Nyack were in a war. A silent, dangerous, escalating war. He gave her a long tight hug and she let him, because she knew what had happened and she understood.

He got up, looking around the room, and suddenly noticed the sleeping bag on the chair at the end of the bed was gone. Gone. His heart clenched for a moment. He needed that sleeping bag. He also needed his toothbrush and pajamas and they were gone too. Dread filled his lungs like a thin fog making his breath short. Tonight was the night of the slumber party and he needed to get out of the house. Badly.

With his eyes wide and dark, he ran into the next room just short of a panic. His mother and aunt were at the kitchen table. "Get on some clothes, Raphael," his mother shouted. "You can't run around here in your underwear!"

"Where's my sleeping bag?" he asked, trying to keep his voice from trembling.

"Where's your sleeping bag?" his mother answered. "It's back with the neighbors—that's where's your sleeping bag. Now take a shower and put on some clothes. You still stink like that milk."

He tried to stay in control as his breath chased away from him. "But Mom, I need that sleeping bag for tonight, you know—for that party tonight, I need it."

"I know, Raphael, but I need *you* tonight to—"

He interrupted, "No, no, but Mom—"

"Raphael, Raphael, honey, listen to me. I need my little helper tonight to—"

"Mom, *Mom,* but—no—but—I need that sleeping—"

"Raphael, you don't need the sleeping bag beca—"

"*Mom-Mom-Mom-no, no, but*—MOM—I NEED TO HAVE THAT SLEEPING—"

"RAPHAEL," she said with a firm shake of his shoulders, "you don't need the sleeping bag tonight because you're not going to that party. Your aunt got a shift at the restaurant with me and you gotta stay here to take care of Tony and Davey."

Raphael turned white. He spoke, but it was as if he was talking off the edge of a sucking abyss. His appeal drifted up into the air like ashes from a burning leaf pile. As he tried, his words became so thin and distant that even he stopped hearing them. He was fading away.

"—be *plenty* more parties to go to," his mother continued, "and besides, we got some movies here and I'll make you some popcorn before we leave and you guys'll have a real ball."

Raphael watched his mother's mouth open and close, hearing nothing.

"—know you were looking forward to going but we need that money, and if your aunt gets a shift, we gotta do it. It's hard, it's hard, I know, but that's the way it is. I gotta do my job, and you gotta do your job. You and me—we're a team, honey!"

Raphael had turned away and was almost in the bathroom by the time he heard "—a team, honey!" as if it was a thousand miles away. With the door locked tight, he stepped in the tub and turned on the shower. The hot jets of water cascaded around him. And he cried.

By nine o'clock that night, the cousins were business as usual. They'd been bouncing on the bed for the past hour, even though Little Davey had fallen and cried twice. Raphael had tried to stop them, but there was really no stopping them from doing just about anything they wanted, since Raphael knew very little Spanish and the cousins knew very little English. And it was a war. Raphael and Nyack were holed up in front of the television and the cousins had control of the rest of the apartment. That's the way it went for the four nights a week that Raphael was mother's "little helper."

At nine-thirty, the cousins were supposed to be asleep. They were supposed to be wrapped in blankets in the dark bedroom lying motionless. Raphael was usually able to get them tucked away on cue, leaving the rest of the evening wrapped in beautiful solitude. He'd planned on calling his buddies after putting the cousins away, for a long, feet-against-the-wall, sweaty-eared chatter. He was so tired of the cousins' shrieking Spanish. He was tired of seeing their tiny bodies fly from room to room—little heels incessantly pounding the floor like rubber mallets. He was tired of their senseless fistfights and their instant tears. Mostly, he was tired of *baby-sitting them*. Throughout the evening Little Davey had been running from the couch to the kitchen table, mustering up a creepy disproportionate strength to lift them a few inches and let them fall with a jolting bump. He'd grunt and whistle through his teeth while making tiny lifts of every heavy thing in the apartment he could budge.

Raphael had given up trying to gain any control over the chaos the cousins were drenched in. With the mothers gone, the apartment had turned into a free-fall of banged heads and jammed fingers, of flying toys and spilled sodas, of bruised chins and fat lips. The cousins played long and they played rough. They kicked from behind, aimed for the groin, and, boy, was that fun. They laughed hard and they cried hard, it was impossible to distinguish when one ended and the other began. Raphael was starting to really lose his marbles, so he did the only sensible thing. He went to the bathroom, locked the door, and sat on the toilet, waiting for the thunder to pass.

And then it happened.

In the midst of the dull roar of destruction, a muffled sound crept through the crack at the bottom of the door. It spilled in, crammed between the savage pig squeals of the cousins, and smashed into Raphael's skull, splattering what was left of his sanity against the white tile walls. Nyack was in trouble. Her piercing howl cried out to the very depths of Raphael's mother bear. His head quickly filled with grizzled fury. He charged for the door and pulled it back, the desperate yowling rattling his eardrums as he stormed toward the bedroom.

Standing in the doorway, he shuddered with a rage far exceeding the load limits of his nine-year-old body. He screamed from adrenaline-soaked lungs but it made no difference. Little Davey reached down and gripped Nyack's tail. He arched his little body and snapped the cat into an atrocious game of crack-the-whip. Around and around she twirled in a white blur encircling the hooting Davey, finally slamming with a hideous crack into the wall. Together they fell to the floor in a puff of fur. The room froze for an instant, filled only with the quiet out-of-breath giggles of the cousins. Nyack lay still, slightly dazed. Davey suddenly lurched toward the cat for a second round, but Raphael stepped in the way and slammed both fists violently into his face. To save Nyack from Little Davey, he hit him with all he had.

That's what the *first* punch was for.

The momentum of the two-fisted punch sent them both careening across the room into a chair. Raphael landed on top of Davey and began a barrage of haymakers. Davey screeched as Raphael's fists arced hysterically through the air. His queer strength was no match for Raphael's festered wound. The fists plunged into Davey's ribs as if into dough and, hey, wasn't that fun. Raphael was starting to feel really good. Suddenly Tony exploded from the bed, coming to his little brother's aid. He landed on Raphael's back and ten stony fingers reached around to find nostrils, lips, and eyeballs to gouge. Raphael stood up with Tony's fingers stretching his face into a hideous fun-house grin, and ran them both backward into the dresser, slamming Tony's head fiercely between his own and the hard wood drawers. Tony's fingers instantly released Raphael's face as they both collapsed to the floor. From behind him, Raphael heard a rasping Davey on the charge. He jumped up and fired his foot squarely into Davey's oncoming chest, sending him sailing backward into the corner of the room. Raphael followed him to the corner and delivered two full kicks across his chest, lifting him against the wall with each blow. Davey's thin body thrashed on the floor as he gasped for enough air to scream. Raphael had made his point and he could've stopped there. But he didn't.

He turned to Tony, who was standing but still shaky from hitting the dresser. He was slowly making his way toward Raphael, and when he was in range, Raphael arched back and with one sweeping motion crashed his fist into Tony's face, sending him floating through the air and onto the bed. Raphael strode like a predator to where Tony lay and planted fists into him, one by one, filling the small room with the sound of smashing pumpkins. The body jumped up from the bed, springing to meet his fists with each blow. Raphael's frenzy showed no sign of stopping as he pounded Tony's limp body with both fists at once. He closed his eyes. He kept planting. His fists grew numb and began to separate from his body. Slowly, he opened his eyes and watched with curious wonder as the fists smashed, like a driving rain, into Tony's neck and chest. They came down and down and down, and Raphael watched them from across the room, not knowing who they belonged to. Whose hands could do such terrible work? His own fists would not be capable of such destruction. They dropped like hammers, bouncing Tony in a mad dance around the bed. There were only fists and they belonged to no one.

What would he say later to those who would ask him what happened? All he could see were the fists.

It may have been the blood splashing in his face that stopped him, but I'm just guessing with that. Only Raphael knows why he finally stopped. Blood did splash into his face and that must've been sort of unexpected. Blood didn't figure into Raphael's intentions. After all, why go through the bother of teaching someone a lesson if you're just gonna pummel them into oblivion anyways? It was safe to say little Nyack would not be bothered again. That accomplished, Raphael felt some small satisfaction—but that *Tony.*

As each second passed with no movement from Tony, Raphael's body filled with dread. He had never seen his cousin's body so completely still. Even when he slept he was always stirring. Raphael's eyes fixed on Tony and begged for just the slightest bit of movement. His fists tingled as they slowly returned to his arms, and Raphael's whole body began a deep, subtle tremble. He looked to the corner, grateful to see Little Davey crying softly. Davey was following the program—a few purple patches, but none of that bleeding—and he was moving, painfully, throbbingly, but *moving,* thank Christ. Maybe if Tony stopped that obscene bleeding he could move, too, Raphael thought, and ran to the bathroom on rubber legs to get a roll of toilet paper. Racing back into the bedroom, he could see a red halo soaking into the sheet under Tony's head. A tiny wellspring of blood poured from his left ear. Raphael turned Tony's head to the side, and gathering a wad of toilet paper, dabbed it into the flooded ear. Blood quickly saturated the paper and Raphael plunged another piece into the swelling red puddle. He continued the useless drill until the roll of paper was almost gone. Overwhelmed and defeated, he stepped back and watched as the little ear filled itself almost instantly and spilled over the insanity of Tony's ballooning face.

8

I WASN'T THE ONE WHO INTERVIEWED Raphael at Bronx Detectives. As soon as he admitted beating the cousins to me, the questioning was turned over to more capable hands. I asked Raphael to tell them the truth and to tell them everything, and he did.

An hour later, Borrero stepped out of the taping room and invited Jerry and me back to his desk where he gave us a long and detailed account of how the perfectly docile and lovely Raphael was transformed into Cousin Tony's killer. By the time Raphael stepped out of the taping room, it was almost 5:00 A.M. Surrounded by detectives, he looked at me through a blur of tears. "Do I have to go to jail?" he asked.

Jerry was filling out a 701-b for the mothers and preparing to take Little Davey. Both women were white as sheets and too far gone to indulge in any purity of emotion. When Jerry informed them of the removal they asked why, Jerry said because, and they left it at that. The evening had beaten all of us beyond the luxury of consciousness.

Two oddball-looking detectives were working Davey over with the largest, most awkward-looking camera I'd ever seen. It was a tangled monstrosity in three huge pieces that looked more suited for 1930s medical procedures than for taking pictures. It took the two of them to operate it—poorly. They stretched the reluctant Davey prostrate on a white table to photograph close-ups of his ripening bruises. In his underwear, beneath the bright lights, he was being handled like a butchered chicken—the detectives flipping him around on the table with the courtesy of meat inspectors. They'd have Davey freeze in the most impossible display of his injuries as they moved in close with the camera only to find the flash units hadn't charged. Davey would strain to hold his position as the men waited for what seemed like an eternity, through the whine of the recharging dinosaurs. The child winced and whimpered as they began, but by the time they'd finished, he had closed his eyes and let them have their way, assuming the wayward positions they put him in like he'd done it a thousand times.

Jerry exchanged a few numbers with the boys and we picked up our things to leave. Davey was wearing only the baggy green underwear he came in, and since the Bronx at 5:00 A.M. is no great shopping experience, I wrapped him in my jacket and we headed for the door. He felt like dead weight. He didn't even look at his mother when she kissed him good-bye, staring aimlessly past her with frowsy rag-doll eyes.

I don't know what happened to Raphael. He had to stay.

As we were heading out the door, Borrero chased us down with two T-shirts in his hand and tossed them to Jerry, saying "Here guys, take these—they're only available to the men on the squad, but you earned them. Tonight you guys were detectives."

Heading down the stairs toward the car, Jerry opened one of the shirts with a big smile. "Look, boss," he said, "we're detectives, man." They were dark blue shirts with the Bronx Detectives insignia brandished in yellow across the chest. I've still got mine.

In the car, I sat in the back with Davey as Jerry began the long drive home. Davey never looked at me once for the rest of the night, but I looked at him. A few feet away from me in the seat, he had the papery transparency of a reflection. I cupped his tiny shoulders with my arm and pulled him to my side. Under his thin gray skin his bones felt as though they'd turned to glass. I gave his weak frame a squeeze and offered a few comforting words that fell into his ears like stones down an old well. Little Davey's eyes remained unchanged as I listened for a splash, but there never was one. The well had dried up and all the animals had died. Releasing his shoulders, I propped him back up on his side of the seat and buckled him in. I'd never seen a kid go so deep. Jerry and I had been at the scene of an explosion and we were bringing back a corpse—gazing forward, the face of a ghost, lost deep within himself along the spiral paths of the zombie place. Less than a year ago, he had played on generous Puerto Rican beaches expansive enough to host the joyful roughhousing with his older brother. But welcome to America, where apartment walls squeeze and single mothers have midnight shifts and bills to pay. Brother dead and mother gone. Welcome.

After a while, the bumping streets of the Bronx lulled me into a sleepy hypnosis. I stared out the window, treading deep within my own spiral paths. If there is a zombie place in the mind, there is one, too, on this earth and it floats through the Bronx at 5:00 A.M. Here the land that was once a wash of starry night sat bathing in the sickening peach haze of sodium lights. Through half-cocked eyes, the blur of the street seemed not unlike a woods at night with its similar crawl of activity—night sounds that rustle just barely out of sight, whole scenes played out in peripheral vision, like chasing a spot on your iris that never comes to where you can get a square look at it. After the long grueling night, in between wandering hallucinations, the memory of a nighttime field in sweet Wisconsin came to take me home.

The crunch of dried-out mustard weed marks each footfall on a cold September evening. The field is a dark blue ocean of waves framed by the skeletal trunks of distant elms. All is quiet. A silver moon casts its cool beauty across the land, turning everything silver and black. Far out on the reaching arm of a distant elm, a silhouetted bird calls out across the night. I carefully sight the front blade of my Winchester pump .22 rifle on the dark bird. The stock feels cold against my cheek as I push the gun off safe, steady its sights, and squeeze the trigger. It fires with a thin crack that echoes distantly in the clear night air. The sharp silhouette muddies crazily before the bird falls silently to the ground. I've made an impossible shot. With my heart thumping in my ears, I put the gun back on safe and run as fast as I can to where it went down. After stepping through the brush in the vicinity of the fall for some time, my foot hits a soft lump in a patch of nettle. Carefully, I reach in to retrieve the kill. It is warm in my hands and as I bring it into the moonlight, I realize I have killed the most beautiful bird I've ever seen. I hold it out against the blue landscape. Its yellow and orange patches slowly cover with dark blood. I set the bird down in the dried mustard and pray for forgiveness. *Please, God, forgive. I didn't know. Please, God. Please forgive, dark little bird. I didn't know. Please forgive.*

With my eyes sorrowfully shut, a growing music fills my ears. The rich bumping tones of Thelonious Monk's saxophone dances through my body as Mulligan and Monk jam a cool tune in the breeze. Floating in on a bed of stars, the moon snuggles in close to the melody and smiles as only the moon can. Tall dark buildings race across the field with their tenement windows blazing. The boys play louder and the moon smiles wider as the buildings crush head-on against the dark silhouettes of giant elms on the horizon.

3

Bad Bad Dream

Hey God
God don't never change
He's God
Always will be God
God in the creation
God when Adam fell
God way up in heaven
God way down in hell
Spoke to the mountain
Said how great I am
Want you to get up this morning
Skip around like lamb

—as sung by Blind Willie Johnson
Tuesday, December 10, 1929

ON THE WAY HOME FROM the zombie place, I thanked God
that the case was Jerry's and not mine. By the time we got to
the office, a pre-sunrise glow had already begun to stain the
night with the promise of the coming day. It was late—or early
really—about quarter after six. Jerry would be ready for breakfast by the time he finished the case write-up. All I had to do
was drop Little Davey into an orange plastic chair and barrel
it on home to my old futon. I would be staring at the piranha
man and listening to a rat convention by the time Jerry was
completing his second page.

All was quiet when I walked into the apartment. Quiet was
everywhere at 6:15 in the morning—babies sleeping, drunks
passed out, insomniacs reading, old barking dogs tuckered out,

and all so quiet save for the occasional worker on the tail end of the night shift casually tipping trash from metal cans into his garbage truck. The sound of quiet in Manhattan is the sound of a metal can bouncing on the lip of a dumper followed by the groan of diesel. Anyone who's been in the city after six in the morning knows this.

I drank a can of beer alone in the kitchen and then I hit the sack. James rolled over as I tucked into my futon and I told him about my night. He didn't say much, but I knew he was listening intently. He was a strong soul and a good friend; it felt good to unload some of the weight on him. When there was nothing left to say, we lay staring up at the piranha man, who was dimly lit by the start of sunrise making its way into the room. I had quieted down after a while, but the rats didn't follow suit. They never did. Rats are like that. I fell asleep finally, as I did most every night, to the sound of scritcha-scratcha and it didn't really bother me that much. Yet.

Just before nodding off, James told me about a black-tie evening at the Roseland dance hall that was being thrown for then presidential candidate Michael Dukakis (anybody remember him?). At the time, James was going out with the daughter of a movie-star mom who invited him to take a friend or two along for what was sure to be a star-studded evening of dance and glitter. James asked me if I'd like to go, and of course I said yes. One of the good things about being in New York is that no matter how plain and unimportant you are, sooner or later you're bound to find yourself squished into company of some pretty impressive caliber. Quite a change from Marsh-field, Wisconsin—where you hear that Hal Holbrook passed through Milwaukee and you think you've had a brush with fame. The event was scheduled for the following Sunday when, with incredibly lucky timing, my college girlfriend was coming for her first visit to New York.

2

BY THE TIME TINA LOUISE stepped from her limo into the glitz of Manhattan's Roseland dance bar, a woman named Regina Jacobs had just begun a nightmare that unraveled her restless sleep in Far Bellpage. She twisted and shook in her bed, alone, as the dream took on horrific proportions. The essential line between dream and reality was obscured by apparitions too perfectly vivid to not be real. It was simply the worst dream she ever had, the worst dream *anyone* could have—finally not a dream as much as a *crisis*. A breakdown after which nothing would ever be the same.

The week at 108th Street had passed quickly. My girlfriend got into the city on Friday night, and twenty-four hours later, we were donning our favorite (and only) big-time duds and sauntering down a red carpet through a minefield of flashbulbs into Roseland dance hall. As soon as we got inside, we were stuck with round green stickers and ushered into a very small sectioned-off area where we stood muzzle to muzzle with some of the biggest names in Hollywood. I did my best to maintain a New York indifference with my eyelids clenched around my eyeballs to keep them from falling out in amazement. My girlfriend and I exchanged amazed whispers: *"Did you see——!!"* and *"To your left—to your left..."* and *"Was that really——??!!"* and *"I actually said hello to——!!"*

Despite our position with so many of the rich and beautiful, I spent most of the night snatching glimpses of the glamorous and still youthful-looking Tina Louise. The swanky sounds of Tommy Turlette's Big Band and the Crooners buffeted the air as she passed back and forth. Her auburn hair still wisped around her sunken cheeks—her eyes still twinkled with the sleepy sexuality they smoldered out every afternoon at four o'clock on Channel 7's own deserted island. I spent many hours of my formative years with the castaways, watching Ginger as she pitter-pattered across the TV into my budding adolescent fantasies, and now she was right in front of me. The opportunity was ripe for picking—I had to talk to her.

Back in Far Bellpage Ms. Jacobs was sweating a kiddie pool in her bed. She screeched with animal intensity throughout the night, creating a racket like a collision in slow motion—like the sound of a fire. As I gazed at the velvety eyes of Ginger, Ms. Jacobs was staring into the furious eyes of a hellhound. The dream continued relentlessly.

... It was cloudy outside with not a patch of sky showing but still the air was bright with sun. Searing wind whipped up black dirt devils that danced across the parched ground. The Jacobss' building stood like an inmate on death row. Everything worthy had been taken by the good Lord to make way for Satan and his army. The good people were now in heaven communing with the angels and saints. With nothing left to balance it, Satan's work was being splattered and splashed furiously across the earth. Ms. Jacobs's mind reeled in panic as she came to grips with the terrible reality. Why were she and her five children left behind? Weren't they good and holy? Once in a while they slipped, but in their heart of hearts, weren't they all basically good? They were. They were!!!! Especially the children. Can children be anything but good? Why weren't they taken???!!! Could they have been forgotten???? Had this been a terrible mistake? Would she and her children be left to burn with junkies and hookers and killers and rapists for eternity?

Yes and yes and yes.

The building suddenly burst into flames. Ms. Jacobs had her head crammed into a bare corner of her living room. A blast of heat and the wail of her children made her turn around. The temperature of the room soared to volcanic. Sweat dripping from her body and hissing on the floor, she got up and ran to the window. The sky was on fire. Trees exploded in front of her eyes. Fire hydrants belched red-hot lava. The entire horizon was a blinding army of white-and-yellow flames thundering forward.

Suddenly, the wail of her children rose in her ears. She ran across the hot griddle of her living-room floor. The choir of five burning children grew louder as she scrambled to their rooms. Her oldest daughter, Shaniece, was tucked perfectly in bed—her mouth and eyes open wide and blazing with orange fire. The child's skin was boiling like Grandma's fudge—the blaze was raging inside of her. Ms. Jacobs was thrown back by the wall of heat radiating from the bed. She clawed her way to the other four rooms, finding each child completely alive, perfectly tucked in, and blazing like wood stoves. Collapsing at the end of the hallway, she tried to scream but produced only a painful rasp from the charred black tunnel of her throat. Furnace air hissed in and out of her lungs. Each gasp stabbed the top of her diaphragm. She reeled in agony.

In an instant, the tortured wail of the children tripled in volume. She looked up as all five of them came bolting out of their rooms—fire dancing madly over their bodies. They turned toward their mother lying at the end of the hallway, and approached with blazing arms reaching desperately for her touch. One at a time, they wrapped themselves around their helpless mother, setting her gloriously ablaze. As they roared in hell's glory, trapped and melting together in a flaming bear hug, the hallway buckled with a loud WHUMP and then exploded, throwing them down into the collapsing rubble of the building. As they fell, the two youngest children were sheared in half. They remained brutally alive, still burning, and still screaming for Mommy. She landed, with a crash of sparks and fire—her flaming children strewn about her in oddly shaped chunks. Shaniece, still burning, hung directly in front of her, speared through her chest by a beam. She twisted in agony around the metal stake. All remained hopelessly alive, screaming at each other. She knew that instant—they would never sleep, they would never rest, they would never die. From now on, there was only watching—they would watch each other burn and shriek in the blazing damnation of their collapsed building for all fucking eternity . . .

Bad bad dream.

At Roseland, the Turlette band played on fabulously. The walls were a blaze of friendly fire—red and golden metallic streamers bathed the crowd in their yellow light. I was having an evening I would talk about with my friends for some time, but I still hadn't exchanged words with Ginger.

The Turlettes kicked up a rousing rendition of Dave Brubeck's "Take Five" and Ginger headed with a date to the dance floor. I figured this was my chance. My girlfriend and I began to dance and I steered us through the throngs of fame, butt first, to Ginger. In between the flickering of other dancing heads and spinning orange lights, she was more beautiful than ever. She was laughing. We were laughing. The Turlettes were laughing. Everyone was laughing. Suddenly in the small sectioned-off area, we were family. With the laughing Ginger to my immediate right, the stars aligned in the heavens and I turned to her buoyantly. "Excuse me please, would you mind if I cu—"

The band stopped instantly. I was left swaying in silence. Ginger looked at me with courteous suspicion. Tommy Turlette was announcing that Mr. Dukakis had just arrived and would be addressing us shortly. Her smile began to fade and our eyes fell apart. If I said nothing else, she would allow us to pretend the previous moment never happened. The carousel began to dismantle itself as we headed back to our seats. Before separating, I touched Ginger's shoulder and said perhaps the stupidest thing I've ever uttered. I looked into the soft pools of her eyes and said, "The little boy in me loves you." She shot me a blank smile that was deafening. I fell dead and was turning cold. A small voice in my head begged for a do-over. She paused for a moment, patted me on the wrist, and then walked away.

In Far Bellpage, Ms. Jacobs lay in her bed as she did in her dream. Trembling. As the Turlettes played their second set at Roseland, the nightmare skipped intermission and began act 2. Ms. Jacobs was sweat soaked and exhausted, but she wasn't dancing. The walls were blazing, but the Turlettes weren't invited.

...Lying on her side, staring at the children, her eyes felt like boiling sacks of molasses. Her chest heaved painfully in shallow cat breaths. Her lungs had been almost completely ruined by the heated air. The family lay in agony—burning but they couldn't burn up—dead but they couldn't die. The children begged her relentlessly to give them relief. Now at their greatest time of need, she was tipped sideways and hopeless, unable to be more than a horrified spectator...

The night dragged on second by second, the dream vividly present and vividly unchanging. She lay flaming in her bed, her eyes boiling themselves dry, while the dawn held out like a true bitch.

Back at Roseland, I was getting tired and tomorrow was a workday. My girlfriend and I found James and his date to ask them if they'd like to go home with us. They were ready to go, too. On the way out of the building I was asked for my autograph. If I'd known who the signature hound thought I was, I would've signed appropriately. Instead, I just signed my own name and gave the book back. She looked at my signature and her eyes got wide. "Thank you, Marc!" She gushed. "You bet," I said, bewildered. It didn't make much sense, but it was a perfect fit with the whole loopy evening. With the hoo-ha winding to a close, James and I hailed a cab and we all headed for home. Back at 108th, my gal and I crawled onto the futon and passed out cold. When the morning alarm rang, I could've sworn my head just hit the pillow.

Ms. Jacobs, rocking back and forth in the flames, had been burning for just under eight hours. She had stopped agonizing for the children and was completely consumed by her own torture. The children were simply *other people*. Other people who were suffering no more than she was. Strangers.

—*Seven-year-old Shaniece had been trying for the past few hours to pull herself off the beam that was puncturing her sternum. She stared at her mother with a hideous dead-monkey grin. Ms. Jacobs stared back vacantly as the child's struggling limbs wrestled dumbly with the red-hot metal. Shaniece had managed to drag her body forward on the beam about seven inches but not without leaving behind a trail of innards sizzling on the edges of the—*

Ms. Jacobs's eyes flashed wide open.

A flat pause. How long? A minute? A month? She didn't know. They shot to her window. The sun was rising silently, its brightness casting yellow threads of light through the blinds onto her sweat-soaked body. Her bedroom walls were as quiet and bored as a midweek church. She looked at the empty white walls of her room . . . *not burning* . . . took a deep breath, and burst into tears. She lay there for some time, crying like a stifled popgun, trying not to wake the children. Glaring at her legs, she groped aimlessly at the squiggles of light as she thought about her rocket ride to hell and how it seemed less like a dream and more like a premonition, a prophecy, maybe worst of all—*a warning*. It was 6:00 A.M. Saturday dawn when she began to realize what she had to do.

I rolled out of bed with seven minutes to get ready for work. I had to do that silent fast-motion thing to get ready in time and not wake the entire sleeping household. The previous evening already seemed like an impossible schoolboy's fantasy. Tina Louise patted my wrist. I looked at my wrist, brushed my teeth, put on my watch, and hit the street. You're allowed to be six minutes late without it officially counting. I just made it.

3

THE FIVE JACOBS CHILDREN AWOKE and scrambled into the kitchen to get the sweet cereal fix they had earned after a week of hard work. It was not a school morning. It was not Cheerios and Wheaties. It was the weekend. It was Cap'n Crunch and Cocoa Krispies. It was Lucky Charms and hallelujah. Shaniece was first into the cupboard. She reached up and grabbed through the school-morning cereals straight to the back where a motherload of sugar awaited her and the siblings. Peering through the colorful boxes, she spotted pay dirt—the box with one last serving of Fruity Pebbles she had stashed away the previous weekend. Hushed excitement shot from her mouth as she clutched the box. "*Yesss.*" She pulled it out and jumped off the teetering chair, racing to the refrigerator for milk. The television crackled on in the next room and the sound of singing began to slowly rise, waking the apartment with the quintessential sounds of Saturday morning. *Now's the time! Hit the lights! This is it! The height of heights—and Oh what heights we'll hiiiiiiiiiiiiiiiiit—ON WITH THE SHOW—THIS IS IT!!*

Shaniece sloshed the milk into her bowl and poured the rainbow of cereal on top. Her brother Paul always gave her hell for doing this. He said Shaniece was doing it backward— that the cereal should go in first, then the milk. He would steal the milk when he caught her doing it and ask her what her husband will think someday if she keeps this up. On several occasions, Shaniece had been forced to eat her cereal dry while

Paul poured the rest of the milk down the drain to teach her a lesson. This morning she could hear him jockeying for the coveted puffy chair, which was best for watching the TV. She knew she was safe, and so at her leisure, she let the Fruity Pebbles fly to the bowl and float gingerly on top of the ice-cold milk. She skipped contentedly into the living room to watch Bugs and the gang. Seeing her cereal, the other kids began a squabble about the unfairness of her clever stashing. The whole tirade of Fruity Pebbles and Bugs Bunny and the puffy chair and the bickering were the fabulously mundane nuts and bolts of Saturday morning.

Ms. Jacobs worked hard to ensure the certainty of these carefree mornings. She and the children's father were separated, she worked like a sled husky all week, and by the end of each day she was too exhausted to enjoy her family. She cooked them supper, but usually fell asleep before they finished eating it. Her oldest daughter, Shaniece, always cleaned the dishes without even being asked. The weekend was relief from the grind, and she used it to sit back and appreciate the health and happiness of her home and the fruits of her labor: her beautiful kids. While most of the other children in the neighborhood woke to bleakness, she took great pains to offer her children something a little better.

On this morning, Ms. Jacobs sat quietly in the corner of the kitchen, barely noticed by the children. She watched each of them with love and devotion in her eyes. Tears trickled from her cheeks as they ran in front of her... *not burning... yet...* She continued to sit silently sweating and digging her nails into the soft wooden edge of the kitchen table. She was a million miles away—consumed by a bullfight raging in her head. She wrestled and begged for an alternative to the inevitable.

"Maybe I should leave. Maybe I should just go far away," she mumbled out loud. Far away would've been good, but she just couldn't move. Instead, she continued to sit, listening with a clenched jaw to the repeated descending whistles of Wile E.

Coyote falling, the anticlimactic thud as he smashes into the ground, followed by the happy sounds of the Road Runner— *Whistle . . . thud . . . beep-beep. Whistle . . . thud . . . beep-beep. Whistle . . . thud . . . beep-beep.* She had seen the future, and now, she had to protect herself and the children from its torture. The responsibility was hers alone. She cried out softly to God and then listened, but heard nothing that might stop her.

The report came in just after three o'clock. *Beep-beep.*

> Mother threw daughter Shaniece out of a 23rd-story window "To save her from the sins of this world." Shaniece expired from multiple trauma. Mother also threw son Paul out of a window and he is in critical condition at St. John's Hospital. Police and EMS intervened and there is concern Mother would have thrown her remaining children out of the window. Currently Mother's three other children are at the emergency room. Medical Examiner will be contacted. Shaniece's body is still at Roosevelt Memorial Hospital. It is unknown if the D.A. has been notified. Mother is currently with the police of the 101st Precinct. If and when Mother is medically ready for discharge, she will be taken into custody. Father's current whereabouts are unknown. Unknown if Father is aware. ADD. INFO—The press is at the hospital

Called in by a hospital social worker, the case first hit the "war room," as we called it. All reports that came into Emergency Children's Services were received from the central registry in Albany on giant dinosaur fax machines, read and prioritized according to severity, and doled out to the grunts. I was sitting at my desk with a bucket of coffee arguing about whether or not Jimmy Page had a life outside Led Zeppelin (I say nay, they say yea) when the case came zinging into my hands. It was stamped all over in bold letters—FATALITY FATALITY FATALITY. My supervisor yelled, "This is a field visit, Marc, get out there right away. Find out what's going on. Don't talk to the media." I called the hospital to tell them I'd be right out. The social worker told me Dad, Mom, Grandma, and Grandpa were all there, as well as Channel 2, Channel 4, and Channel 7.

4

THERE IS NOT A MORE APTLY NAMED AREA of the city than Far Bellpage. Far Bellpage is far. No matter where you're coming from, it's far. It was the only place we had to go, save some areas of Staten Island, where you felt like kicking off your shoes and getting car food. And once you were *in* Far Bellpage it *felt* far. It was bring-your-passport and where's-my-pocket-translator far. Siberia. I was paired up with Yvette, the woman who'd watched Willie stab the pit bull. She was with me for moral support and to keep the kids we removed from riding my shoulders on the way back. Yvette was a shrewd thirty-year-old Haitian with an eye for good jewelry and cool shoes—the kind of woman who's more comfortable in a set of thigh-highs than a flannel nightie. She was also a workout queen whose killer body had gotten us out of more than a few tight jams with pissed-off homeboys. Her hard curves and tight skirts afforded us safe passage through many dark stairways and midnight halls, and she knew it. She was from the sex-is-a-tool school, and I was from hey-whatever-works. When shit hit the fan, she could douse a fire like no man, and I was grateful for it. Unfortunately, she was also a little unpredictable and could be mean as hell, but I was able to keep her at arm's length and that seemed to work well for both of us. We usually spent the long trips to case addresses with me doing imitations of various people in the office and her hitting the dashboard cackling wildly.

I gathered my things, and we jumped into a car to check it

all out. I had put an ink spot on my map at the location of the hospital; anything to make traversing the mazes that were New York City streets more manageable. The far reaches of some of the outer boroughs, especially Brooklyn and Queens, had to have been designed by some city planner on a dare. I learned street navigation in my hometown of twelve thousand people, where Main intersects with County Road C at the north end, and County Road E at the south. Except for a couple of long straight back roads that was about as complex as it got:

"Say, is the Kentucky Fried south of C? ..."

"North."

"North?"

"Yep."

"All right, great thanks."

Yvette and I barely spoke on the way out. Twenty minutes into the trip she broke the silence. "What are you gonna do on this one, Marc?"

"I don't know," I said. "Talk to Mom, Dad, ... Grandpa ... talk to the kids, I guess ... you know."

"Yeah," she chuckled through a thick Haitian accent, "I know I'm glad this is your case."

We didn't say much else. She wouldn't be much help on this one, but she wouldn't get in the way, either, and she didn't smoke in the car.

We finally got to the hospital—surrounded by cameras and news vans with satellite dishes raising their hands to be called on. Reporters were scurrying about. We got inside, identified ourselves to security, and were immediately pounced on by the social worker. "HI, I'M BENNY ... THE SOCIAL WORKER? ... I NEED TO KNOW WHAT YOU'RE GONNA DO."

"Right on it, Benny," I said. "Right on."

He looked at me blankly. I knew he thought I was one of those crazy civil servants you read about in the papers. I told him I was gonna go as I go, and I'd let him know what was up as soon as I knew myself.

I spoke to the doctor first. Shaniece was DOA. EMS had scraped her off the sidewalk and put her in a bag. Paul would die if he was lucky. The twenty-three stories had left him with a headful of jam that was telling his heart to beat and his lungs to breathe. He was plugged into a maze of life-support machines—chest rising mechanically; eyes too dark, staring off into eternity—*dead but he couldn't die.* The other kids, seven-year-old Blein, five-year-old Tisha, and three-year-old Keisha, were okay. They were on another floor with police. Mother was in the Psych ER with police. Dad and Granddad were in a hallway with police. Friends and neighbors were in the waiting room (no police).

I spoke with Dad first. He had been at the hospital for some time but still had his coat on and was standing near an exit like he wasn't completely there. He was neatly dressed with an unreal calmness swimming across his cheeks. A razor-sharp line of a beard closely trimmed his chin and lips. He hadn't been crying. His father stood a little shorter than him and directly at his shoulder. His coat was on, too. He didn't say a word, but did manage to release a few tears from his walnut eyes as Dad and I spoke. I introduced myself and we shook hands like salesmen.

He didn't see it coming. That was the heart of what he told me. Mother had a job. She had friends. She led a life that was as normal as the next-door neighbor. She laughed and cried and went to restaurants. She rented movies and returned them late. She had tried to lose weight and was saving up for a new couch. Dad had seen Mother and the children five days ago and everything was bliss. He and Mother had a cordial relationship that they kept up for the sake of the children. He had visited weekly. On his last visit he didn't notice anything strange or out of place about Mother—she wasn't particularly sad, or nervous, or anxious, or depressed, or anything. She had been fine. Just fine. Maybe a little depressed, but only a little, nothing unusual.

"Why did she seem just a little depressed?" I asked.

He took a long pause stroking his lips. "I don't know... she just did. I mean now that I look back on it...her voice just sorta sat lower in her or somethin'...I don't know...I'll never know...I didn't see it coming."

With that I was whisked upstairs by "BENNY...THE SOCIAL WORKER?" and into a dimly lit room in pediatrics where a big cop in full gear was sitting on the floor playing with Tisha and Keisha. Blein was sitting on a tiny chair at a small low table. He didn't look at us when we entered the room. I unbuttoned my coat and sat down. With my knees at my ears, I introduced myself to Blein. He looked at me without expression and asked, "What do you want?"

Blein was sharp. I could see this. He was not going to go for the typical "Hi buddy—do you like school? Any girlfriends? Who's your favorite teacher? What kind of ice cream do you like? You think those All-Star Wrestling guys are for real?" He knew why he was here and he wanted to cut to the chase.

"I want to talk about what happened to Shaniece and Paul today," I said.

He looked up from his hands. "Mom told them to jump out the window."

The other kids continued to play with the cop. They were stacking some dirty-looking hollow plastic blocks covered with the spit and tears of a thousand sick children. Tisha and Keisha played silently, but the cop did not. The pauses in my conversation with Blein rang with husky imitations of buses and cars and shoppers and poodles from the big boy in the corner wearing a gun.

"What did your mom say to Shaniece and Paul before they went out the window?" I asked.

"She said all of us were going to jump out the window... but I wasn't gonna. I was just mad at her...I wasn't gonna jump out that window." Blein looked angry. It was strange to see a child's face laced with the anger of a full-sized man.

"Why did she want all of you to jump out the window?"
I asked.

He answered with an appalled sound in his voice, "She was
saying she had a bad dream and it was from God and she was
saying everything was gonna burn up in a fire and so we had
to go to God so we wouldn't burn up in that fire. But...but I
was just mad and I wasn't gonna do it. And I was looking at
Paul and he didn't want to jump out that window and Mom
was saying that he *had* to jump out that window and then she
was saying that when he jumped out...that he wouldn't hit
the ground. She was—she told us that God would catch me
when I jumped out that window. But I was just saying no and
I wasn't gonna."

"You weren't going to jump," I said.

"*No,*" he answered quickly, "and no one wanted to."

"Then what happened?" I asked. Blein paused, scratching
at the table. The officer was barking softly in the far corner
with a block in each hand, "...*ruff...rrrooo rooo rooo...*
Hey you...you stop that!...Hey you...hey you, big dog!...
Rooo rooo rooo rooo..."

"Blein...Blein, what happened then?" I asked.

"Then she was saying for us to all be quiet and God was
gonna tell us to jump out that window...and then we were
all just sitting there...but *I* wasn't gonna close my eyes."

"She asked you to close your eyes?" I asked.

"*Yeah,* she did," he answered. "She told us to all close our
eyes and so everyone was closing their eyes, but I didn't 'cause
I was just mad, and also Keisha didn't either 'cause she was
just playing," he continued with a disgusted suck of his teeth,
"*Tch*...I was just mad 'cause I was thinking that God
wouldn't tell none of us to jump out that window..."

He paused. The cop was trying his best to distract Tisha
and Keisha with that silly unfunny voice adults use with children, "...Hey you, big dog!...don't bite me!...Hey you...
hey you, shopper!...what'dja buy, shopper?..." He kept it

going but it had little effect on the girls as their attention shifted to Blein, their new oldest brother.

"Shaniece?" Mother asked. "Go over to the window." Shaniece went to the window, which was wide open. Tears fell from her cheeks as she looked straight ahead to the blue sky. Mother was sitting on the floor with the other children. They could see only a silhouette in the window, like the shadow drawings they had done in art class with a slide projector. Shaniece's shoulders quaked with emotion and fear. Through her own tears, Mother asked one more time, very slowly, a thousand tons on each word, "Did you hear God tell you to come to him, Shaniece?" The air was still and heavy as eight little eyes watched their oldest sister set an example for the rest of the family. Shaniece's head slowly nodded up and down. *"You are my dearest heart,"* Mother whispered to herself. Shaniece stood shaking in the window as Mother continued her instructions. "Climb up on the windowsill, Shaniece." The children watched in silence as Shaniece climbed to a crouching position where she teetered on the windowsill—her toes pointing over the twenty-three-story drop. She continued staring straight into the sky, never looking down. "Shaniece?" Mother's voice trembled with emotion. "When you step off the sill, you won't hit the ground. You know that, right? Don't look down. God will reach his hand in front of you and take you up to be his most special daughter." Mother squeezed her eyes shut in prayer. Tears gushed out as she begged for God's mercy. She opened her eyes.

Shaniece's body became suddenly still. Then with her head up and her arms outstretched, she stepped forward and silently fell.

Mother shot up screaming Holy Jesus. Shaniece had been saved from Satan's fire. "We're *all* going to be saved," she said as she turned around and looked to her four remaining children. They were huddled together on the floor while shouts floated up from below. "Paul?" Mother asked. "Stand up and walk to the window, Paul."

"Paul didn't want to go to that window," Blein said to me as Tisha and Keisha abandoned the cop and the blocks and wandered over to the tiny table with us. Keisha sat on my right knee as Blein continued.

"Paul was scared but he walked over to it anyways," he said. "I was thinking I would just get up and run out the door 'cause God wouldn't tell me to jump out no window, so I would just run away."

"Did you try to run away, or did your mother tell you to stay in the room and to not leave or anything like that?" I asked.

"No," he said, "she was just talking to Paul then. I think she could tell Paul was really scared so she went up by the window with him." Blein's eyebrows looked as though they would be permanently pushed down from this day on.

"What did God say to you when your eyes were shut, Paul?" Mother asked as she stood looking straight out the window. The shouts from below were growing louder. Paul stood stone-faced at the window with his mother close to his side.

"What did he say, Paul?" She asked again. Paul looked over his shoulder to his little brother and two sisters.

"Paul?" Mother whispered.

"I don't know," Paul mumbled.

"You don't know? You don't know, Paul?" she asked. "God told Shaniece to come to him, Paul. Shaniece is with God. We're all going to be with Shaniece and God. He wants us all to be there together so we can be safe. Paul . . . . *there's a fire coming.*"

Paul looked straight out, not letting an ounce of emotion escape from him. Blein could see through the poker face and prayed for God to take their mother first and decide later about all of them. It felt like the fire was already here and they were in the thick of it.

"I love you, Paul. You know I love you," Mother said. "Climb up on the windowsill. Don't look down."

Paul was a big eight-year-old. He might have been able to overpower his mother, but he was also a good boy. Good boys don't overpower their mothers; good boys listen to their mothers. Paul climbed reluctantly onto the metal edge of the sill. Mother stood behind him, helping him up. The outside air whipped his shirt around, making it ripple and tickle on his back. It sounded like there were a lot of people below, and they were all shouting. Now he was very scared.

"Look straight out, Paul," Mother said. "Don't look down. When you step out, look for God's hand. It will come out of the sky and he'll take you up to be at his side with Shaniece. The rest of us will be coming right after you . . . We'll all be saved, Paul . . . we'll all be—"

Frantic pounding on the front door. Harrowed screaming from below. Paul looked down. People were screaming. People were screaming at *him*. People were screaming at him to fall back into the house. People were *begging* him. It looked like there was a lady crying. Suddenly he saw Shaniece, who was nowhere near the right hand of God. She was a red lanky heap on the sidewalk. Good sense smacked him hard. He arched his shoulders backward in terror, grabbing at the edges of the window, but it was too late. His mother had already *pushed* him off the sill. Reaching back, his fingers clutched whistling air. He landed on top of Shaniece, who broke his fall. He did not die instantly.

Mother stood with her head gyrating on her shoulders. Her arms clutched the sides of the window as she screamed a painful praise to Jesus. The pounding on the front door became furious, blending with Mother's frenzied praise in a lunatic thunder. The three children jostled to their feet. Mother whirled around from the window, setting her sights on them. Blein and

Tisha bolted. Three-year-old Keisha stood in tears, frozen, her little mind fibrillating with confused fear. Still rattling praises to her savior, Mother raced over in a panic and swooped the child into her arms. By this time, Blein had made it to the door, which was heaving savagely. Blein and Tisha could hear frantic shouting from would-be rescuers on the other side, but they were just a confused blur. There were three dirty brass locks on the door and Blein's little fingers raked ferociously at them as Mother headed with Keisha to the gaping window. Hysterical spectators galloped senselessly around the crushed Shaniece and Paul as Mother stood in the window with Keisha held forward in her arms. The child was a frozen block of wood staring out at the sky. Her eyes fell back in her head as Mother moved her to the very edge of the window's open mouth, still hollering to God and angels. Keisha did a dainty ballerina tip-toe on the edge of the sill trying to hold on. Suddenly she let out a siren burst from her pinhole mouth as Blein tossed the last lock open and police flooded in like water through a submarine door. The first officer plowed to the window and grabbed Mother and Keisha, throwing them across the floor and into the cupboards. Instantly the room filled with large blue-shirts, and the screaming praises of Mother were drowned out by a static barrage of police radios.

Keisha was getting heavy on my leg and as I switched her to the other one, Blein talked about sister Shaniece, his favorite.

"Shaniece's not gonna come back no more... and I know that Mom threw her out that window—God didn't do that. I liked Shaniece the most 'cause... 'cause she would always play with me—always. She was the best one to play with... She said, 'And I'm always gonna play with you, my little Blein... And I'm always gonna play with you.' I'm gonna miss that Shaniece sister... I miss her right now..."

Blein's head bent and he cried. He hissed two lungfuls and stopped abruptly, twisting his fists into his eyes. Tisha patted him on the back and stared at me blankly. Keisha played with my pen. Keisha the window ballerina.

I told the children I was going to talk to their mother and then come back and take them with me.

"Where are we going with you?" Blein asked, instantly suspicious—the new little man.

"I'm going to take you to my office and we're going to try to find a place for you to stay that will be safe. I'll be back," I said.

Eyebrows down, he stared at me silently as Keisha rolled off my knee and pumped her legs busily over to the cop with the blocks. I left the room feeling like Blein had filled my head with lead.

I opened the door and walked out into the hall with silent Yvette. "BENNY...THE SOCIAL WORKER?" was leaning against the wall and sprang forward as we stepped out.

"WHAT'D THEY SAY?" he asked.

"In a nutshell?"

"WELL, YEAH...I HAVE TO KNOW FOR THE CHILD WELFARE REPORT."

"I'm *with* Child Welfare, Benny."

"OF COURSE, I KNOW THAT."

"So you already gave a report. That's why I'm here."

"WELL...I KNOW, BUT I STILL HAVE TO CALL IT IN."

"But I'm here already."

"RIGHT, RIGHT—BUT I STILL HAVE TO CALL IT IN TO CHILD WELFARE."

"But I'm *with* Child Welfare."

"OF COURSE, I KNOW YOU ARE."

"So I'm already here, Benny."

"WELL, I STILL HAVE TO CALL IT IN."

"But you already did. That's why I'm—"

And so on.

Benny finally led me to where Mother was being held after

I promised I'd give all the details for him to CALL IN THE CHILD WELFARE REPORT. We walked through a maze of hallways and doors guarded by security and an occasional cop until we reached a large white door. As we approached, Benny pointed to it, keeping his arm held close to his chest and his eyebrows raised, mouthing, "That's it. In there."

Benny left and I stood with Yvette at the big white door.

5

IT'S PROBABLY WRONG TO BELIEVE then or now that there is any way to imagine the terror Ms. Jacobs had experienced. A dream that had turned black, a black so rich and pure that darkness begot darkness until the black covered all that was normal and routine. The most terrifying question for all of us is, How near are we to the pure black at any given moment? Of all the abominable dynamics of the black, there is nothing that rivals the insanity when it comes to visit out of context. On a sunny day. At a wedding. At a ball game. At a barbecue. *During a restful sleep.* And when it strikes, it only strikes hard. How much can our minds take while still maintaining sleepless vigil of relentless sanity? How far can we go with the black visiting our own living rooms before it's all upside down and children start to drop out of windows? As important as the answer is, there is only uncertainty.

What does it take to convince a mother to throw her children out a window? There's comfort in believing a person who would do something like this is a complete lunatic and nothing like the rest of us. But I think that might not be entirely the case here. All indications pointed to the fact that prior to that morning, Ms. Jacobs had done a stellar job as mother to her kids. Prior to her actions, it seems, she *was* just like any of us. Her home was neat and well furnished. She and her ex-husband got along nicely. She didn't use drugs, according to friends and neighbors, and had no radical religious beliefs or practices. She had no prior record of child abuse and according to the hospital, no history of mental problems. It was the dream that broke Ms. Jacobs, I'd soon find out. She revealed a few of its details with the words, what she left unsaid was communicated well enough through the shuddering lines of her face and the incoherent quaking of her throat. To understand her actions, I've tried to re-create the intensity of that dream so that it might, in the smallest way, explain her actions when she woke up. I'm not saying we'd all throw our children out a window after a dream like hers—everyone is different. What I'm saying is that we all hold, in our minds, the ability to create images that would break us in half.

I took a deep breath and let it go. I looked to Yvette, who stared blankly back. Then, with a dry mouth and the hairs on the back of my neck slowly rotating in their follicles, I reached for the door and pushed it forward. It scraped heavy on its hinges as it opened wide, and I was confronted with a bleak sight—the empty neon-white room with one blank-faced cop, and the wet, sputtering face of Ms. Jacobs. Each of her wrists were handcuffed tightly to the ambulance stretcher she was lying on.

"You need me to stay here?" the cop asked, immediately concerned.

"I think we'll be okay, if you don't mind," I said, indicating the door.

"I'll be right outside if you need me," he said. "I'll just be right here if anything happens."

"Right. Thanks."

I'm thinking, *What's she gonna do to us handcuffed to a stretcher like that? Where's the danger?* He looked back at me as he was leaving, with his eyes asking, "Are you poooositive I should go??" The concern was thick and it gave me the spooks. The room closed behind him and we were with her.

Silent, Yvette stood with her back on the door. I stood one step closer.

To look straight at her was chilling. A person that has done something so terrible has a power that's intoxicating. You get the feeling that they might do anything because, in a way, they already have. If someone has the constitution to toss her kids out a window, what's to stop her from following up with any of the worst possible acts imaginable? *This is a person with no boundaries,* you think, *who can go all the way, a person who can get intense.* She gave me the creeps, plain and simple. The room was so tight that there was no way to be anywhere but *near* her. It was a stifling little place and it was *her* place. I thought if she suddenly moved, or shouted, or even just said my name, I'd drop everything and bolt right through the big white door.

"Hello?"

Nothing.

"Ms. Jacobs?"

She turned her head like a beaten dog. The handcuffs clinked against the side rails of the stretcher. She looked at me through badly mucked-up eyes, paused without expression, and started to make a quiet popping sound with sticky lips, "*pup pup pup pup pup pup pup pup puppuppupupupup . . .*"

Gooseflesh broke out over my arms and cheeks. "Ms. Jacobs? . . ."

"*. . . pup pup pupp pu pu pu pupupupup pupupupupu-pup . . .*"

I looked back at Yvette. Nothing. I turned back to Ms. Jacobs who was pup-pup-pupping away. Her lips struggled to stay glued together as her jaw flapped madly. We hadn't even started and I was feeling lost. Her eyes beckoned me through the muck to join her. I struggled to stay with it; just to stand there and ask a few questions.

"What are you doing?" I asked her stupidly, "Are you trying to say—are you..." I looked to Yvette. Her skirt wouldn't get us out of this one. Her shoulders went up, and then they went down. Nothing. Ms. Jacobs continued pupping uninterrupted. The sounds sped up and evened out.

"Ms. Jacobs?...My name is Marc Parent. I have to ask you about what happened with your kids earlier today."

She's just really so curious what my name is, I absently thought. *Now she knows me and we can be great friends.*

"Ms. Jacobs?...," I continued. My voice was trembling badly. I was trying my professional best, but I knew I was giving myself away. This was one of those times where being professional seemed almost insincere. I was at a loss—so many things to ask, such a small room, so much pupping. My mind jumped away from me. *You repulsive, vile—I could twist your Medusa head right off and you'd probably enjoy it—*

"Ms. Jacobs?...," I begged for a moment of clarity, from her, from me, from Silent Yvette, from the cop outside, from anybody. The room was getting tighter and louder.

"PUPUPUPPUPUPUPUPUPUPUPPUPUPUPPPUPPUP..."

My mind began its own rampage—*Fucking shut up, you filthy, revolting*—as I struggled to stay with it. "Ms. Jacobs," I pushed on, shouting over the pupping. "Why are you here right now? Why do you think you're here?"

Her cuffs squeaked and chattered against themselves and she barked, "*I gotta use the bathroom.*"

Bingo. Sweet clarity.

"Ms. Jacobs—please, if you can wait—"

"I GOTTA GO TO THE BATHROOM," she shouted.

Well, let's just drag this out as long as we can, since we're getting along so famously.

"Get the cop," I told Yvette. She opened the door and leaned out.

"He wants you," I heard her say.

Well done, Yvette—nice shoes.

The cop bounced in, ready to rock.

"She's gotta go to the bathroom," I said. His chest deflated as he looked over to her.

"She's gotta take a pee?" he asked.

"Well...I don't know," I said.

"I'll get someone," he said, and jangled off.

The door shut behind him as he left. I stood motionless in the tiny room with Mother and Yvette.

"...*pupu pupupuppu...upupu upupupup...*"

I stared at Ms. Jacobs's toes curling over the end of the stretcher. They lunged painfully forward to look around without the slightest connection to the rest of her body. What a peculiar sight it would be from underneath the stretcher with her toes peeking playfully about. I thought absently about this while waiting for the help to arrive. *At least I don't have to help pull down her drawers, I just have to talk to her. That's impossible enough.* The person helping Ms. Jacobs with her drawers hadn't talked with the children. I should've really talked to Mother before talking with the children. Some of Blein's anger had seeped into me, and it was now *my* eyebrows that were pushed firmly down on my forehead.

"...*pup pup pup upupupup upup...pupupuppu...*"

"Let's wait outside, Yvette," I said. We stepped out and stood a few feet from the door. I took a deep breath and relaxed my shoulders to waist level. The cop came clattering back with a nurse in tow. They pushed Mother down the hall and around the corner.

After a few moments, Yvette looked at me and asked, "What in the hell was that lady trying to say in there?"

"You think I have any idea?" I asked.

She humped her shoulders and shook her head. "That lady is fucked up."

"I'm gonna call the office to let them know what's up," I said. "They're probably bumping their heads on the ceiling wondering what's going on."

I went to the nursing station to begin the long wait on the phone. There were at least five people in the office being paid full salaries to answer the phones and direct calls to their proper places, but God help me if I didn't spend a year and a half of my four years at ECS waiting for someone to pick up. After one hundred and one rings, the phone was answered as always—

"Emergency Children's Services."

"Hi, this is Marc, I'm at th—"

"MARC—where are you?"

"I'm at the hospital. Everyone's here. I spoke with Dad—he didn't see it coming. I spoke to the kids and I'm just about to speak—"

"MARC—did you speak with Mother?"

"Right, I spoke briefly with her but she had to—"

"What did the mother say, Marc?"

"Well, not much, she had to go to the bathroom. I was just calling to let you know what's happened up to this poi—"

"MARC—did you *see* her?"

"Yes."

"Then what did she say?"

"Well, nothing yet...I kept trying to speak with her but she just kept making like a 'pupping' kinda sound."

"What do you mean 'a popping sound'?"

"No, no—a *pupping* sound—with her mouth. I don't know, she was just going 'pupupupupup' whenever I asked her—"

"What was she trying to say, Marc?"

"...Well, I'm not exactly—"

"MARC,...Marc—listen. You have to try a little harder, okay? I understand you're upset and have a lot to think about—this is a *challenging case,* but you've gotta try to relax...okayyyyy?

"Bu—"

"Marc?...listen to me—"

"Yup."

"The mother may be trying to *tell* you something."

"Okay."

"And you have to try to read the *visual cues* she's displaying to understand the situation. Remember to use all of your resources. She may not be communicating with *words,* but that doesn't mean she's not giving you *a lot* of information by other means! Try to pick up on the *nonverbal signals* she's putting out—Are her emotions appropriate for the situation? Is she depressed? Is she sad? Is she angry? What's making her angry? Is she capable of identifying her situational dynamics?"

"Can she identify the major *stressors* in her life?" I added.

"*That's* it. Get her to answer these questions so you can root out the appropriate coping mechanisms that might be at her disposal. She can then use these to deal more effectively with this difficult time in her life. Is she being admitted?"

"I don't know."

"Well, you have to find that out."

"Okay."

"I know you can do it, Marc."

"I'll do my best," I said. "I gotta go."

"Don't be afraid to call again for help—oh and also, don't be afraid to use Yvette—*she's a resource too!*"

"All right. I gotta go."

"Call me back, Marc. You're my eyes out there!"

"Yup. I gotta go now."

Situational dynamics?

I walked back to speak with Mother, and ran into "BENNY...THE SOCIAL WORKER?"

"YOU GOING TO TAKE THE KIDS?" he called out.

"Looks like it, Benny," I answered. "Did'ja call in that Child Welfare report yet?"

"I WAS WAITING ON THAT ANSWER," he said. "I'M CALLING IT IN NOW!"

"Good job, my man," I shouted back as he flipped me a thumbs-up.

Yvette looked at me flatly. "Marc, that man don't gotta call in a report to Child Welfare—we're here already."

Back in the suffocation room, Mother looked a little rejuvenated by her pee break. She was still cuffed by each wrist, but was now sitting upright at the end of the stretcher. Her legs dangled over the edge with her curious toes still dumbly flexing around. They were a terrible distraction. Mother's head was still wet with grief, but the pupping had stopped and it looked like I had a window to get a few words with her. She swayed gently as we spoke. The cuffs tinkled like wind chimes.

"Ms. Jacobs," I began, "if you're able to, I'd like to hear your version of what happened today... Ms. Jacobs?"

"... okay," she gurgled.

"Can you tell me why you're here?" I asked. She paused and then began crying lightly, still swaying. I could tell she was trying to stay with me. "What happened to Shaniece and Paul?" I ventured.

"Shaniece... Shaniece was my good sweetest... she was my heart... that's a good girl... that is such a good girl," she chirped through tears. "Shaniece is my dearest angel." Her voice suddenly went low. "Someone should've called me... why didn't... *if only someone called me*... someone should've—*SOMEONE SHOULD'VE CALLED ME... I might not have—it might not... NO, GOD—OH PLEASE ...OH GODDD...*"

"What happened to Shaniece?" I asked.

"Shaniece went out that window, my heart," she said, quickly shifting to a little-girl voice—a little Shaniece voice. "She is so so good. Shaniece is my best one..."

"Why did she go out the window?" I asked. She looked around gingerly. There was a real fit going on inside her as she struggled to keep on. She looked at me sweetly. "She went out because I *asked* her to ... I asked her to and she did it ... she is such a good girl."

"Why did you do that? Why did you have her do that?" I asked.

She cleared up for an instant, looked at me sternly. "What are you saying? You think I don't know what you're saying? You think you're so smart ... *I love that girl* ... you don't know ... don't you even think—I know what you're thinking ... that girl's my *heart* ... MY HEART ... I love that girl more than you'll *ever* know ... more than you'll *ever* know ... I know what you're saying."

I bet you do, I thought.

"Where is Shaniece now?" I asked her. It almost felt like a cheap shot. Her crying got thicker as the window began to close.

"Where is my Shaniece now ... where is my sweeeeet ... where is my SWEEEEEEEEET ..." Her voice soared to its highest register; I was losing her fast.

"Why did you tell her to jump?" I erupted. *"Why did you do it?"*

She looked at me startled and still wheezing, "I HAD TO SEND HER TO GOD ... I SENT MY SWEETEST CHILD TO GOD ... I DON'T KNOOOOOOOW ... UUUAAAUUGH-OOON'T KNOOOOOOOW ..." She tried to bring her hands to her face, but the cuffs clanged against the steel railing of the stretcher, holding them at least a foot away. Her torso lurched forward, desperately straining to bring her head to her hands. She clenched her teeth, growling as she pulled with a mighty burst against the cuffs. They crashed loudly and bit into her wrists, pulling her skin impossibly backward. Her face remained naked in the light.

"They were burning ... I had a dream ... God was saying ... all night ... all night ... WE WERE BURNING ALL NIGHT ... The whole building—everything was ... I watched them burn to pieces ... burning little pieces ... I couldn't, I just

could NOT ... *keep* ... *do that* ... *I love them all—you'll tell them, okay?* ... *I will always love them* ... I will ALWAYS love them ..."

She looked squarely into my face and swung her wrists sharply upward causing the cuffs to make a chilling squeal against the rails. "—*you try to put THAT in handcuffs* ... *you tell them their mommy LOVES THEM* ... *dearly dearly* ..."

She sputtered off, fell back exhausted, and mumbled prayers to God. The window shut tight and she was gone— maybe for a day, maybe for always. I'll never know. Perhaps she'd come back for brief periods and slip away when reality came bearing down. I don't know how many times she opened the window to come back, or if she ever came back at all after that last "dearly dearly," but I did give Blein and Tisha and Keisha her message.

6

IT WAS AFTER MIDNIGHT by the time we hit the road. Yvette played in the back with Tisha and Keisha until they fell asleep. Little man Blein sat up front with his eyes popped wide and suspicious. I got friendly enough with him that he could trust me for the ride, but not so much so that he would be crushed when we separated, which would be soon. No matter what you had just been through with the kids you removed, as soon as you hit the front doors of the office, they were swooped away by the staff of the newly formed nursery and that's the last you'd see of them without a glass between you. The system demanded that you keep the children at arm's length while at the same time fighting for their well-being as if they were your own. It was a tough line to walk. One of the many mistakes made by new workers was getting close to the kids to soften the initial blow of removal. As soon as they got to the office, they'd be ripped apart and it would be another scream-fest at the front door.

Just before reaching Manhattan, we stopped at a Mc-Donald's for a little pick-me-up. It had been a long evening for everyone but it was far from over for the little Jacobses, and while the office was great at removing kids, it wasn't so hot at feeding them. The more french fries they ate now, the less bologna-and-mustard sandwiches they'd have to slag down later. Blein and I ordered and brought it all back to Yvette and the girls. The two of us had Big Macs and medium Cokes. The girls had Happy Meals and split a strawberry shake. Yvette had a large diet Coke and a box of McDonaldland cookies. The girls put on their Happy Land paper hats as we finished, and wore them the rest of the night. We got to the office and were separated at around 2:00 A.M.

I was coffee drunk at four when I finally finished the write-up. As I was gathering my things together, the night manager came running over with a case flopping in his hand. "Better run out and check on this, Marc," he said with a smirk as he tossed it on my desk, "called in by this Benny guy—social worker at Far Bellpage. Looks like some lady just threw her kids out the window."

I called my girlfriend to tell her I'd be coming home. She met me on the street and we slipped into the Jack and Jill Diner for some scrambled eggs and home fries. Across the booth, I nuzzled against the soothing folds of her palms. The familiar din of after-hours clubbers with the munchies was comforting. In one moment and in two loving hands, I was a million miles from Far Bellpage. The eggs arrived and turned cold sitting in front of me as I rambled on about the evening. She listened with puffed, squinting eyes and hunched shoulders—eager to get back to bed. I shut up after a bit and we picked at the cold home fries until they were gone, leaving the eggs lonely on the plate.

I had a hard time getting to sleep that night. I took the next day off and enjoyed Sunday coffee and Dutch Mill doughnuts with the roommates. We laughed at how good they tasted and how cheap they were, and agreed we'd all pay a lot more for them. My girlfriend picked up the morning papers and on the cover of each one was the tragic story of the Jacobses. All the articles were pretty much the same: mother threw kids out window—motive unclear—surviving children taken by Child Welfare. The next two evenings in the news were filled with numerous accounts of what happened. One channel featured an especially chilling version of the moments before Shaniece's and Paul's jumps. The reporter had managed to get into the Jacobs home and repeatedly jabbed the camera over the edge of the window, giving all of us a look at their final moments.

For the remainder of the week, I listened to my girlfriend fall asleep, the sound of her breathing ushering me through endless, infuriating valleys of insomnia. The Jacobses were evicted from the headlines after a few short days. Not forgotten—who could forget a story like theirs—but definitely out of the spotlight of public consciousness. Filed away in the brutal-world-but-what-are-you-gonna-do-about-it archives. You never forget—I didn't forget, *you* won't forget. But at some point, you do stop thinking about it, and that's the whole problem.

4

Gruff Robby

THUNK-WHUMP. TIME CARD. One year later—November, and the days were really getting short. Even though ECS was called the nighttime office, we all tried to cheat Mr. Dark as much as possible. During the summer you could get out quick and handle two cases in Queens before night shut out the lights, but in November, dusk teased the skyline at about four o'clock. After punching in and downing two coffees, it might as well have been midnight. Not that taking someone's kid away in daylight made things any easier, it wasn't like—*"Oh since there's still daylight, let me get the door for you. Bye-bye Johnny—be good in foster care!"* It's just that the dear blue sky made getting to the cases seem a little less like a daredevil sport.

I walked to my desk and tossed my jacket on a chair. *Thunk-whump. Thunk-whump.* Willie Samuels. Two time cards, one paycheck, right, Will? One card would go to the clock and the other was slipped into the side pocket of his wine-colored leather trench.

"No money, no honey, my brother," he'd always say. "No money, no honey."

He strutted back to his desk and threw down a battered briefcase with a bumper sticker on it proclaiming I'M A CHER-OKEE with a big-titted squaw in a mini and high heels tipping her feathered headdress howdy.

Willie slapped the briefcase onto his desk and snapped open the clasps. "No money, no honey—and that ain't no funny for the Superfly."

A shout came out of the back of the office as six-foot-eight, 250-pound Jesse Knight lumbered into the room. "Get off the radio, Willie. You ain't on the damn radio now—you're at your damn job and you ain't no Superfly. You're a Super-Sucker-Sorrymotherfucker and you punched in twice."

Willie had already stopped at the deli outside. He tossed two bags of fried "hot 'n' spicy" pork rinds, a can of mackerel in oil, and three coffees on his desk.

Jesse looked at me with mock disgust. "My man Will callin' himself the Superfly. What about that shit, Money?"

Jesse and the gang would call me "Money" but it always came out "Moany." Jesse was especially good at tossing out little phrases that demanded a response and yet at the same time were impossible to follow up. Little things like, "What about that shit, Money?" or "What's fat, Homes?" He and Willie would stare at me and I'd drop the ball with a dumb smile and a halfhearted, "I don't know, man." I finally realized after some time that all they really wanted from me was a " 'ts fucked up" to keep the rap going.

Jesse kept it up, pointing to me and shouting to Willie, "Money says he ain't down with that—right, Homes?"

"I don't know, man," I said.

He looked to Willie, laughing. "Money don't buy that, Homes. He says if you the Superfly, then he's the Freaky Freak. Ain't that right, Money?"

"I don't know, man," I said.

Willie began twisting the tin off the can of mackerel, filling the air with the smell of greasy fish. "I *am* the Superfly," he said and turned to me. "Pleased to meet you, Freaky Money."

"AEYOOOOOOOOoooooo," Jesse chimed and clapped five with Willie.

This kind of thing could go on for hours and it usually did, but when the situation demanded, they could turn it off like a faucet and assume a professional facade complete with "how-do-you-do-sir"'s at all the right places.

After a few minutes of trying to find my tongue, I made an awkward "I-don't-know-man" exit and went to get the daily dose of memos and announcements stacked in my mailbox. I took them back to my desk, cracked open a cup of coffee, and started the look-crumple-toss machine. There was nothing unusual: minutes from the last union meeting—three hours of motions to decide the color of union mugs; a two-day training in Queens on spiral fractures and failure-to-thrive syndrome—let your supervisor know when you'll attend; unit meeting to discuss vacation schedules—someone's got to work on Christmas; party for Wilda "I AM TAKING DE CHILD" Hidalgo to celebrate twenty years on the job—bring a dish to pass and ten dollars for a gift; finally, a weekly howdy-do from the commissioner of the agency accompanied by statements about how hard our job is and how great we're all doing.

At the bottom of the pile there was another letter from the commissioner, but this one was different. It lacked the telltale black streaks of Xerox indicating agencywide distribution. It was on thick cream-colored paper, probably the commissioner's own. It was urgent. It stated in effect that it had come to his attention that phone calls had been made out of the ECS office to various "chat" lines in the area. Seems someone had been chatting up a real storm. They'd racked up a bill of twelve thousand dollars over the past two months. Twelve thousand dollars. I wanted to stand up and just shout "All right, who the hell did this?" but I didn't. No one did. At least not publicly. We all speculated privately among ourselves about who could've had a twelve-thousand-dollar "chat" in the lack of privacy the office provided. Sure we had our own desks, and sure there were partitions, but that was it. Even for the supervisors, it was the same. We were all connected in a collective murmur and none of us could remember hearing any twelve-thousand-dollar chat.

The commissioner kindly informed us there would be secret monitoring of our phones and that in the future, conversations with Kiki and her Wild Friends would have to be on our own time with our own dime. Did this mean, we all speculated, that if the bad apple in the bunch was discovered, he or she might be *fired*?? They would actually attempt to *fire* someone? This was more amazing than a twelve-thousand-dollar chat. Believing that someone could actually get fired was like believing in a UFO landing—you know it could happen but you also know it never will. We'd all become convinced you'd have to take a crap on the commissioner's desk singing "New York, New York" for them to even *think* about "starting an action" against you. Fired. Excellent idea. We were in desperate need of some slight staff adjustments. On the whole we were a good machine, but there were some annoying knocks in the engine and job security was becoming a real pain in the ass for quality control.

They never did find out who to bill for the nights with Kiki, but after a lot of discussion and debate, we all figured it was Giles. He was a strange guy, but that didn't make him much different from many others in the office. When supervision decided he was so strange that they couldn't use him to work on cases anymore, agency heads began sharpening their ax. Here was a man who was not allowed to work, even though he was allowed to punch in every day. They tried to fire Giles for the next seven months.

He was an unusually tall man with a tiny goatee wrapped tightly around the rim of his small mouth. Pinhole black eyes peered through his darkened, very thick glasses—contrasting sharply with the pale whiteness of his skin. He was one of the few people in the office who always wore a suit, though usually without a tie. He kept strictly to himself but was always polite when spoken to. At the end of the night when everyone was chattering away while waiting for the time clock to hit the end of the shift, Giles would sit in his chair looking at his fingers or at the phone or at his shoes or at a pen. For the most part he seemed completely detached from the world as we know it, but there was a sliver in his head that was wide awake and didn't miss a lick. It was the sliver that made him scary.

He'd only been in the office a few months before people started refusing to go to the field with him. Often, when the supervisors gave a field visit to a bad worker, they'd send them out with someone who was capable as a kind of insurance. The thinking was to put the good bucket under the one with holes and call it solid casework. Never officially admitted, this happened all the time with Giles and a few other rusty buckets. Although I could understand and even agree with the thinking, some of us old pails were getting tired of catching the spills.

The last straw came when Giles went out with one of the better spill catchers and asked if he could get something from a friend's house on the way to a case. They stopped in front of the friend's house and Giles ran inside with the car keys in his hand while his partner waited in the car. An *hour later* he came out and gave up the keys, saying he couldn't drive because he was feeling "a little funny." After that, everyone refused to go out with him. For the next month or so, supervision sent him out by himself on low-priority cases that couldn't

possibly be botched. But letting Giles drive a city car on city
gas and city time was like turning a kid loose in a candy store.

Giles was given a case, one night, requiring a visit to a
home located just over the Brooklyn Bridge, about twenty
minutes from the office if the traffic was bad. He went out at
five o'clock and punched back in around eleven-thirty. His case
write-up stated plainly, "Visited case. Knocked on apartment
door. No answer. Case referred for follow-up." Giles had taken
six and a half hours to do this fine bit of work. When he
handed the case in to his supervisor, she told him to sit down.
There was some mumbling between them but soon the volume
increased—the supervisor's, not Giles's. He had a way of
remaining completely expressionless and totally unflappable
through the harshest criticism. The supervisor did her best to
turn up the heat, but Giles sat as calm and happy as a loaf of
bread.

"There was no answer at the case address?"

"Oh, no," Giles answered earnestly.

"You knocked on the door?"

"Yes."

"And there was no answer."

"...Oh, that is correct."

"So where the hell were you all night?"

"...Oh, I was at the case."

"And no one answered the door."

"...Oh, that is correct."

"You're going to have to do better than that, Giles."

But he didn't have to do better than that. He never had to
do better than that. He'd throw out the most poorly conceived
lies with no explanations or apologies. It was like if he said it,
it was just true, because he knew no one had the time or energy
to *prove* he was lying—and everybody knows you've gotta
prove someone's lying if you're even thinking of suggesting it.
His supervisor waited for a response, but Giles just raised his
eyebrows and shrugged.

"C'mon, Giles, you were out all night. What took you so long to get back?"

"...Oh, the traffic was bad."

"Why didn't you call me and tell me the traffic was bad?"

"...Oh, I didn't have any money to call."

"Giles, you're suppose to take money with you so you can call. Everyone in this office calls when they're in the field. I told you to call me."

"...Oh, I'm sorry about that. I think I forgot all about that."

"Look, just tell me if you even went to this case. I have to send someone else out right away if you didn't."

"...Oh, I visited that case," he said with his bread-loaf expression.

"You visited the case."

"There was nobody home."

"And you got stuck in traffic...Giles, get out of here. Go back to your desk."

She ran back to the war room and flagged the case for an immediate visit on the next shift. Giles wasn't sent to the field again.

He kept coming to work though! Seven months they tried to can him. Every day, I'd be up to my nostrils in cases and glance over at Giles, who'd be sitting at his desk looking at the ceiling or looking at his hands or *talking on the phone.*

Having a chat.

Get it? I got it. But I couldn't prove it. *Giles, say hi to Kiki for me. I'll do three cases for you if you send her my love.*

After the commissioner's memo, I started to recall how many nights I'd seen Giles hunched forward in his cubicle with the phone pressed to his ear. Once I had to use the phone next to him and I could hear him cooing, with the only smile I ever saw on his face, "...Oh, really?...Oh, would you?...Oh, that, too?" It didn't seem too strange at the time, but three hours later, I had to use the phone again and Giles was having the same conversation—"... Oh, really?... Oh, you would?... Oh, that, too?"

They never succeeded in firing Giles. Instead he was transferred out of our site and into a daytime field office. Two years after I quit ECS I bumped into him, one afternoon, at the Nathan's Hot Dog in Coney Island. He smiled across the metal tables and said hello to me as if we'd been talking just ten minutes ago. He complained about still being in the field office.

"The people in this office are assholes," he said through a mouthful of french fries, "but the job is pretty good, though. They give me a car and I can just cruise around." He bounced his eyebrows at me. I smiled and we raised our hot dogs to each other.

"Good seeing you, Marc," he said as I turned to leave. "I think you lost some weight. You look good."

I made a muscle and we both laughed. I hadn't lost any weight.

"It's the truth. I'm not lying," he said with a smile. A sort of bread-loaf smile.

2

BY FOUR-THIRTY, EVERYONE was clearing their desk of useless memos and tucking away the ones they needed. A few folks straggled in late and began to complete tardy forms before even taking off their coats. Barked coffee orders filled the office and quarters changed hands. People were cleaning their phones with rubbing alcohol and plugging in their radios. From about four to five was the limbo time of the shift, when there was no telling if the night would bring a sprinkle or a hurricane. I could hear cases churning into the war room but that didn't mean anything. Many of them were forwarded directly to the field offices to be picked up in the morning. The emergencies were pulled from the conveyor belt like factory rejects and set aside to be prioritized and assigned.

My first coffee slid down a little too quickly so I decided to head out to get another before being covered with work. By the time I had my jacket on and was heading to the door, I had five additional requests for coffee along with an order from Jesse for a cheeseburger with fries. Downtown Manhattan, where the office was located, is pretty boarded up by five o'clock, but there were two places in the area that remained open. One, a larger restaurant, was bounced off my favorite places in New York list after I came across an unidentified object in a chicken salad sandwich. The other was a lovely little diner that looked like it was plucked straight out of the Midwest and smacked into the base of a skyscraper complete with boothfuls of old folks dribbling cold cereal and milk down their chins. Fake wooden planks spelled out the name above the door, SQUARE DINER. It was a much more humble diner than the other joint, but there weren't any wigglies in their chicken salad and the Cokes were bigger. While waiting for Jesse's cheeseburger, I enjoyed an order of mashed potatoes served up in an I ♥ NY coffee cup.

When I got back to the office there was a case placed squarely on my desk marked "field visit."

> Mother is a drunk. She is drunk every day. Her child Robby, 11 yrs old, is alone with her now. Robby has been seen on numerous occasions dragging his mother into their building after she has passed out on the streets. Mother is believed to be a prostitute. It is unk. if mother uses any other drugs. Robby is mother's only child. Mother is drunk now.

The source of the report wished to remain anonymous, so there wasn't anyone to call to clarify the allegations. Once in a while, cases generated by anonymous callers proved to be true, but not usually. Reported crack houses with children locked in small crates covered in bruises and urine often turned out to be buildings with doormen and well-cared-for children tucked tightly in bed. The toll of false reports was exhausting. It was sickening to visit families in the middle of the night, make parents wait outside, wake up children and strip them naked to look for bruises that were never there. More often than not, victims of false reports turned out to be people in the midst of completely unrelated feuds with a neighbor or two. Strange coincidence.

"Marc, did you get the case on your desk?" The shout came from a supervisor cubicle. "You'll be going out with Dana. She's got a case uptown but I want you to visit yours first."

Dana was one of my favorite people in the office. She was everything you'd want in a partner to run through pockets of hell with—smart, tough, funny, agile, clever, dependable, a pretty decent driver, and she knew all the best rice-and-beans places. You could be in Satan's own bedroom and Dana'd make you grateful to be there with the rice-and-beans place she'd find. Food so good it scrambled down your throat before your teeth could get ahold of it. Flan for dessert with warm sugar syrup dribbled over the top and a hot Cuban coffee on the side. Good eats. On top of all that, Dana was also a lesbian, which meant more than anything else that during lunch breaks at Manhattan sidewalk cafés, we could watch the summer-hot pedestrians and appreciate the same daisy dukes—tight as they could be, the shortest shorts on the planet.

Although there were no official field partners at ECS, the preferences of workers were generally respected. It did, after all, make a big difference in the course of the night and sometimes in the course of safety. There were workers whose style was so abrasive and inflammatory that it was amazing they ever finished their shift without two fat lips. It was also helpful to have another set of eyes you trusted when huge decisions boiled down to a few very fine judgment calls. Dana and I were sent out together frequently and we'd become familiar with each other's styles.

She cleared my case through the computer while I was out harvesting Jesse's burger, and found three previous reports on my drunk prostitute mother—all generated by anonymous callers, all investigated, and all unfounded. A slow night. This wasn't the kind of case that would get a prompt visit on a normal night when every mother was reported drunk at the very least, and visits went only to the ones playing naked party games with their children. It looked like a quick in and out and Dana's seemed like more of the same. We weren't complaining.

I ran into Dana on my way to the bathroom. She was putting some things into her locker but stopped to give my shoulders a quick squeeze.

"Looks like a cakewalk tonight, brother," she whispered with a big white smile and a devilish curl to her nose.

"Looks like it," I said. "Looks just like it. Looks almost exactly like it."

"Did you eat?"

"Not really," I said. "Just a cup of mashers from the Square."

"Oh man—I told you already to knock it off with those nasty potatoes. They're no good there. Is that how your mom's potatoes tasted? Those things are so full of shit—you're gonna get yourself sick on a cupful one of these days."

"They're good," I said.

"They serve them in a coffee cup and they're not good," she said, stuffing the rest of her things in the locker. "You can't tell me potatoes served in a coffee cup are any good. Let's get out of here and get some serious good uptown, all right?"

"How 'bout we knock off the cases first so we can relax."

"All right, fine, but I'm hungry," she said, twisting the padlock shut.

"These are gonna be nothing, Dana. Let's just get out and get them done. I'll hit the bathroom and I'm ready to go."

"I'm ready now," she said. "I'll wait for you in the front."

I signed out a car and we parted into the dimming streets. Cruising uptown, we celebrated finding a real song on an AM radio, hollering at the top of our lungs to "Train in Vain" with the Clash blaring out of car #603's straining dash-mount speakers. After a bit of tooling around peering at building numbers, we found our case address. I pulled up and stopped the car just to the right of the building's awning, which ran across the sidewalk to the street, proudly proclaiming the building name—THE MAPLEWOOD. A doorman rushed out immediately and told us we were not allowed to park in front of the building. When we walked inside and told him we'd be going upstairs unannounced, he quickly forgot about the car.

"I have to announce all visitors," he recited in a thick Indian accent.

"We go up unannounced," I said.

"But I have to announce all visitors," he repeated, glancing briefly at our clothes. We were better suited for a mid-Bronx visit than an opulent Midtown lobby. The beat-up leather jackets that had seen us through many sticky neighborhoods unnoticed and unharassed were not serving us as well at the Maplewood.

"We're not visitors," I said as we pulled out our IDs for his inspection. The ECS ID never had much of an effect on people. They were flimsy plastic cards with a picture and signature. You can get one just like it at any arcade or amusement park. For the four years I was at ECS there was continuing debate among the higher-ups about adopting a more impressive-looking identification, but this issue, like so many others that would very much help the workers on the job, was constantly discussed and never resolved.

"What is this card?" the doorman said, turning it back and forth, looking for the smallest trace of a stamp or official seal. Even the commissioner's signature was a Xerox.

"That's my ID. We're with the city and you have to let us upstairs unannounced."

"This is no good," he said, shaking his head. He hated us now. "I have to call the supervisor. We will see what he says."

"Listen," I said, stopping his phone call. "We're going upstairs now. Unannounced. Call whoever you want, but if you call apartment 507, I promise I will contact the police and have you arrested for obstructing a mandated city investigation."

I don't know if he believed me, but he did put the phone down.

"Give me your names," he demanded, looking through the top drawer of his desk for a pen.

"We'll talk on the way out," I said as Dana and I headed around the corner to the elevators.

"Nice building," Dana said. "Hope he doesn't call the apartment."

"I hope he does."

"Easy there, tiger," Dana chuckled as we stepped into the elevator. "I love it when you try to be a big man. Just don't do it in front of anybody for too long or they'll figure you out."

The elevator glided up like it was on glass runners and came to a gentle rest on the fifth floor. We stepped out and scanned the numbers on the doors to figure out which way to go.

"This way, Marc," Dana said proceeding down the hallway and around the corner. I scurried to catch up. When I rounded the bend, Dana was still up ahead, clomping past doors, pointing to each one, and counting them down. As she went farther she stopped saying the numbers aloud but kept pointing until she reached the door we were looking for. She stopped there, glancing back at me while pointing silently at the door. I reached her and we stood for a moment in front of apartment 507.

3

THE BUILDING WAS complete stillness. My heart drummed softly in my ears. Condition yellow. I always found it hard to bring my fist down to the first knock. Even in a nice building. Even on an anonymous call. Even if there wasn't a scrap of truth to the allegations. It was like opening a dam with no knowledge of what's on the other side and knowing that once the water starts, there would be no getting it back in. At the very least, I'd have to tell Mother that word has it she's a drunk whore.

I straightened my jacket, took out my ID, drew in a breath, and knocked on the door. There's so much in a knock really. You didn't wanna go too hard and spook everyone inside. Too soft wasn't any good either. You had to hit it right in between, ready to attack and ready to apologize at the same time. And not too many knocks, either. Incessant weasely knocking would really start a case off on the wrong foot. About four medium knocks were good, or seven with a small pause between the fourth and the fifth—the last three being a little slower and slightly deliberate in tone. You'd have to knock in a way that says, "I have the right door, I know you're home, and I'm not moving...Thank you." I got so I could say that with about four and three good clean knocks.

My fist fell, telegraphing its message through the door, and we stretched our ears forward to listen. If we heard so much as a pin drop, we'd stay at the door all night until it opened. On the other hand, a series of knocks sandwiched with silence meant go to lunch and let the next shift give it a try. Just after my second go at the door, we heard a loud bump from inside. After a pause there was another bump, followed by a crash, followed by a woman's moan, followed by a series of smaller bumps, followed by another moan, followed by the sound of unsteady slippers approaching the door.

"...fLAgeEetTeg...*Sha*...*d*...*faaaak*..." Two arms fell against the door and slid to the floor. "Who ti *faaak*... whOOoiiisiit..."

I turned to Dana, whose head was tipped back. She slowly turned to me with a blank gray stare as the sound of drunken babble rose behind the door.

"...fuck..."

She turned back to the door and after a few moments, I knocked again. Forcefully. Carefully. Politely.

"...Ooooo's at the door...WHHO'S THAT AT THE DOOR?!!...ROBBY!!!...C'MERE..."

"Mrs. Hayes?"

"ROBBY??!!...someonz aadhe door, Robby..."

"Mrs. Hayes?"

"*ROBBIEEEEEE*..."

Dana looked at me blankly. "Robby's home."

"Sounds that way, doesn't it?" I replied, giving a few more sharp knocks.

"*ROOOBIEEEEE*..."

"Mom's drunk," Dana continued.

"Mom's wasted."

Then came a small gruff voice, "Who is it?"

"Robby?" I called to the gruff little voice inside. "Is this Robby?"

"Who's there?" the gruff little voice answered.

"Robby," I said, raising my ID to the door. "I want you to look through the peep at my ID, all right?...I'm with Child Welfare, Robby, and I have to come inside to talk to your mother about a report we just received...Robby? Can you tell your mom we have to speak with her?"

There was some mumbling and then another bump at the door.

"...hooo dhe hell izz dhis?"

"Mrs. Hayes?" I continued.

"—bezides hooever id iz OOOOOOOOOOOOOOOOO..."

We both jumped back a little as the sound behind the door faded into the apartment.

"*Jesus,*" Dana said with her head cocked back. There's really nothing quite like the sound of an irrational wail to get you feeling jumpy.

The gruff little voice returned. "My mom says to come back tomorrow."

"Robby—is this Robby?—listen, Robby—tell your mom we can't come back tomorrow. You have to let us in so we can talk right now."

"My mom says that you weren't announced and we don't have to let you in."

"Robby, tell your mom to come to the door."

"She says she can't come to the door because she's sleepy."

I started to get the sneaking suspicion Robby wasn't delivering my messages and his mother wasn't sending any. His mother was passed out—wasted in the kitchen as she probably was most hours of the day. Robby was a one-man show— waking up for school on time, making them both dinner, tucking himself in for the night, and trying to shake the aggressors at the front door.

"Robby, please open the door. We want to see if you're okay."

"My mom says sorry to please come back tomorrow," came the curt reply followed by steps trailing into the apartment and then silence. I knocked a few more times but there was no answer.

Dana stepped back, letting out a long sigh. "Oh man, not tonight. Please, not tonight. How old's this kid?"

"Eleven."

"...shit..."

"You still hungry?"

"You're a real funny guy, Marc."

I looked over the report again. " 'Mother is always drunk. Mother and her eleven-year-old are at home now. Mother is a prostitute.' Well, two out of three so far. You think she's wearing yellow five-inch heels?"

"Not with the buzz she's on," Dana answered. "Well... you wanna wait here and I'll get the cops?"

"Damn it..." I really didn't want to bounce things out of control just because Mrs. Hayes was playing peek-a-boo at the door. "Let me give it one last shot."

This knock was, as you can imagine, quite different than the previous variations and not unlike the sound of cruel teenagers beating a birdcage in a pet shop. With the back of my boot I gave ten serious blows to the bottom of the door.

After a moment of quiet, there was a mad shuffle behind the door followed by the slightly more lucid voice of Mrs. Hayes. "What in the hell are you goddamn people banging on my door for—"

"We're banging on your—"

"—and who the hell let you up here?"

"We're banging on your door because we understand you're sleeping and we need to talk with you," I shouted to the peephole with my ID, that impressive-looking plastic card, held to the right of my face. "Now you can let us in so we can talk like civilized people, or we can scream at each other like animals while the police break your door down. I'd prefer to sit down and quietly discuss this report I have on you and Robby, but it's your choice."

I waited for a response but there was none. After a moment we heard those unsteady footsteps again fading back into the apartment.

Dana nudged my shoulder. "Listen, you wait at the end of the hall and I'll get the cops."

I put my ID back into my pocket as we turned to leave. We'd only gotten a few steps away when the lock on the door of apartment 507 began to jangle, ringing loudly through the empty manicured hallway. As we stopped and turned around, the door swung suddenly back and there was Robby. He stood defiantly in the entrance in a short-sleeved T-shirt with large blue and white stripes running around his stocky frame. His stomach hung slightly down over the top of his pants, looking just a couple of years shy of a beer gut, a 19" Zenith, and a football game. He stood firmly at the door, the little gatekeeper, and spoke in his gruff voice, "What do you people want?"

4

BEHIND HIM THE APARTMENT WAS DARK, but I could make out a short hallway that led into a dimly lit room. I glanced quickly inside and could see Mrs. Hayes lying on a couch with her eyes blaring straight at us.

"Robby," I said, creeping forward with one eye on him and the other on his mother, "we need to talk with your mom."

"She's on the couch," he said, stepping back from the door and into the apartment.

We walked in and Dana closed the door behind us. It was hard to get a take on the place because everything was so poorly lit. Robby walked ahead, leading us into the living room and to the couch where his mom lay. He stopped at the end of the couch and faced us with a look in his eyes that said *your move*. His mother's eyes were still half open. As we were walking in they seemed to be staring straight at us, but standing at the side of the couch it was clear they had merely fallen open and were drying out in a drunken haze. I called her name out softly, but her eyes remained fixed on the bare wall behind me. The three of us gazed at her for a moment like a bunch of country kids looking at a roadkill gut pile for a good spot to poke with a stick.

"Well, Robby," I said, looking up to him. "Can we talk with you then?"

Robby nodded and we went to the table, but no sooner had we sat down than Mrs. Hayes bolted up from the couch in shock. She came screaming at us, asking who the hell we were and what the hell were we doing in her house and so on and so forth. We tried to calm her down, but she suddenly had no recollection of our previous exchanges at the front door, so from her shadowy perspective, a rough-looking man and woman had just been zapped into her apartment and were now sitting at her table trying to talk with her Robby. With Robby's help, we managed to calm her down enough to exchange a few words.

It was always a good icebreaker to read the report straight off to make parents aware of exactly what allegations have been levied against them. Mrs. Hayes was seated with us at her kitchen table and had sobered a little with the dump of adrenaline rushing through her veins. She shook her fingers through her hair, trying to tame it into composure, long ice-pick nails scraping over her scalp as I read the allegations. The other hand was busily trying to make her green silk robe do its job. A skimpy silk robe is an unruly garment to wear on a drinking binge with strangers visiting. It thoroughly failed its purpose, sliding rudely off her large breasts and vehemently opening in the middle, flashing the small triangular swatch of her red panties. Simple words like "How 'bout you slip into something a little less comfortable?" are so hard to find when you really need them. The little red swatch was like a flashbulb going off in my peripheral vision, and was about as easy as a flashbulb to ignore.

FLASH "Mrs. Hayes"—*FLASH*—"we're here because of a report we received tonight with the"—*FLASH*—"following allegations." I read from the report, but when I got to the "Mother is drunk now" section, she stopped me with a snort, standing up and almost tipping over.

"I ave ad a Godthamn drinks!" she said with all the im-
petuosity of a World War II vet declaring he's a Goddamn
American. "I ev ada drink...now izzat againzt tdeh law?"

"No, ma'am," I replied.

FLASH "...izzat againzt de law?...I ave ad eh Godthamn trink," she said again with righteous certitude. *FLASH*
"One Godthamn tdrink..." Robby watched intently from the
other room. "—en you peeble come to my howze becuza one
Godthamn trink?"

"What've you had tonight, Ms.—"

"—en there'z peeble all over beading their chilren—an you
peeble come to my howze—"

"What've you ha—"

"*One drink of my Black Label,*" she proclaimed, again the
proud flashing vet. "Izzeh perzon allowed that?...Izz at
againzd the Godthamn law?"

I looked over at Robby in the other room and saw in his
face he knew exactly what was going on.

"Arrezz me then," she said, thrusting her wrists forward
for handcuffs. "Arrezz me or gedod of my Godthamn howze."
BIG FLASH

"Mrs. Hayes, do you have any friends or relatives in the
building or in the area?"

Her eyebrows raised up in a clown mask. "Why do you
wan...I don think thaz any of your Godthamn buzinezz...I
don think I have to tell you that."

"I'd just like to ask them to come over until you're feeling
better."

"Ohhh *pleazzzze,*" she said, standing up and tripping over
to the cupboards. "I'm fine. I know why you peeble ar here—
look," she said, frantically opening and slamming closed her
cupboard doors. "Look—I ave food, see...look." Her boobs
tumbled out of her robe and food fell off the shelves sending
her groping for both.

"And look," she said, continuing into the living room,

grabbing Robby by the arm, lifting up his shirt, and pulling down his pants. "Look...an look here...heez fine—see?... look here...see?"

"Mrs. Hayes," I pleaded. "That's not necessary. Just tell me if you've got a friend to—"

"No no no no no," she said, stumbling into the next room. "Look ad diz." She began pulling Robby's dresser drawers out and tossing his clothes in the air. "He azz clothes...see?... look ad thiz...looka theeze clothes...look ad all theeze clothes...all right?"

"Mrs. Hayes, could you hang on a minute and just please talk with me?"

"Talk—talk, go ahead an talk," she said, collapsing onto the living-room couch, out of breath and pawing again at her hair and robe.

"Do you have anyone that we could go get to come stay with you until you feel better?"

"NO," she said with a crooked stare. "Now yoo can zee everting is fine so I don't know why you're sill standing in my howze." She stood up and wobbled to the front door, opening it and gesturing out. "Pleezs leeve."

I begged pardon for the intrusion, thanked her for letting us in, told her everything would be fine, and informed her the daytime office would follow up as a formality within forty-eight hours. She was still upset when we stepped out of her apartment, but she also seemed reassured, which was exactly what we wanted her to feel. She was still drunk, and even though we weren't sure about what to do next, chances were more than good that we'd be skipping supper and getting to know Robby a lot better than we cared to. It was no time to scare Mother into a disappearing act.

Dana and I walked down the silent hallway without saying a word. Halfway down the elevator glide, Dana spoke up. "So what do you think?"

"I don't know," I said.

Dana pushed her hands in her pockets, looking at the floor. "Call the experts?"

"The office?" I asked.

She nodded with a smile.

"Yeah," I said as the elevator humped gently to a stop. "Call the experts."

The doors slid smoothly open and we stepped into the lobby. The doorman and a few other men around him gawked at us like we were naked as we gave them our names, which were hastily scribbled on paper. We left the lobby feeling as though we were stinky intruders of the worst kind and stepped into the darkened street.

The dark had no effect on the endless river of New York pedestrians. We trudged along with the faceless mob until we found a pay phone about a block away. Dana flipped me a quarter and went to get a slice of pizza next door while I made the call. By the time she came out with it in her hand, I was still ringing. Three bites into Dana's pizza, someone finally answered and put me on hold. A few bites later, I finally had a supervisor. The sound of the office behind her voice was a roar.

"What's wrong, Marc, what's up?" she shouted.

"The mother on my case is drunk."

"Is this the prostitute?"

"I can't say for sure she's a hooker," I said.

"How old's the kid again?"

"Eleven."

"And Mom's drunk?"

"Mom's wasted," I said.

"This is the prostitute?"

"Can't say for sure."

"So take the kid," she said, ready to call it quits.

"Well, that's the whole problem," I said. "You see, the kid seems basically all right. I mean, I have a feeling this isn't a one-time thing for the mother and it looks like Robby's learned to do pretty well for himself when his mom's on the bottle. In fact, if we did a removal, I bet she'd miss him a lot more then he'd miss her. He calls the shots around there, you know what I mean? Man-of-the-house stuff."

"But she's drunk."

"Yeah, she's drunk," I continued. "But it's like, Robby probably gets along better in his house with his wasted maybe-hooker mom than he would in foster care, you know what I mean? What've we got tonight for placements?"

"How old's the kid?"

"Eleven."

"For an eleven-year-old? Let's see, tonight he'd have to go to one of our group homes."

"Oh, that's no good. Any chance of getting him into a private house?" I asked.

"Not tonight," the supervisor yelped over the clamor of the office. "We got busy after all. I swear everyone that went out is bringing in kids—a lot of four- and five-year-olds too. No relatives on yours, huh?"

"None."

"Now, the report says Mom's a prostitute. What d'ya think? Yeah?"

"Can't say."

"Pretty nice world, huh, to have hooker for a mom at nine years old—"

"Eleven."

"Well, Marc," she went on. "That's a tough one but I trust your judgment. You seem to have a handle on it—you make the call, I'll back you up. I got someone on hold for another case so I gotta go. Call me back if you decide to bring him in. Oh, and Marc, listen—you can't go on record that the mother's drunk if you don't take the kid, all right? Good luck!"

She hung up.

Dana gave me the last bite of her crust and we finished off her soda. We were in the middle of the wilderness, the supply plane had just made its life-sustaining drop of goods, but when we opened up the bundle, all we found were blow-dryers. When you're asking for help on whether or not to do a removal and you get "You make the call, I'll back you up"—this is a blow-dryer. We could take Robby or leave him. It was amazing to realize that we could just forget the whole thing—*You on your own tonight, Robby, but you've been on your own for a long time; your mom's a drunk, but so are a lot of moms, and you'll probably be okay.* We'd been given permission to forget the whole thing and make a beeline for that thick, sweet cup of Cuban coffee and a warm piece of delicious flan to loll across the tongue—"just don't go on record that Mom's drunk." Blow-dryer, and not even a good one. With that realization also came the crushing weight of being the bottom line. After all the policy makers and expert fact checkers make their conclusions and draw up their guidelines, after all the headlines and the holy golden words of politicians, the blood-saving work still boils down to the people at the bottom line.

I wanted to leave. I wanted to leave badly, but not because of the hot coffee and flan. Not because of the unbelievable rice 'n' beans. I wanted to leave because poor Robby was one of a million children tucking their passed-out parents into bed, and because somehow and in most instances, the Robbies of the world survive. I wanted to leave because there were no emergency foster-care homes for the night, and because I've seen group homes that resemble Turkish prisons. I wanted us to leave because *Robby* wanted us to leave, and I was feeling at the moment that he should have some say in that, being the man of the house and all. Hadn't the fact that he was silently running the house given him at least a fraction of that right and a moment's consideration? I thought maybe. But there was no way to write all that up in a case summary—*Eleven-year-old Robby was left at home to tuck in his wasted maybe-hooker mother because they have developed a system that, however dysfunctional, seems to work, and because the New York City group homes resemble Turkish prisons and can only*

be used as safe havens when reported children are at imminent
risk of amputation or the like.

In order to leave Robby undisturbed, I'd have had to write
something like "Mother appeared *drowsy* but otherwise fine."
I could leave Robby at home if I lied, but I had promised myself
I wouldn't ever do that even though we were given permission
to do so. Of course it was never called lying, it was called
"interpretation." Within certain limits, you could *interpret* a
situation to suit just about any purpose; Cuban coffee, Turkish
group home, or otherwise. All I had to do was document how
things *seemed* and indicate that a supervisor was consulted,
leaving out the fact that she heard every third word and threw
me a blow-dryer.

"What'd she say?" Dana asked, wiping her mouth with a
napkin then stuffing it into the empty soda can.

"She said it's our call."

"*What?*"

"Yeah."

"She said it was our call?"

"Uh-huh."

"She said that?"

"Yup."

"That's all she said?"

"She said, 'It's your call.' "

"She said, 'It's your call' and that's it?"

"She said, 'You seem to have a handle on it' and then she
said, 'It's your call.' "

"Oh man," she said, tossing the can into the trash. "I was
afraid of that... You know that—Wow... That really pisses
me off. I mean that's what she's paid for, isn't it—to take the
heat for these kind of decisions? Her *job*—right? When it's an
infant in a crack house she says 'Take him' but when it's like
this, she says 'It's your call'—right? Like we need her help to
figure out whether or not to take a kid out of a crack house—
but with this, 'It's our call'—right?"

"Dana, you'd get pissed if she told us we had to remove, or that we had to leave the kid—I mean they don't give most people in the office any leeway at all to make these kind of decisions."

"Oh, so you mean we're supposed to take it like some huge compliment that our supervisor is so comfortable with our judgment that she doesn't have to do her job when she talks to us—right? Like she can talk about the latest cute thing her poodle did when we're on the phone, right?"

"She said she'd back us up," I said.

"You know what I'm talking about."

"Yeah."

"C'mon, Marc."

"I know," I said.

"Right?"

"Yeah, right."

"Well," she said, "what's the call?"

I thought about that for a moment, leaning into the booth and bumping the back of my head against the receiver.

Dana chased off a person who was waiting to make a call. "We're using it," she barked. "We're using it." The man scowled at us and trudged on. She followed the man for a few steps then turned back to me. "Well? What's the call?"

"As a normal person," I began, "as a normal person on a hypothetical situation about some faceless kid, I'd say leave him, you know? I mean, there was food, he was dressed, the house was clean, right? He wasn't *bleeding*, right? As a normal person, I'd say he hasn't got an ideal home life, but spending a few months in a group home wouldn't be doing him any favors, either. You know?"

"As a normal person."

"Right—as a normal person. But as a *caseworker*—"

"Right."

"As a *caseworker*," I continued, "I mean, the bottom line

here is that Robby has probably had more than a few nights like this with his mom—"

"Right," Dana said, adding, "and he'll give her hell for it later."

"Sure he will, definitely—when he's around seventeen or so—"

"Kid's gonna be pissed at seventeen."

"Right," I said. "So he's used to this though, you know? I mean he didn't seem shocked or anything to see his mom falling out of her slip and all over the floor—"

"It happens all the time," Dana said.

"But as a caseworker, right? . . ."

"I hate this."

"As a caseworker . . . I gotta say we take him."

"This is gonna be a bad one."

"Am I right?" I asked Dana.

"This is how it'd go," Dana theorized. "We'd leave this kid because we know he'd be okay, then he gets a paper cut, right? And it's front-page news—ROBBY WAS VISITED BY CHILD WELFARE AUTHORITIES ONLY HOURS BEFORE BEING INJURED."

"And we say, 'Yeah, mother was wasted but Robby seemed okay,' " I said. "And we get hung."

"This is gonna be a real fucking scene," Dana said, shaking her head. "This is gonna be bad. You know she's gonna freak, right?"

"They all freak, Dana."

"No, Marc, this woman is going to completely freak."

"Yeah."

"C'mon, Marc, you know what I'm saying."

"She's the type."

"Right?"

"So let's do it."

I dialed 911, unable to imagine what was to follow, completely unaware that we'd only seen the tip of the iceberg and not even a glimpse of the freak hidden beneath it.

5

WE WENT BACK TO THE MAPLEWOOD and waited in our car for police to arrive. A light rain began to drum against the windshield. We didn't talk. Dana hit the wipers every few seconds so we could watch Maplewood dwellers in nice coats rush from the building into waiting cabs. I really had a bad feeling about the removal, not about whether or not it was going to happen—they always happened once they were initiated—I had a bad feeling because my heart wasn't in it. It was difficult to take a child from his home even in the most dire circumstances, but to take a large unwilling Robby from his warm bed with your heart not in it, I had a bad feeling about that. I had called the office back to tell them I'd be bringing Robby in and was cheerfully informed that the light rain was not bringing out the best in people. The office was full of wet angry kids eating bologna-and-mustard sandwiches. It would be a while before a placement for Robby could be secured.

After about five minutes, the cops pulled up in front of the Maplewood awning. We stepped out of our car and into theirs, quickly exchanging IDs and badges. The role of police in a removal is strictly to keep the parents from shooting or stabbing or otherwise causing the need for immediate hospital visits as we take their children away. It wasn't necessary to involve them in the details of the case, but I always offered to tell them anything they needed to know. Sometimes they were interested, but in most cases they'd just say something like "Hey, whatever. You say they're out of here, they're out of here—I got kids!" They almost always had kids and the flash of imagining their own little ones in the same circumstances as the reported children always made them more than willing to do whatever was necessary to facilitate a removal.

Not so with these guys. Although I had no doubts about

their willingness to help us, they let us know in no uncertain terms that they had their own rice 'n' beans with Cuban coffee to attend to and so after a quick call to their sergeant to let him know the apartment we'd be going to, they grabbed their nightsticks and headed into the building.

We breezed through the lobby, leaving the front-desk guys with their jaws bouncing on the floor. I completed the 701-b removal form as we stepped into the elevator and slid up to the fifth floor. We had told the cops we anticipated a straight removal—no need for much discussion. We shouldn't be in the home for more than five minutes, enough time to give Mrs. Hayes a few phone numbers and have Robby put on some warm clothes and grab a favorite toy. At the front door, they pulled out their nightsticks and bounced them on the door— not at all the firmly polite "I'm here and I'm not leaving thank you" but more on the lines of "open the fucking door or we'll bust it in and push our boots against your neck." The sharp nightstick blows coupled with the fuzzy chatter of their radios did a much better job on the stubborn door than my three-and- four knock and plastic ID. The door flew open and Mrs. Hayes stood before us, completely dressed, sporting a very unsur- prised look on her face. We all stared at each other for a mo- ment and she spun around and walked staunchly into the apartment, wobbling slightly as she did so. We followed her inside to the living room where, upon reaching the far wall, she spun back toward us with her arms folded. She looked angry and defiant, but mostly scared and still drunk. Robby stood like a pillar behind a couch. He looked angry.

"Is this Robby?" the first cop asked with a forced friend- liness in his voice. "Hey, how you doin', little guy?"

Robby stared at the cop from behind the couch. His small dark eyes radiated pure heat that burned away the soft dew of kindness offered. Who needs kindness when it comes from a cop standing in the middle of the living room on a school night? Robby was all business.

"Aren't you gonna talk to me?" the cop continued. "Give me a hello or a how-do-you-do?"

Robby didn't say a word.

"That's okay, Robby. You don't gotta talk to me. He doesn't like to talk to me, either," he said, indicating his partner, who was casually stepping in and out of the other rooms, looking around corners and in closets. "But you don't gotta stand behind the couch like that, c'mon out—nobody's gonna get you."

The irony of that really rang out. The cop had probably said that to distressed kids in the past as a comfort, but spoken to Robby, it wasn't a comfort. It was a lie. Robby could smell it. He didn't move.

"Apartment's clear," the other cop said to his partner as he returned to the living room. Mrs. Hayes glared at us, her eyes darting back and forth in her head like fish in an aquarium when you slap at the glass.

"Mrs. Hayes," I said, offering her the 701-b, "this is for you."

"What izzit?" she snapped with her arms tightly shut across the chest that only moments ago was so badly misbehaving. She'd finally gained some control of her body, barely resembling the flashing vet we'd seen earlier. The 701-b dangled between us in my outstretched hand.

"This is a form that tells you how to follow up with our agency after we remove Robby from the apartment tonight." Silence sat between us for a moment, silence so thick and fat I could've sat the 701-b on it. I broke the air with a final clarification. "We're taking Robby with us tonight." I held the 701-b closer for her to take it, but her arms remained shut.

"You should take the paper, lady," the first cop chirped with his artificial tenderness. "It tells you how t—"

"I don nee dhat," Mrs. Hayes snapped as I laid it on the table beside us. She picked it up instantly and shoved it in my face. "I don nee dhis paper," she said matter-of-factly.

"Robby's not going anywhere tonight." When she could see I had no intention of taking the paper back, she walked through us and flung it out her front door. "I don nee dhis," she said again as it flew into the hallway. "Robby," she called out, suddenly the good mother as she closed the door and returned to the living room, "Ged ready for bed, baby, izzza school night."

Robby didn't move. Still behind the couch, he began embroidering his fists to the cushions.

"Robby, did you hear your mother? Ged ready for bed, young man."

"Mrs. Hayes," I began. "Can I talk to you alone for a moment?"

"*Do you mine,* zir?" she said as she passed me and headed for the couch to get Robby. "I'm trying to pud my zon to bed."

"Mrs. Hayes, hang on a second, Mrs. Hayes," I pleaded with her as the cop reached out—

Crossing the line.

—and grasped her arm.

"*Don you touch me,*" she said, suddenly snapping her arm out of the cop's gentle grip.

"Mrs. Hayes, could I ple—"

"*Don you touch me in my howze,*" she continued, focused on the cop, who was skillfully positioning himself between her and Robby.

"Mrs. Hayes, please," I said, trying to get her attention. "Could I just talk with you alone for a min—"

"And I don needa zpeek with you alone, either," she said, turning sharply to me. "You can zpeek ride 'ere. I'm not leaving Robby alone with any of you. He can hear anything you have to zay—if you have to zay id to me you have to zay id to him."

"Mrs. Hay—"

"WILL YOU PEOPLE PLEEZE GED OUD OF MY HOWZE—I HAVEN'T DONE ANYTHING WRONG, PLEEEEZE..."

"Mrs. Hay—"

"Robby—go ged your coat, we're going to zee your aunt."

"Mrs. Hayes—"

"ROBBY," she roared, suddenly jumping around the cop standing between them and seizing her son's arm tightly. *"Go ged your coat."*

The cop swooped around and grabbed onto Mrs. Hayes's arm, giving it a few shakes as if checking for loose supports in an old house, but her grip was firmly planted on Robby's wrist and held fast. Both cops instantly dropped their forced courtesy (in that Jekyll-and-Hyde flip-flop that cops can do so well) and began tugging on her arms and shoulders while she screamed at Robby the whole time.

"Go ged your coat, Robby," she implored as the cops filled the apartment with shouts of "Ma'am, ma'am" and "Lady, lady."

"GO GED YOUR COAT ROBBY... GOGEDYOUR-COATROBBY"

The four of them shook like ragged sails in a hurricane from Robby's mast.

"GO ... GED ... YOUR ... COAT—NOW!!!"

Through the frenzy, she begged Robby to do the impossible. Even if he was able to drag the three of them to his coat, he'd never be able to get it on with them coiled so tightly around his arms and showing no signs, any one of them, of letting up. He looked silently at the adults, and stood his ground.

"ROBBY ... ROBBY—" She suddenly wheeled her head around to the cops and screamed, "SHOOD ME GOD-THAMN IT—JUZ KILL ME RIDE HERE BECAUZ I AM NOT LETTING GO OF THIZZ CHILD—SHOOD ME IN DE GODTHAMN HEAD AN YOU CAN HAVE 'IM ... SHOODMEE ... SHOODMEE ..."

There was a sharp knocking at the door. I ran over and opened it to find the very concerned faces of what looked like neighbors.

"POLICE," one of the cops shouted up from the living room. The faces peered nervously in and the cop yelled again from the rubble of noise, "POLICE—go back to your apartments."

"Police," I said awkwardly to the faces. "Go back to your apartments."

By the time I'd shooed them away and returned to the living room, the scuffle had stopped with the score one to nothing—Team Robby. He stood behind the couch in ready position with his mother's arm clutched around his shoulders, waiting for the next volley. Dana watched the tussle from a detached eight or ten feet and had a look on her face that told me she was chewing back the same bits of nausea I was. The cops approached me as I returned from the front door, wearing the expression of two surprised wolves who've sadly underestimated the tenacity of an agitated badger.

A little winded, the first cop put his hand on my shoulder, the wise father at the fireside chat. "Listen, this lady isn't gonna give up her kid—I mean it. You saw us, right? We gave her a good couple shakes, but she's not gonna let go." He gave me a look like I should've known better. I wondered if he could imagine any mother calmly trading in her son for a poorly xeroxed list of Family Court offices.

"Well...," the cop continued with shrugged shoulders and a shake of his head, "wha'dya wanna do?"

"The same thing I told you in the car," I responded.

"*Guy*—I just told you this woman ain't gonna give up this kid."

"Well, I figured that's how she'd feel," I said. "That's why we called you."

"*Guy*—hello? She's not goin' for it."

"Yeah—I didn't think she'd be goin' for it, they don't usually go for it unless they're unconscious. That's why we usually call you guys, for a little help."

"Well, wha'dya want us to do?"

"You're asking me what we want you to do?"

"*Guy*—this lady's not gonna give up this kid, I just told you that—it's like, we'd have to sit on her while you drag him out of here."

And that's exactly what they did, and that's exactly what we did.

The most vivid moments in memories are never moving pictures. The times when you think back and can almost feel the carpet through your shoes—when you can taste the air on the back of your tongue—these moments are always captured in a snapshot. I remember a snapshot of the big cop riding like an urban cowboy on the hips and shoulders of a shrieking Mrs. Hayes, looking back at his partner and saying, "Recheck these people's names before they take the kid and make sure they're spelled right—the paperwork for this better be spotless."

I walked around to the side of the couch where Robby was standing, and begged him to come out to get his coat so we could leave, but he'd have no part of it. As much as I tried, I couldn't steal his attention from his mother who, with the inexhaustible constancy of a 25¢ ride in a shopping mall, continued bumping and bucking the cop airborne. Finally, after numerous failed attempts to win Robby's focus, I grabbed his shoulders firmly and gave them a shake. He looked at my hands on his shoulders and looked up without expression, focusing his eyes tightly on mine. Over the bouncing clamor of Mom plus cops, he spoke with the calm authority of a forty-year-old man, "You can take your hands off of me right now. I'm not going anywhere with you people."

The lunatic momentum of the moment carried Dana and me into the unthinkable. We clamped onto each tight fat arm of Gruff Robby and heaved him rudely over the back of the couch, sending the three of us tumbling to the floor, where we rolled about for a while before tipping upright with Robby in our control, now bumping and bouncing on our own 25¢ ride at the Hayes amusement park. Robby hated us. His mother really hated us. The doorman in the lobby hated us. I think the cops were starting to hate us. Worst of all, I started to hate us. *As a normal person, right??...as a normal person, I say we leave him...but as a caseworker...* My normal person was despising my caseworker. It felt like growing up. I'd joined an adults-only club with an enormous roster of normal people who hate their professional self. Riding on the shoulders of an eleven-year-old was my initiation to the club, after which I was eligible to wear my I'm-Just-Doing-My-Job! button on my Ask-Me-If-I-Care! T-shirt.

Robby shook his shoulders from our grip as we stood up, and made a try for the back of the couch again, but we caught him by the thighs and hauled him back to the floor. The cop on the back half of Mrs. Hayes was having a hard time hiding his anger at the fact that we'd just bitched up his whole evening. He glared at us. "Will you people stop juggling the kid around already and just take him if you're gonna take him."

"Robby, Robby," I said to him sternly. His face was on the carpet and Dana was on his shoulder. "You have to cooperate with us, okay? Robby? Are you going to cooperate with us?"

"Sure," he said into the pile of the carpet with controlled smoothness.

"If you promise not to run," Dana said, leaning close to his ear. "If you promise not to run—"

"Will you just get off me," Robby interrupted with an appalled sound in his throat.

Dana made him promise not to run to the back of the couch and began to help him up, but a young boy's promises are easily broken when made in the sulfuric air of a mother's screams. As soon as Dana released him, he made another mad dash for the back of the couch only to be tackled again and hoisted back into our tight fists.

"Where are your shoes, Robby?" I asked.

"I don't have any," he said, staring blankly forward.

"Robby, it's cold outside. Where are your shoes?"

"I'm not going outside."

"Where's Robby's shoes, Mrs. Hayes?" I shouted to the tangle on the couch.

"*FUCK* you—", she screeched through struggling grunts.

"Mrs. Hay—"

"*FUCK* you—"

"*Guy*—will you just get out of here already?" the cop begged us.

I held Robby from behind in a tight bear hug while Dana rummaged furiously through the closets for shoes and a coat. After a futile search for a coat, Dana did return with shoes, which Robby refused to put on. With Dana and me on each fat foot trying to jam them into their respective shoe, the cop barked again, "C'mon, people, this ain't no Buster Brown, let's move it."

"Hey, listen, we are trying to move it—"

"*Guy*—will you just get out of here with that kid? We can't hold this lady like this much longer—she's gonna bust a gut."

With that we heave-hoed to the door with the barefoot, hanging out of his T-shirt Robby, where, upon reaching the doorway, he made his best and final all-out effort to stay. His arms shot out from his sides and grasped either side of the doorjamb. The sudden commitment of his entire force caught Dana and me off guard. Robby had a fat little Hercules in his round red biceps. Dana and I pulled on each arm, but they held fast to the doorjamb. I thought about stories of people lifting cars over their heads in panicked distress. Both Robby and his mom had us beat hands down in the adrenaline department. I heaved firmly against Robby's arm but it barely moved. Back in the living room, the cops wrestled against the almost spooky stamina of Mrs. Hayes, who continued nonstop, practically bouncing them against the ceiling. Dana and I managed to loosen Robby's arms by using the palms of our hands like chisels to pound his wrists free, but no sooner did we have control of the arms than his legs kicked firmly against the baseboards.

As soon as we'd chipped his legs loose, we were back working on the arms and back to the legs and back to the arms and so on and so forth in a sickening little drill.

We yanked on every part of him, pulling on his young round body, stripping him of any trace of child; yanking his arms, yanking his fingers, pulling the back of his neck, then pushing on it, then just holding it in a tight pinch, knocking on his legs and pounding on his wrists, pushing on his skin, pushing his back, pulling his shirt, all in a grand home-wrecking frenzy—and we were getting nowhere.

Dana began to shout at Robby, who was huffing and puffing against my hold. Up to that point, as much as we were pulling and tugging on him, we were doing it ever so gently, a courteous manhandling of sorts, politely gripping and releasing him in every possible hold. But anyone who has experienced even moderate roughhousing, even in a playful context, knows that something in the pushing and pulling calls to an inner animal that's always more than happy to respond. The simple dynamic of skin pushing on skin leads to relentless and certain escalation the longer it takes place. Cops know this, bouncers know this, jailers know this, madcap wrestling brothers know this. If they don't, they find it out soon after the first concussion. Our skirmish was quickly going the way of all skirmishes, and there was nothing we could do about it. We were just doing our job.

I grabbed Robby's arm hard. I mean *really* hard: Marks and Bruises Hard—Too Hard. Somewhere tucked in that grab was the same magic that was in the sharp blows of the police nightstick. One grab was all Robby needed to understand that his escape would not be won with straight resistance. One grab was all he needed to see that we were willing to mark and bruise him in the process of the removal. One grab told him there were more to follow. So because Robby was not as strong as two adults, and because Robby was no dummy, he surrendered to brute force and stepped barefoot into the hall.

"You don't have to hold my arms," he said in a disgusted voice as the three of us trudged awkwardly down the hall. "You're embarrassing me."

"I'll let go of your arm if you promise not to run," I said.

"Just let go already—you people are humiliating me."

"Promise not to ru—"

"I have to live here," he said, cutting me off. "I haven't done anything wrong."

"Marc, let's just get him into the elevator," Dana said reasonably. Suddenly, Robby bolted from my grip, his arm sensing the smallest degree of looseness as we neared the elevator. Dana and I pounced and quickly had Robby back in our fists, where we held him again. Hard. Harder than I've ever held a child. Harder than I should have.

Dana hit the down button for the elevator and the three of us stood, waiting with the dull faces of teenagers in church— only the clenched whiteness in our fingers against Robby's red arms to give us away. The door breezed open and we stepped inside. A nice-looking couple in their fifties stepped to the side to make room for us. The woman wore a fur. Dana hit the lobby floor even though the button was already lit, and I knew her heart was beating against her molars as hard as mine was. The elevator began its smooth glide down and I could feel the weight of four eyes to our left. Then very calmly and with the earnest stare of a boy half his age, Robby turned to the couple who were just noticing his bare feet and said, "These people are taking me against my will. Please help me."

The couple looked at us in shock with the fear every New Yorker has that they will one day witness a *New York Post* headline in the making. "Please," Robby continued, "I don't know who these people are—they're taking me against my will." The elevator stopped and the doors parted mercifully to reveal the lobby. I tightened my grip on Robby and the three of us stepped out as he pleaded calmly to the couple again, "Please help me. They're hurting me."

The couple ran past us to alert the doormen but that became quickly unnecessary as Robby delivered his calm, urgent plea to the people throughout the lobby. As we picked up the pace to get outside and into the car, the crowd began to close on us.

"CHILD WELFARE—GET OUT OF THE WAY," Dana blared over Robby's "somebody-help-me"s. The people looked to the gathering of doormen and saw their disgust but also saw they were allowing the abduction. We were followed outside and when we shoved Robby into the official city business car, they backed off some to marvel at their city tax dollars at work. As I rounded the car in the rain, I heard shouts of "What's wrong with you people—couldn't you at least have put some shoes on him?" and "Where's his coat?" along with a couple of "Heartless—totally heartless"s tossed in for good measure. Dana sat in the back with Robby to make sure he wouldn't make any sudden moves to rip my ears off, and we got the hell out of there.

6

WE DROVE FOR A FEW BLOCKS without speaking, the air around our heads ringing with the sound of car #603's fat wheels whining against the wet street. I could feel Robby's eyes pointed at me from the corner of the rearview mirror like intense penlights. I didn't look at him but I could feel him. I could feel his feet, probably wet and cold and with a few small stones and dirt from the street crammed between the toes. I could feel the clammy cold of adrenaline sweat rising from his neck. I could feel his red arms still pulsing from my grab. I could feel his stomach burn on the border of a child's fear and a man's rage. I didn't look at Robby, but I could feel him. Car #603 never felt so small.

Rain came down hard and the wipers slammed back and

forth on the windshield like useless strips of bark. I sat low to peer through the only space of glass not streaked with the glare of Manhattan. The windows began to fog and Dana cracked hers. We drove in silence a few minutes longer and then Robby broke the air with his gruff little voice. He spoke slowly and carefully as if to plant the words in us where they would do the most damage, "You enjoyed that back there, I was looking in your eyes and you were having fun." I didn't say anything; I couldn't say anything. I felt like the scum of the earth. Robby knew, and he was playing chopsticks on it. The thing that was really making me sick was that Robby believed what he was saying. He wasn't taunting us, he was calling it like he saw it. As he continued his voice grew deep in texture. "You were really getting into it, weren't you? I could see it in your eyes, you *loved* it."

I looked up at Robby's eyes framed in the rearview mirror. They were dull and smiling. "It's over now so you can just tell me," he continued. "You two get off on this, don't you?" He looked to Dana and then back to me. "You're both sick. What you do to kids is sick."

"C'mon, Robby," I mumbled. "Take it eas—"

"Fuck you." The words were foreigners in his mouth but they kept their effect.

"Don't do it, Marc. Don't even go there," Dana said. Robby turned to her with a cool rage. "Fuck you, too."

"Whatever you need, Robby. Whatever you gotta do," Dana said, leaning back into the seat.

With the rain driving down like anything and the bark wipers doing their shitty best, Robby leaned toward the back of my head to hammer in the last nail. "Hope you crash," he whispered, "*I hope you crash.*"

The rain came down and it came down and down. Thick streams of water spilled over the windshield in sudden rivers. Huge puddles leaped over us at 50 mph, flickering our vehicle from car to submarine and back to car. Wet round blobs smashed against #603's metal lid in a dull roar. It lullabied the three of us into silence and into ourselves like only rain on a car can do. Where was Dana? I didn't know. Where was Gruff Robby? Maybe visiting a bruised Little Davey at the front gates of the zombie place. I went back to Wisconsin. Always back to Wisconsin—such a quick trip from what-the-fuck-are-you-doing-in-New-York-you-big-dumb-country-fuck-in-Manhattan. Brilliant distraction washed over me like a lover and I fumbled my fingers through her hair while tinkering the blinkers of #603. A road, a gut pile. A field, the shot night-bird. The piranha man, the hallelujah coon, a meat scream.

I flicked on the crackling AM radio but couldn't find a thing. Not that it mattered. What mattered is that I had grabbed a good and decent kid harder than I ever thought I'd grab even a bad kid. Harder than I've ever grabbed an animal. Harder than I should have. That's what mattered and that was the night. I made a vow in rain-soaked #603 to keep my normal person at the controls and throw my caseworker to the shredder, and to hell with it if it gets me fired. I made a promise never to grab a kid that hard again. I wish to God that I could've turned to Robby's penlights in the rearview mirror and apologized. I wish I could see him now and tell him that the way I grabbed him wasn't right. The whole damn night wasn't right. It still drives me crazy when I think about it. I pray Robby's forgotten, or if he hasn't, that I'm only a fuzzy recollection playing a bit part in a bad play. I still can't get over it. I hope Robby has. I think there's a good chance of that. The injustices we commit against others always end up falling harder on us than on the ones we've hurt. Time brings everything back around on life's karmic carousel. Robby's probably forgotten the way my hand felt on his arm, but I can't forget the way his arm felt in my hand. Robby's forgotten the squeeze, but I can't forget the squeezing.

By the time we made it into the watery desolation of lower Manhattan, a small dripping had begun on my left shoulder where #603's door met its body. A distinct smell of canoe rose from the rocker panels. We went left off the West Side Highway and sloshed by the World Trade towers, which looked like simple low-rise units, their majesty hidden from view by thick gray storm clouds. Another left and we were pushing like a barge in a canaled city up Church Street to where the office was located. I stopped at the front of the building to let Dana and Robby off before parking. They ran in to avoid getting wet. Robby waddled on the outsides of his bare feet, his arms flying awkwardly in the rain to maintain balance. Dana held a clipboard over his head as they dashed up the stairs and into ECS.

After several blocks of circling, I found a place to park. I locked up #603 and made a mad sprint for the office. By the time I got to the front doors I looked a little better than a shipwreck survivor. Inside, the office was the loony bin our supervisor had promised. The place was crawling with kids and reeked of wet hair. I whisked past Robby, who was sitting on a plastic chair in a cleared-out corner of the office called the nursery. The only thing that was nurserylike about the place was that it was *called* "the nursery." There were no nurses there. There was a small staff of tired old ladies who looked hauntingly similar. They churned out bologna-and-mustard sandwiches for those who craved them and poured Kool-Aid for anybody dying of thirst. The person at the helm of the nursery was a very large disheveled woman who looked like she had a specific pain for every bone in her body. She moved with a purposeful shuffle and permanent whining eyes. For as long as she was there, I never saw her without a large black purse slung across her shoulder. It was amazing to watch her bottle-feed several children in her arms while the purse fell against her back like an attacking animal. The image of the nursery would float through the mind of anyone contemplating a removal. It was not a comfort to know that after gashes were inflicted on children in the field, they'd have the salt of the nursery to roll around in while waiting for placement in emergency foster care. There was a separate room for babies—well equipped and very clean—but if you happen to be a kid past the crib stage, at ECS, you were out of luck.

I punched in and quickly made my way to the back where my desk sat next to Will and Jesse's. I could tell they had spent the evening in-house because of all the litter on their desks. Junk had even made it to my desk; orange soda and ginger ale cans skittered away as I threw my clipboard and paperwork down. Jesse was kicked back with his size 13½ Nikes resting on his desk like the flippers of a giant friendly walrus. He was plugged into a Walkman that scratched out the heavy driving rhythm of house rap. As soon as I threw my things down, he jumped up and hustled his six foot eight inches over to my desk.

"Pardon me, monsieur," he said with a mock of dainty sophistication, drawing out his s's and r's to their utmost goofy effect. "The good Master Samuels and I seem to have soiled your work area. Our most gracious and humblest of apologies to you, finest of marvelous sirs." He made an exaggerated move to clear my desk, and paused. "Do you mind?" he asked, with his eyebrows to the ceiling. I waved my open palm in a be-my-guest gesture, and Jesse commenced to bat the garbage to the floor with the back of his hand, laughing in a high giggle as he did so. When he finished, the area looked like a tornado-ravaged trailer park. I took off my coat just as he was pulling out my chair for me.

"Please, most humblest of finest sirs," he implored through oafish giggles. "Allow me." With that he made a few quick sweeps on the seat of the chair with the back of his hand, and then stepped back in an awkward jester's bow.

William remained intently focused on a phone conversation through all of the flying garbage. A few cans skidding across

the desk were nothing to Will. He'd have continued with the
Rockettes doing a kick line from his shoulders. What can I
say—the man was intense. When he worked, he slaved. When
he played, he romped. When he laughed, people left the room.
When he got mad, people left the building. He was good when
he was good, and bad when he was bad, and it was all about
focus. When Will did something he *did* it. Whatever it was. He
was the type of guy that could finish a beer while his arm was
on fire if he wanted to. He could make a stripper say, "I love
you" and mean it. He could win a stare down while being
punched in the face. He was Paul Bunyon in the city with an
afro. He was the guy from *Shaft,* only better. He was an AM
DJ for Jesus. He was all that and more. He was the *Superfly.*
I never found him on the radio ("Jesus Is 'cause he just *Is*—
dig?") but man, could that Superfly rap with someone on the
down and out:

"My brother," he spoke with hushed intensity, hunched in
his cubicle.

"My brother"—I threw my rain-soaked jacket to the side
of my desk.

"My brother..." Willie was a racial Everyman. A bit of
this and a bit of that. He called everyone "my brother."

"My brother. First, chill. I listened to your rap and it's just
okay. So now you gotta take a kickback and chew on mine—
you dig-dang?"

Willie could get away with the most antiquated jive,
because it wasn't an act with him—he'd speak to his own dog
alone in the bathroom with the same seventies funk that would
sound like showing off in anybody else's mouth. And Will
wasn't a young guy. I don't know how old he was, but he
wasn't a young guy. His trite rhymes and phrases were oratory.
He did it as a living historical monument. The man was groovy.

"Hey, Sleepy Sid. Sleepy Sid. That's right, my brother, I'm
calling my man Sleepy Sid 'cause you gotta be on Mr. Nod
time if you ain't down with what I been tellin' you this whole

night. Look at you now. You got the cops sitting on your furniture. The shit is blowin' down from the top of the mountain and I'm ridin' on it in a big boat to your front door—you copy? Your shack is sinking, Sid, you're sinkin' in the stinky, and you're takin' your family with you, and that ain't right.

"But I'm gonna throw you a line—you down with me, Sleepy? Everybody gonna chill so my man and me can rap. I arranged that, Sleepy Sid. The cops are gonna chilly but we gotta dance for one tune or this show's over and we all get stupid—I get the kids, your son gets the can, and the mouse gets the cheese."

Willie gave me a glance and held out his fist for me to bump, which I did. He knew I was listening. I knew he didn't mind. From what I could make out, it sounded like some guy beat the shit out of his wife and caught a few of their kids in the cross fire. After the drum solo, Elvis left the building. Will was talking to the father of the guy with the busy fists, who also lived in the home, and who could probably direct the cops to his son's whereabouts.

At my desk with my jacket off, I was all set to get busy. I had unlocked my drawer and retrieved my pen. I grabbed a pile of history sheets to write up Gruff Robby. I was ready to go and could've started writing but the clock was already on overtime—or what-the-hell-time, as we'd sometimes call it. Rushing to finish and get home wouldn't make it any earlier—the hour was already miles from decent, so I decided to idle a bit and take in the world's only rapping doo-wop Cherokee.

"There's only two ways to skin this pony, Sid." Willie listened for a moment before continuing. "Look, look, look, look—I don't care what she did. I don't care if she slept with everyone in the building and sang the 'Ave Maria'—you listening to me? I don't care what she did. He don't own her and he can't hit her. He can't beat on his woman and he can't beat on the kids and he's not gonna get it until he gets it. But I'm not waiting around. Now, *you* know which couch that cat ran under, and you gotta tell the cops, my man. You gotta tell the cops so they can lock him up. You got it, Sleepy? Those cops ain't shankin' your shack without a prize—either they take your son to the slam, or they take your grandkids to me...

"I don't care if it's not right. Listen—you're tellin' me what's not right when your son's playin' hopscotch on his woman and your grands? This is your son, Pop. You have a man-to-man with him. You tell him what's not right, and I think we both understand what I'm talkin' about here—'bout a little girl named Lisa and her little brothers Richie and Eddie... 'bout how fucked up they look right now... 'bout their mother cryin' in the bathroom... 'bout the cops sitting on your furniture—am I right, Sleepy Sid? And your man out braggin' about it with his wildcats, right? So you got to man-to-man with him and you gotta tell him what's not right. Tell him what's not right. I don't care what she did to him. Tell him what's not right. You're his father. Act like it. Your man's goin' down. He's goin' to jail 'cause he's a coward and he slammed on his wife and kids. Every man's old lady and kids drive him crazy. Every man wants to crack it sooner or later. There's not a man alive who don't know about that. Someone says he don't know about that, that man's lyin' to you, am I right, Sid? But the difference between a big man and a big baby is the man just takes it and the baby just cracks it. Crackin's for babies, Sid. Your man's goin' to jail 'cause he couldn't hack it and he had to crack it—he's goin' to jail 'cause he's a big baby. You know where he is. Tell the cop on your couch. Tell him where he is. Tell him, 'cause if you don't, I'm taking these kids from their mother—"

Willie hesitated as a tinny voice rang through the receiver. He gave it a moment before jumping in. "I don't give a rat's asshole if it ain't right—if the cops don't—Hey Sid... Sleepy Sid—you're sleepin', Sid, you just keep sleepin'. Listen, if the cops—hey... HEY—YO, SID—Listen up and I'm done: If the cops don't find your son, they can't lock him up. If they can't lock him up, the kids are at risk. If the kids are at risk, they come with me. End of story. Finalmente, Sleepy Sid. Think about that. Put the cop on..."

The tinny voice in the receiver raised in pitch and I knew the father was giving Willie his all-out and final everybody-go-home-so-we-can-forget-this-ever-happened appeal. Willie cut him off. "That's it, Sleepy. I don't care about that. I ain't hearin' it. I don't care what she did. Put the cop on. I'm done already. Hey...Sid—Put on the cop, Pop. Put on the cop, Pop. The cop, pop, put him on, Sid."

Willie glanced at me, "Acting like she whittled his dick off."

"What'd she do?" I asked.

"I don't give two shits what she did."

" 'T's fucked-up man," I said.

"His grands like patchwork fuckin' quilts and he won't give this shithead up"—Willie returned to the phone to speak with the cop.

"All right, ask this fuckin' guy where his son is, then come back. I'll hang on."

A minute passed. Willie tried to swig at two soda cans that were empty. The cop came back and Will leaned into the phone to listen. After a moment, he looked at me and shook his head.

"Well I guess the apple don't fall too far from the tree," Willie said into the phone. "So the kids gotta be cleared at the hospital before you bring them to me. You got our address? All right, I'll see you soon. Tell the mother we'll be in touch— oh and don't forget to tell her this guy's fuckin' up her life. She's gonna have to lose him to get the kids back."

Willie hung up and pushed his stubby fingers into his eyes, rubbing them tiredly. "What's it look like for placements tonight?" he asked when he was done.

"Not too good tonight," I said.

"There's a lot of kids in the nursery, right? Sounds like a fuckin' playground back there."

"Yeah, as a matter of fact, there are a lot of kids back there."

"You bring one in?" he asked.

Yeah, I sure as shit brought one in—put up a fight though. Practically had to tear his arms off, but yeah, I brought 'im in all right. Nice one too—'bout an eighty pounder. Nearly ripped him in half, but I brought him in. He never had a chance. By the way, did I get to tell you yet that I'm the scum of the earth?

"I brought one in," I answered.

"So what's it look like for placements tonight?"

"You just asked me that, Willie."

"I just asked you that, right? Fuck, it's getting late. No good for placements, right?"

"Not too good tonight, Will."

We both returned to the papers on our desks to scratch out a night of events—so different but somehow the same. Just like the children in the nursery; representing every race and from every corner of the city, all so different but now, somehow, the same.

7

BY THE TIME I FINISHED THE case write-up on Robby and his maybe-hooker mother, the kids on Willie's case were being brought in. There were three of them. The oldest was about eight and the other two looked to be under five. The cops came clamoring in with the little ones in tow. You gotta love the cops. They start the night ready to shoot someone's eyes off and at the same time ready to carry a child with a grandmother's tenderness. Ready to shatter and ready to soothe at the touch of a trigger, a good cop is an amazing animal. I've been with more of them than the average career criminal and I got nothing bad to say. I love a good cop.

These two came in and gingerly set the kids down on seats

not far from where Robby was still sitting. The two younger children looked okay, but the older one was sporting a puffed-up left eye. I don't know what happened with this family, but I will say that it wasn't unusual to find the oldest was the one in the worst shape. This was often the case because the oldest was the one responsible for protecting the household from the ravages of an attacking paramour—even at eight years old. In the course of jumping on the shoulders of scumbag boyfriend or scumbag husband, it wasn't unusual for the little protectors, God bless every one of them, to catch a fist in the eyeball or an elbow at the very least, and chalk it up to a rough childhood. This eight-year-old watched her younger siblings as they ran to play with dirty nursery toys. She sat quietly on her chair with her black-and-blue badges and the look of the protector in her eyes.

The sad fact of emergency placements was that you had to take what you could get, even if it meant separating the protector from the sheep. Willie had secured placement for the younger children in the same foster home, but hadn't yet found a bed for the eight-year-old. Separating a child from her siblings was a thing too unjust to imagine but in the name of getting kids into beds, it wasn't unusual. It drove me crazy. The biggest rub for me was that it always seemed so unnecessary. I'm certain every group of kids I pried apart would've been better off falling to sleep in the ECS chairs against one another's shoulders and waking to bologna-and-mustard sandwiches for breakfast than in the beds of foster homes with boroughs separating them.

I passed Robby on my way out the door. I hadn't been able to find a placement for him at the usual places so I flagged the case for follow-up by the head manager of the office on the midnight shift. It would be up to him to twist the arms of various other agencies and homes until Robby had a place to put up his wet dirty feet. Children who filled the nursery when Robby arrived were now gone. Getting placements for children had more than a few dynamics in common with picking teams in grade-school gym class; captains making their choices quickly and slowing up by the end when there's only the fat kid, or the clumsy kid, or the short kid, or the skinny kid. The end of the night at ECS was no different, with kids like Robby twiddling their thumbs as they watch the babies get whisked to foster homes and the older kids railroaded into group homes. Robby's kind was too old for one and not old enough for the other, so it was up to the bosses at the agency to play the gym teacher and make the captains choose among the rejects.

He sat in the nursery on the same chair where I'd left him. He was in dry clothes, given to him by the nursery boss with the attacking animal purse. He wore socks but still no shoes. He looked tired and vacant, not at all the empowered little man at the front door from a few hours ago. Where would Robby ever find his peace now that the moat that surrounds the family had been so easily crossed? Where would Robby ever feel secure in a place where city government pays to have twenty-five-year-olds in beat-up leather jackets take children from their homes against their will and in their bare feet? Sitting on his chair, Robby had the look of an old man beat to shit by the tumult of a lifetime's worth of raw deals. I could barely stand the sight of him. Part of me wanted to return to the office in a ski mask to steal him back to his home and to his probably very sober mother. What an amazing turn of events that would've been. What a wild car ride back uptown with a terrified Robby in the backseat. What relief when I tear off the mask and what laughter would fill #603 when I tell him he's going home. What wonderful noise—#603's fat bald wheels whining at 70 mph across small lakes up the West Side Highway, and me and Robby in coyote howls all the way home.

Yeah.

Even more simply, I wish I could say that as I passed him our eyes met, I leaned in to him, had a man-to-man, told him what's not right, apologized, and left him with a smile and a wave. I wish for even just the smile, if only for selfish reasons, like the pediatrician who coaxes hesitant grins from his young chemotherapy patients only so he can go home, eat dinner, and fall asleep without losing his mind. My eyes did meet Robby's, but nothing was said between our glances. I didn't allow it. I couldn't take it. I felt I had wronged him so sharply and I just couldn't take it. I had to look away. I couldn't take it, so I had to crack it, and this big baby hightailed for the rain-soaked streets. It's not as though Dana and I shouldn't have removed him—it's that we couldn't *not* remove him. Now that I look back on it. Maybe that's obvious by now. I'll never forget Robby. *Hope you crash.*

I hope he's forgotten me.

5

The Hex

THE DEPTH OF WINTER IN MANHATTAN is evident mainly in temperature. Since most of nature's handiwork has been eradicated from the city, there are few signs to indicate the icy season is at hand. Even the hardiest snowbanks are trampled flat in a matter of days. When I got up in the morning wondering how to dress for the weather, it wasn't the thermometer or the wind in the trees I looked to. A quick glance at the coats humping along on the street below gave me all the information I needed and was as good as any forecast. The city's people are its nature.

It can get pretty cold in the city. Not Wisconsin cold, but chilly nonetheless. The cold in Manhattan always catches you off guard. In Wisconsin people are prepared for it. Most households have an entire attic bursting with snowmobile suits, subzero parkas, snow boots, and the like. New York's weather may warrant that type of protection one week out of the year—not enough to justify a complete Arctic wardrobe. When that one week hits and the mercury goes into hiding, it's a sorry sight around here. The heaviest Manhattan clothes are no match for the bitter air. The people look good, but they're cold as hell.

At eleven-fifteen on a Sunday morning in January, I walked a block north to 109th Street and Central Park West to catch a downtown subway to work. Thirty-five minutes later, I stepped out at Canal Street. The sun shone as brightly as a heat wave in July, but the wind was stiff and it was freezing cold. Six steps out of the station I broke into a stiff-legged jog. My leather jacket was a bully to the wind but it caved in completely to the cold. It was too snug to accommodate an underlying sweater or down vest. A good chamois shirt was about the most I could get under it. Impractical as it was, that jacket was my armor. I felt like I could get the devil to beg for mercy when I had it on. Matte black, chopped straight at the waist, 100 percent horsehide with a yellow-and-black plaid wool lining, it was my passport through some of the roughest buildings in the city. I picked it up at a vintage clothing store in the Village. The guy who sold it to me said it was an old police jacket. It was a beauty, but on really frigid days I had to pay for it. I looked good, but I was cold as hell.

The office was unusually quiet. People who came in at nine were mostly out on field visits and there were only a couple of us on the noon-to-eight shift. A few supervisors huddled in their cubicles sharing sections of the Sunday *Times*. One of the two bosses of the office, a large man in his midfifties, waltzed out of the war room in his customary thick plaid shirt. He always made the office feel like his living room and you were stopping by to drop off some hot dish and exchange a neighborly howdy-do.

"Afternoon, Marc," he said, cheerfully smacking on a pipe. Sam was the kind of guy who'd lay in wait to snare you in a thoughtful conversation about anything from cut roses to prostate cancer, haircuts to old jazz records. He could turn a discussion about Chinese take-out into a fireside chat.

"How are you, Sam?"

"I'm okay today, Marc," he replied.

"It's too cold out there," I said. Sam took his pipe from his mouth and pondered this for a spot.

"It is cold today. Now, I wouldn't think this type of weather would bother you, Marc," he said, returning the pipe to its resting place on the corner of his mouth. "Canadians don't seem to mind the cold."

"I'm not from Canada, Sam."

"Okay, Marc. Cold in Minnesota, though."

"I'm from Wisconsin."

"I know that, Marc." A small blue band of smoke lifted from his mouth to his nose. "Wisconsin gets cold, I imagine."

"Yup."

"Now, I've been in the Adirondacks...," he began, then took his pipe out to think about it for a while.

"Yeah?"

"It gets cold up there, Marc."

"I bet it does."

"Pretty, though."

"Is it?"

"You've never been up there?"

"Never been to the Adirondacks," I replied.

"Well. That's too bad, Marc. Guy like you would enjoy himself in the Adirondacks. That's a place where Man can commune with Nature. Cold, though," he said, putting the pipe back. "You'd like it, Marc. Probably a lot like Canada."

"Wisconsin?"

"I've never been in Wisconsin, Marc. Gets cold there, I bet."

"Yeah, it does."

"Now, I had a buddy used to live in *Maine*. Said it used to get cold up there. And they got that snow, Marc. Seems to me I remember him saying they'd get upwards of seventy foot of snow a season."

"I don't think they get seventy feet."

"Oh, I think they do, Marc," he said, trundling off to the bathroom. "That's serious business up there in Maine..."

2

LAURA WAS ALREADY SITTING AT HER DESK when I came in. She was reading *People* and *Harper's* at the same time and slurping an extra-large iced coffee.

"How on earth can you be drinking an iced coffee when it's this freezing outside?"

"I know," she said, looking up and taking another slurp. "It's weird, right?"

Laura and I began working for ECS at the same time. We were in training together. She, too, was from Wisconsin and a recent college grad/New York transplant. We hit it off famously from the moment we met and often saw one another outside of work. She was connected to a large extended family of Wisconsinites so it almost felt like going home when we went out with her friends. She stood on the shorter side, with long dark hair, and a keen eye for good clothing. Everyone loved Laura. Almost anyone would fall for her after a five-minute conversation.

"You know when you start to get into something and you just have to have it? It doesn't matter how crazy it is, but you're just into it? Like: it's so cold outside and I'm drinking iced coffee. I have a chill even."

"It's called a craving, Laura," I said.

"You're right. I crave iced coffee. I have a craving."

"I craved olives once."

"I have a craving. That's what it is."

"Couldn't get enough of them," I went on. "Must've tried every kind."

"I can't believe I really have a craving."

"—had these little containers all over the fridge with every kind of olive I could find."

"Do you think it's okay, Marc? It's so cold outside and I'm drinking iced coffee, it's a little weird, don't you think?" She took another slurp.

"I think it's just a craving."

"It's weird, Marc. It is."

"The whole thing *about* a craving is that it's weird. It has to be weird if it's a craving."

"Right—if it wasn't weird, it wouldn't be a craving. It would be like a—"

"It would be a hankering."

"Right. So I'm not crazy. I have a craving. People get cravings. Cravings are usually weird."

"There you go."

"So I have a case already. It's in Staten Island," she said. "You wanna go with me? You can get a burger at Wendy's. I'll get a chicken or something. They have the best fries."

"You got a case already?"

"It was sitting on the desk when I walked in," she said, tossing it to me. "Have a look."

Mother believes she and her children are under a hex. Mother is not feeding children because she is afraid of the food. The children are hungry now. Mother is behaving strangely. She is not answering the phone and will not open the door for anyone. Last week Mother reported seeing "strange men" outside of her apartment window. Mother lives on the 16th floor. There are bizarre

sounds coming from the apartment and it is believed
that the children are at risk.

I handed the case back to Laura, who was finishing the iced
coffee with a final slurp. "Bizarre sounds from the apartment."

"I know," Laura said with an overwhelmed wind in her
voice.

"And the mother's 'behaving strangely.' "

"Nice, right? You think it's for real?"

"I don't know," I said. "Anonymous source, so maybe not.
But it's almost like it's strange enough to be true, you know?"

Laura exhaled deeply and leaned back in her chair with
her eyes shut. "...oh man...," she said, running her hands
through her hair. "I hate it when the allegations are vague and
all weird like this. I mean, who would call in and say stuff like
this? I can't believe they took the report without getting more
information. It's crazy not knowing what to expect. I mean, is
it like this is some sad little woman who sits in the dark, or is
she some lunatic sharpening her knives for the next visitor? Do
we go alone or do we bring the cops? You know?"

"Right...A hex. Wow...you call the house?"

"No answer."

"Probably tough to hear the phone with all those 'bizarre
sounds,' " I said.

"Marc—"

"And you pick up the receiver and the earpiece starts spinning and vomiting pea soup."

"Marc, c'mon, I'll get the car," Laura said.

"This woman's like, 'I'm home but I'm *floating* so I can't
get to the phone'—right? 'I'd love to talk but I'm too busy
behaving strangely.' "

"It's cases like this that make me wanna quit this job.
I mean, I don't want to visit some woman who's 'behaving
strangely,' you know? You think about the kids and that gets
you to the front door but then it's like—good God, right? Who

knows what this woman is doing? I'm looking at this name on a piece of paper and some very vague allegations, and in an hour I'll be sitting on a couch wondering what's crawling into my clothing and praying that she doesn't suddenly decide I've been sent by the devil and go for my neck or something. I'm looking at this paper and I'm like—*who knows* what *this is*. I mean—'a hex.' It's Sunday. I don't wanna go to an apartment with a hex for God's sake. And I don't care if they're not real—people say they're not real. They're real enough to the ones who believe in them— have you heard about the people who kill chickens and dogs or something or other to lift a hex? They find these dead animals all over Central Park in the summer—like they've been *sacrificed* or something? There's people out there who actually sacrifice animals for gods or something or other—can you believe it? These people are the real thing. They're serious. It's a gas to read about it in the paper; some woman who thinks her husband's turning into a horse, right? But who wants to sit on their furniture, you know?"

"I'll go out with you, Laura."

"It's—I don't know, today I'm just not up for the craziness."

"Happens to everyone here."

"It doesn't happen to everyone here. Some people are cut out for this. William Samuels."

"Willie was born for craziness," I said. "You think I don't go insane about nine out of ten days—wondering what the hell kind of mess I'm in the middle of?"

"Some people can just go and do a case, you know? They focus on the kids or something. They get in there and work."

"Yeah, but everyone's got a freaker, Laura. Yours is a woman under a hex who's behaving strangely. So let's just go and do it."

"The poor kids, if it's true, right?"

"Let's go see if they're all right."

"I'll get the car," she said, tossing her empty coffee cup into the trash and heading into the war room where the keys are kept. I went to Sam to tell him I wanted to go with Laura on her case.

"Okay, Marc," he said with his pipe bobbing on his lip. I turned to go and he stopped me. "Oh, Marc," he said taking the pipe from his mouth. "That's the hex case, isn't it?"

"Yeah."

"Serious stuff, Marc. Those people go all the way with that." He paused, looking briefly to the ceiling. "Kill chickens...dogs and cats...lizards, I believe,...rabbits maybe... find 'em all over Central Park—beheaded mostly. Now I'm pretty sure the thinking with that goes, they have to sacrifice the blood of an animal to lift the hex, and it goes—I think— the bigger the hex, the more blood it takes. I might be wrong on that, but I might not be."

"Yeah," I said. "Read about it in the *Times*, I think. A while ago."

"I read about it in the *Times*, Marc. We may've read the same piece," he said. He took a pair of reading glasses from his breast pocket and put them on. As he sat down, he cocked his chin to his chest and looked over the half lenses into my eyes, speaking in a somber tone, "Marc, you gotta see if those kids are all right. Serious business out there—take the cops if you need 'em. You two be careful."

I left Sam to his newspaper and headed back to my desk. Laura swung out of the war room with the keys in her hand and headed for the bathroom to empty some iced coffee from her bladder before the long drive to Staten Island.

"Marc," she called over her shoulder. "Would you mind doing a clearance on the family while I get ready here?"

"No problem," I shouted back. "What car did you get?"

"603."

"Number 603 smells like a canoe," I said. "It leaks."

"601's the only other car available and I'm not even gonna

say what it smells like. I had it out last night. Something died in the trunk."

I went to her desk, grabbed the case, and headed to the computer. After logging on, I ran a check on our woman but found nothing. Whoever she was, as far as the city was concerned, she wasn't a child abuser. I also ran a check to see if she was on welfare. Nothing came up for that either. This was a woman who'd not crossed the waters of HRA. She was an unknown. Delia Gammon was a mystery woman with a big problem. A hex. A hex on her home, a hex on her head, and a hex on her children. You tell her they're not real. They're real enough to the people under them—real as a tingle in the neck bones. Real as a pinprick in the worst possible place. Real as a strange man lingering outside the sixteenth-floor window. Real as a beheaded Doberman in the woods of Central Park.

3

WE GOT IN THE CAR TO head out to Staten Island. Laura set her seat to its farthest back position and we bumped and rumbled over the Brooklyn Bridge across the East River. I liked to get to Staten Island via the Brooklyn-Queens Expressway, though many would argue that the BQE isn't the quickest route. It didn't matter to me, the BQE is one of my favorite highways in the city and a sure shot to the Verrazano-Narrows Bridge, New York's own Golden Gate done in pale blue and leading straight to the heart of Staten Island. When you enter the BQE eastbound off the Brooklyn Bridge, there's a spectacular view of Manhattan to the right with the power to render the most callous New Yorker slack-jawed in wonder. Brooklyn Heights is to the left but on the passenger side there's nothing but blue water and a glittering forest of steel. I've heard that this short stretch of road has more than the average number of traffic accidents due to the breathtaking cityscape. At 50 mph, you get about a twenty-second shot at it—about three if you're driving.

Immediately after, brick walls rise on either side of you and the driving gets a little intense. Some sections of highway on the BQE were designed for drivers with telepathy. On- and off-ramps appear like sucker punches—the walls that force their changes, decorated with assorted scrapings of paint and bumper. The road signs lie. Pylons appear from nowhere. There's no speed limit. Dividing lines suggest a method to the madness, but even they can't always be trusted. The left lane is for daredevils, and criminals. The right is for the elderly, the foreign, and people with new cars. The middle is for families. Additionally, some of the stupidest drivers are in the middle lane: the ones too frightened of the left lane and too impatient to deal with their own kind in the right. They take the middle as a kind of security, with the left and right lanes keeping the walls at a comfortable distance. Graffiti-covered delivery trucks wobble and sway to the whims of demonic fates, spiriting themselves between speeding cars like fat men at a high-speed disco. Ninja bikers could be anywhere, and they usually are.

I was a left-laner mostly—pushed from my natural inclination to the middle by the slow drivers who should've been in the right. So I drove like a criminal and #603 was happy to oblige. What the car gave up in appearance, it more than made up for in power. 603 was a driving car, if you know what I mean. It was an ugly old canoe but it *drove*. While every cosmetic aspect of the vehicle was in disrepair, the city went to great efforts to put a spit shine on the gas and the brake.

After about twenty minutes in hell, you take the Belt Parkway exit and the road opens wide, giving up another breathtaking view on the right. Just when you forget that New York is a city on the ocean, the Belt offers its stunning reminder as it rounds the southeast perimeter of Brooklyn. Even with the windows shut tight, the smell of the ocean hits you, just before the awesome view. In one suck of salty air your mind shoots to carnivals by the sea—the Zipper and the Double Wheel, the Scrambler and the Bullet, franks and fried clams and candy and more candy, and butter—butter and glittering lights covering everything. 603 soars over a swell in the road and—bang, there's the ocean. Flat gray water in chilly November reaches from the frenzy of the city to the emptiness of a pale horizon. Freighters and ocean liners the size of small islands lumber silently into oblivion's haze. There were always five or eight of them either coming or going along that stretch. The ones on the horizon looked almost cartoonish—colorless and jagged, floating mountains drawn by a lazy illustrator.

Laura and I gabbed on for most of the trip. When you see someone almost every day, as Laura and I did, you've got about thirty minutes of small talk until you're used up. With the hey-how-are-ya done for the day, we sat quietly looking at the sea and listening to the conversation between the fat wheels of #603 and the open road. The silence between us was comfortable. The highway breezed along the edge of the ocean for two miles or so before the exit to the island. We wound the lazy loop of the exit, climbing high above the water and looking into the awesome expanse of the Verrazano Narrows Bridge. Passing quickly through the toll, we entered the upper roadway, whose five lanes were almost empty on the chilly midafternoon Sunday. I moved 603 to the farthest right lane and slowed down so we could enjoy the view.

"I know it sounds crazy," Laura said, staring over the water to the tiny gray cluster of buildings in the distance that was Manhattan. "But the whole idea of a hex freaks me out a little. I mean, it's easy for me to just say they're not real, you know?—but the hair on my neck stands up a little just the same. A hex—you know?"

"It does make your stomach get a little shiver in it I guess. Doesn't have anything to do with whether or not you believe in them—it's like a muscle memory. You hear 'hex' and your mind shoots through years of bad TV movies with voodoo themes, the ones you made fun of while they scared the shit out of you."

"You think they're real?" Laura asked.

"Do I think hexes are real?"

"Yeah—do you believe that a person can throw a hex on someone?"

"Laura—I can't even figure out if I should keep going to church or not."

"C'mon, Marc. You think there's something to them?"

"I don't know . . ." I thought about it for a while. "A couple of years ago I would've said no way, but . . . jeez, I don't know . . . it's a big old world. Right? Who can say?"

"You think they're real," Laura said, her pupils wide and dark.

"No, no, no, no, I just—I guess I'd just say I'm open to it—you know?"

"That's creepy."

"What?"

"You're open to it?"

"Well yeah—you know? I mean I can't say they don't exist."

"You're 'open' to á hex?"

"No, Laura."

"That's what you just said. You just said you were 'open to it.' "

"I don't believe in hexes—okay? All I'm saying, the people who believe in them—right? Who can say they're not real for the people who believe in them?"

"It's creepy, Marc. This whole case could be nothing, but it's creepy all the same. I'm a little creeped out by it."

"I don't believe in hexes, Laura."

The bridge descended over the island and it suddenly felt much colder than in Manhattan. The streets were empty; the cold had shut everybody inside their homes to wait out the day. As I knocked 603's heater up a bit, I could almost hear the stern warnings of Wisconsin weathermen back home: *Do not attempt to go out-of-doors unless you absolutely have to. There's a killing cold in our area. Remember: freezing and irreversible tissue damage can occur in as little as two minutes.* They always said "out-of-doors" when they meant business.

"Hey, this car does smell like a canoe," Laura said after a brief silence.

"It leaks," I said.

"So let's not spend more time in the house than we have to," Laura said with a shiver. "If the kids are all right, let's just leave, okay?"

We had our hopes, but this was something a little too strange and a little too specific for an anonymous caller's fiction. We had our hopes, but past experience cast a shadow on that. The intuition was familiar. We both knew the two young boys in the Gammon home were not all right. Not all right at all.

4

IT WAS A NICE BUILDING; one of the city projects but a good one, as yet unaffected by the ravages of tenants on drugs. The elevators worked. Black spray paint wasn't scribbled across every surface. The lights in the hallways worked. There were no large unsavory gatherings of men at the front doors. It looked to be a project that worked. The people in a good project tend to be an entirely different lot from the ones in the war zones. In fact, when a project was working, as they typically were in Staten Island, there wasn't much to distinguish them from any other dwelling in the city—except that apartments in the projects were usually bigger.

I stopped 603 directly in front of the building, and Laura and I gathered our things, tightened our collars, and stepped outside. Freezing air rushed like water through the zipper and down the collar of my old police jacket. Laura shot ahead of me in a vain attempt to outrun the cold. She cursed under her collar as she ran with her head dug into her chest. We both hustled up the walkway to the building, jumping and weaving to avoid slick patches of black ice that could put you on your back in a blink. Laura heaved on the heavy metal door to the building and we stepped into one very cold lobby. Ten steps inside and I could still see my breath. The building felt deserted. We hadn't seen a single person since leaving the car.

"Where on earth is everybody?" Laura spoke through her scarf. A typical project lobby was a roiling metropolis of children.

"It's like the whole of Staten Island has been evacuated," my voice echoed against the shiny cinder-block walls. "Ghost town stuff."

"Creepy, right?" But this time Laura was joking.

"Incredibly creepy," I said as Laura hit the elevator call, chuckling through her scarf. "The creepiest thing on earth— it's so entirely creepy that it's more than creepy. It's over-the-top creepy."

"Cold as hell, too." She hit the elevator call again.

"You think it's cold in hell, Laura?"

"I don't know . . . I think it might be."

"I've heard different."

"You've heard different?" The elevator door rumbled open and we stepped inside.

"Sure. It's gotta be pretty hot, I think," I said.

"You *heard* it's pretty hot in hell?" She hit the number sixteen button.

"Sure, Laura."

"That's creepy." The elevator humped to life and pulled us slowly upward. Laura arranged her papers and silently reread the report as the floors rolled by like years. On year five she undid her scarf and I loosened my jacket and pulled off my gloves, stuffing them into my pockets. I had developed the habit of taking in a deep breath just before getting into an elevator and holding it until I got out. There must be something about living in a housing project that makes you want to urinate in elevators, but I could never figure that one. Most every project elevator I've been in carried a noxious array of odors, but the essential fragrance from which all else sprang—the stock in the soup, the dirt in the forest, the hot sauce at the Taco Bell—was the smell of urine. Three-day-old urine. By year ten, with six more to go, I couldn't hold on any longer. I rationed out a few small exhales until my lungs were empty and there was nothing left to do but cautiously inhale and thank God the Strep A virus isn't airborne. With the first whiff I was relieved by the reek of industrial cleaners. The elevator had been recently scoured. I can barely stand the smell of cleaners; the pine and the fresh spring scents are as far from a gathering of fir trees as a bull-fight is from Girl Scouts singing around a campfire. I hate the smell of "spring violets" but I hate the smell of three-day-old urine more and in a project elevator, nature in a spray can plus ammonia-D was as good as it got, so I was grateful.

In the time the elevator took to reach the sixteenth floor, Laura and I could've had a small family of three, sent them to college, paid for the weddings, and had our first argument about where to retire. We stepped into the hallway, which was empty and quiet, and turned right, walking nervously toward the end of the building. The passage was lit every twenty steps or so by an occasional fluorescent light mounted into the corner where the wall met the ceiling. At the end of the hall in front of apartment 1606, the final light flickered with a single orange band of dull luminescence. The band coiled and rolled like a fat worm in a test tube, buzzing and snapping to an electro-cution whirligig. It looked evil as hell, but I didn't want to admit it. We hadn't gotten to within three feet of the front door and I was already trying to convince myself that a fluorescent light on the blink wasn't really a glass tube holding the world's largest earthworm. The thing cast an awful glow, making

Laura's face look as if it had been soaked in old cherry Kool-Aid. We both stared at it, but neither of us made a comment.

Laura held the report close to her face to check the name of the mother again and to make sure we were at the right apartment. She squinted and tilted the paper to get a good look at it—a fat blinking worm is no halogen reading lamp. When she got what she needed, she looked back at me, rolled her eyes, and gave a small shake of her head. I gave her shoulder a squeeze and she knocked on the door. There was an immediate response from a very frightened voice on the other side. "Aww noooo..." The voice was almost crying. "...Who is that?—oohhh pleeease..."

"Ms. Gammon," Laura spoke. "We're with Ch—"

The door snapped open against two inches of security chain on the inside. Laura and I both jumped at the suddenness of it. It was dark inside—not a bit of light fell from the apartment. Two eyes emerged suddenly, peering at us sideways from under the chain. Before Laura could say a word, the eyes drew back into the darkness and there was a bloodcurdling scream. We jumped away from the door against the adjacent wall; our shoulders pressed flat against the smooth cinder block. Short of breath and suddenly trembling with adrenaline, our eyes fell once again on the fat worm, jiggling and snapping in its tube, as the screaming inside apartment 1606 thunderclapped into complete madness.

5

EXACTLY TWO WEEKS BEFORE the scream at the door, when the world was right side up and the light in the hallway at 1606 gleamed cheery and white, Delia Gammon and her two boys, Rick and Chucky, stepped up to their apartment with armfuls of groceries from the local market. As she groped the bottom of her purse for the apartment keys, Ms. Gammon noticed a curious red smear on the wall facing the front door, directly below the fluorescent light. It was at eye level, about seven inches long and four inches wide, solid red at the center, and tapered out to a swirl at either end. The head of a small creature with horns maybe, deliberately rendered for sure. With her hand in her purse and groceries hanging from both arms, Delia Gammon leaned toward the smear for a better look. A brief inspection sent her eyebrows pushing down against a wrinkle across her nose. Blood. No doubt about it. Definitely blood. Bright red and shining wet—still fresh. *No matter,* she thought. It was the projects after all. She'd send Rick out with a bottle of Windex and a paper towel as soon as he unloaded his bags. Her hand found the keys and pushed one into the bolt lock, giving it a turn and pushing the door with a kick of her foot. The boys rushed into the apartment ahead of her, and she followed, pulling the door shut behind them. She hadn't taken another step before the shouts of Rick and Chucky stopped her in her tracks. Rick came running from the kitchen waving his blood-soaked right hand like a red flag. With the bags still hanging heavy on her arms, Delia Gammon rushed to the kitchen, where Chucky stood with eyes wide and fearful. Her hands covered her mouth. Tears welled in her eyes as she slowly collapsed against the wall. Her bags slumped to the floor on either side of her as she fell to the floor, her knees trembling and a rash of gooseflesh racing over her shoulders and across her back.

Blood was everywhere—splashed on the cupboards, pooled on the floor, dribbling down the fridge, and splayed across the counters. Arcing galaxies of red stars covered the walls and ceiling. All of it bright red and shining wet—still fresh. Most of it seemed to originate from the sink, which was entirely covered—as if a blood volcano went off in the drain, spewing its gore like a happy murderer over the entire area.

"Get back from there, Chucky!" she barked, pulling him to her chest. *"And you go into the bathroom, Rick. Go to the*

bathroom and you wash that hand off right now." Her face shook wildly as tears ran down her cheeks. "Use the alcohol. It's under the sink. *Oohhh God!!!!!!* USE THE ALCOHOL, RICKY!" She buried her face in Chucky's head, shivering uncontrollably. "OOOOOOO...scrub it good, Ricky—scrub it good—oh God...SCRUB IT GOOD, RICKY—IT'S BAD... IT'S BAD THAT IT TOUCHED YOU—SCRUB IT ALL OFF."

Delia squeezed Chucky tight to her heaving chest. In the haze of her shock, her mind wrestled with questions of who and why, but deep inside her, the answers waited patiently to rise to the surface with each wipe of a Clorox sponge. Her ex. He said he'd do it and by God he did it.

6

A MOUTH IS A DRY PLACE in a scary season. Laura and I stood in front of 1606 with tiny gaping deserts below our noses and orange worm light blinking all around us. The screams behind the door were quickly replaced with dreadlike moaning. Waiting for clarity in a situation like this was usually an exercise in futility. Blind initiative was the only vehicle to move things forward, so Laura and I tightened down our helmets and moved it out.

"DELIA—" Laura leaned into the door, shouting. "It's okay, Delia—we just want to—Delia...Delia?..." She knocked on the door again softly. "Come back to the door,... there's nothing to be afrai—"

The door cracked open and the eyes reappeared beneath the chain.

"Delia, is that you?" Laura asked gently.

"...who is it? Who are you?" The voice was just about crying.

"I'm Laura. This is Marc...Are you okay? Is this Delia?"

"Who sent you? Did he send you? Oh please..."

"Did who send us?"

"Oh God help us. Oh please not this now..."

"Did who send us,...Delia? Is this Delia?" Laura asked again.

"Why are you looking for Delia?" The voice was high and teary.

"We have to talk to her," I said. The eyes shifted from me to Laura and back to me.

"This is Delia," she said finally.

"Can we come inside and talk with you, Delia?" Laura asked. "There's no need to be afraid. It's just the two of us."

"Who sent you here?" she asked, her voice still wet with fear.

"We're with the city," Laura said. "We heard you were in some kind of trouble and we wanted to make sure you were okay."

"You're with the city?" There was instant relief in the voice.

"We just want to see—"

The crack in the door closed and the chain rattled on the other side. Laura and I looked at each other and back to the door that remained shut.

"Delia?...," I called out. There was no answer. Laura put her hand to the door and it fell slowly open. A bit of rolling orange light spilled into the apartment from the hallway, but we couldn't see a thing inside. I could feel someone watching us from the darkness as we stood fully visible. Laura looked back at me, shrugged her shoulders, and stepped inside. I followed behind her. Going first into darkness was an awful chore we traded between ourselves. We silently kept track of whose turn it was without ever talking about it. You knew when it was your turn and you took it.

"It's awful dark in here, Delia," Laura called out as we went forward. Pulsing Kool-Aid light from the hall illuminated a few feet ahead of us and kept time with the heartbeat in my neck.

"I'm so sorry," the voice said in the dark. "It must be terrifying enough to walk into a strange apartment—but with no light! I really am sorry." She opened the shades on two large windows and the apartment filled with outside light. "It's been a problem with the window shades open," she said like an embarrassed housewife to a guest who found a hair in the coffee.

Laura and I looked around us. The room was a complete wreck. Two couches were pulled away from either wall. The cushions were turned up and strewn about. Several of them were neatly cut open and the inner padding torn out. Clothing was piled in small islands covering the floor and flowing into adjacent rooms. Framed pictures sat on the floor beneath their hooks. The drawers of a large dresser and all the kitchen cupboards were pulled out and turned upside down. They leaned in stacks against each other wherever they could fit, their contents scattered on the floor around them. It wasn't your average mess, not the kind of thing that can happen on a busy week with no time for cleaning. It looked as though the place had been raided.

"I know—this place is a mess! We've had to do a major cleaning—couple of small problems... *Anyways*...," Delia said with a chuckle.

"It's okay," Laura assured her.

"Well, would you like to sit down or something? We'll have to clear a spot," she said, pushing a pile of socks and underwear aside and putting a cushion on the couch.

"Are the kids home? Two boys, right?" Laura asked as she sat.

"That's right," she said, and then with a look that was flustered and dismissive at the same time, she put her arms on her hips. "Hey how did you know that? *Anyways*—Rick, Chucky—come on out, it's okay." The two boys tromped out of their room and stood side by side in front of us as if they were on display. With their chins at their chests, they looked at us through their eyelashes.

"How you doin', guys?" I said. They stared at me quietly.

"It's okay, boys," their mother said. "You can say hello to the man." They both chirped cautious hellos and ran back to their rooms. Delia was smiling the whole time like we were favorite neighbors come for a visit. I was dying to ask her what the business at the front door was all about, but she suddenly seemed so normal and already completely embarrassed that I decided to let it ride for the time being.

"They're shy," Delia said apologetically. "But we've all been through a lot the past two weeks."

"What's been happening?" Laura asked.

"Well, their father and I recently divorced and there's been a lot of friction with that. It's been especially tough the past two weeks." She stopped herself suddenly with a polite chuckle. "Wait a minute! Why am I telling this to you two? Who are you again? You're with the city?"

"We're with Emergency Children's Services," I said.

Delia's voice lowered. "Wait a minute, I've heard of you guys. Is that the agency that takes people's children away?"

"Well, yes it is," Laura said. "But it's not the only thing we do. We really just came out to see you because of a report we got this morning. We wanted to see if you and the kids were all right."

The two boys were peeking at us from around the corner. I bounced my eyebrows at them and the younger one smiled. They both disappeared back around the corner.

"You got a report this morning and you're here already?"

"Right," Laura said.

"Oh my goodness...well, do you have some kind of identification or something? I guess I should probably see that, if you've got any."

"Absolutely," I said, and we took out our IDs. She held

them in either hand, glancing at their sorry fronts and backs.

"Okay then," Delia said, handing the cards back to us with a shrug of her shoulders. "I don't even know what these are supposed to look like."

Laura read the report to Delia, who listened quietly, a small smile sticking to her mouth as tears filled her eyes. When Laura finished reading, Delia quickly wiped her face and gave another go at her cheeriest expression. "Well...," she said. "With a report like that I can certainly see why the two of you came out so quickly."

There was a moment of silence between us. No one knew where to start. The youngest boy appeared again from around the corner. He held one of his toys, a red plastic action figure, in front of his face. He was looking at me and smiling. I made a silent "Ohh!" with my lips. He thrilled and ran back to his room.

"He's playing with you," Delia said.

"He's a cutie."

"He's a good boy," she said. "They're both good boys."

"So why was it so dark when we came in?" I tried to ask casually. There were several lamps in the room and a ceiling fixture all with their lights missing.

"*Oh that,*" Delia said with a laugh and a shake of her head. "It probably looks pretty strange, I imagine." Tears welled in her eyes again. "I don't know—there's been some sort of electrical problem in the building, I think. I've been, umm..." She struggled to control her tears. "...the lights...they just"—she held her head back for a second—"I'm sorry...they just—well you can put one in and see for yourself. They're not working right. I don't know what it is—like the one in the hallway out there?—like that. I don't know what. The lights don't work anymore. I don't want them to break or something so—... every time I put one in it just—I bought new ones and everything."

Laura put her hand on Delia's arm as she did her best to shake off the tears.

"To tell you the truth," Delia said after quickly whipping a hand through her hair, "I'm actually very glad to see the both of you. Someone from my family probably called you but I don't care—I'm glad you're here. It's been so completely horrible. I mean—I shouldn't be telling you this because you'll take my children, right? But listen, I beg you—I'm not going crazy. *There's things that are happening here.*"

That was suddenly the most chilling thing I'd ever heard. Delia wasn't a maniac. Her eyes gleamed with truth. If she became any more convincing, standing in one place was going to become a major problem.

"I can't explain it without sounding like I'm losing my mind," Delia continued. "But I'll try. These things are *happening*—I swear."

7

DELIA BEGAN HAVING TROUBLES with her ex-husband, the father of her two boys, almost immediately following their divorce. She had hoped their separation would loosen the grip he held on her and would allow her to finally take control of her life. She and the boys had begun their slow climb on the mountainous journey to independence faced by so many single mothers and their children. Big Rick was seven years old. Chucky was five and well into his first year of kindergarten. With both boys in school, Ms. Gammon had begun training at a local technical college to become a legal secretary. Problems with her ex were frequent, but she was persevering.

Things got bad when Delia's ex found out about the new boyfriend she'd met at the tech. He didn't want her going out with another man—nothing new here. I used to carry a list of secret shelters for women trying to escape the sticky web of a once-loved monster. I've sat for hours singing the "He'll Kill You Someday" theme song so familiar to those who deal with women in peril. It's a door I've painted more times than I care to say.

Delia Gammon and her ex were engaged in an age-old dance, only this guy was *creative*. He had a power over Delia, as guys like this always do, and he knew it. Fists and heels and kicks and punches were primitive as far as he was concerned, and hell, they could get a guy in trouble. Breaking someone's arm is just plain stupid if, with a little more cunning, you can make them lose their mind.

The day he found out about her boyfriend, Delia got home from the tech at her regular time, about an hour before the boys—just enough time to finish an errand or two and start supper. As she stepped out of the elevator and began walking toward her apartment, she saw her ex standing by the doorway. There was nothing entirely unusual about that, almost every day since their separation he'd hung around the building late afternoons to see the boys. Only, this time he was early. And he looked angry. Delia put on her calmest demeanor and walked directly to the door without even looking at him. Rummaging impatiently for her keys, she kept her head down. Her eyes fell to his shoes.

Just as she found the key and put it to the lock, he said, "Don't disrespect me." Delia could feel the words on her neck. His breath was warm and sour. Without the masking scent of affection, she found it just short of repulsive.

"You're early," she said, still looking at his shoes. "The boys won't be home for another hour—you know that. They're in school."

"Don't disrespect me," he said again. He spoke slowly. His voice could rock the ocean. Its dark resonance attracted her to the man in the first place. Now it was rumbling like the growl of a mountain lion about to strike. "I said don't disrespect me," he said after another pause.

Delia looked up from his shoes to his eyes. He stared back at her calmly. "What do you want?" she asked. "Why are you here early?"

"Are you respecting me now?" he asked her.

She looked at him confused, "What's wrong with you?"

"Are you respecting me right now?" he asked again.

"Yes, I'm respecting you . . . what? . . . I have to go inside." He stopped her. "What's wrong with you?" she asked again with a quiver in her throat. His voice was melting her calm demeanor. He was holding her.

"You're respecting me now?"

"Yes—what?"

"This is you respecting me?"

"I'm respecting you. Let go of me. What's wrong with you?"

"You are respecting me right now?"

"What are you talking about?"

"You make it worse."

"Please—what's wrong?"

"You make me say it. You push my face in the shit."

"What?" she begged him. "What are you talking about?"

"I'm talking about him."

"Him? Him what?"

He slapped her.

"You make it worse now. I'm not as stupid as you think."

"We're divorced."

"This is you respecting me?"

"I'm not seeing him anymore," she lied.

He slapped her again. She grasped her face this time, giving in to the sting of the blow. In one move, he tumbled the lock open, threw her inside, and flung the keys at her face. She ran to the bathroom and locked herself inside. He followed her and broke through the door. Easily. The lock popped its hold on the frame like a cheap dollhouse. For the rest of their discussion, Delia respected him from a seated position on the toilet.

"You slept with him?"

"I didn't," she lied.

He slapped her.

"Look at me." She was crying. "Look at me," he thundered again. She looked at his face through a kaleidoscope of tears. "You sleep with this guy?"

"We're divorced," she cried. "Please don't . . . please . . ."

"You feel this guy? You kiss him and feel him in you?— Look at me." Her head was bent. She cried. He grabbed a tight fistful of hair and brought her head smartly back, twisting her neck toward him. With his other hand, he grabbed roughly on her breast, giving it a terrible shake. "He touch you like this, you bitch? He touch you here? He touch you like I'm touching you?" He released her breast and pulled back harder on her head. She arched her back to relieve the pressure on her neck. He shook her head with his fist and she burst into an attack of coughing. He held her head back as she strained with each cough to curl it forward.

"See what I'm doing to you now?" he screamed over the hacking. "I'm doing this to you. I'm the one scratching in your throat because you lie to me." Delia could barely breathe. Every suck of air was bulging with his sour breath. Her throat went into a spasm and she began to gag. He pulled her head back as far as it would go. "I can make you cough to death, you bitch. I can scratch your throat till you bleed from your mouth. NO MORE LIES!" he screamed. "Only the truth now. You sleep with this guy?" He let her head go and with her throat relaxed, the spasms subsided and the coughing stopped abruptly. "Only the truth," he said once more. "You sleep with this guy?" He already knew she had slept with him. He wanted to hear her say it. He was pushing his own face in the shit. She didn't care. She bobbed her head yes.

"Look at me, my wife," he said, grasping her cheeks softly. His hands were wet. She allowed his fingertips to pull her face to his. His breath caressed her cheeks with foulness. His eyes stuck to her skin. She suddenly felt exhausted.

He prayed.

His lips formed deep sounds that flowed over her like hot poison. His lids fluttered shut on his eyes. She didn't know what he was doing or what he was saying but she didn't move. He looked as though he'd crack in half if interrupted. His tongue lolled back and forth in the stench of his mouth. A rhythmic clatter began to take shape. His fingers trembled and swayed against her cheeks. Head thick and throat on fire, she followed the movements. Tears fell from his cheeks now, too. They shook and wept together in the bathroom until he bowed his head like a lover to her breast and fell silent. He rose slowly after a moment, and looking into her eyes, asked her almost sweetly, "You have to look at me when you say it. Did you make love to this guy? Look in my eyes and say you didn't. You have to say it to me. No lies, my wife."

He was so close she could taste him. Her stomach riffled with the answer before she could speak it. She felt him looking into the depths of her. He already knew the answer but he wanted to rub his face in it. She indulged him. "I did," she said with a crackle in her voice. "I made love to him."

That shook him. His voice quaked. It looked as though he would fall over, but he gained the strength to rise slowly and back into the doorjamb with a hand against either wall. "*Then I throw a hex on you,*" he said in a low snarl. His eyes got dark and began to shake. His arms pushed against the walls and began to flutter. Balls of sweat joined and raced down the shuddering lines of his face. "*I THROW A HEX ON YOU, YOU FILTHY ROTTED BITCH!*" he screamed. Delia wanted to turn away but she couldn't move. His head reeled on his shoulders as his jaw flapped with demonic incantations. She was mesmerized by the sight of the man she once loved

conjuring the evil forces of the universe against her. Veins rattled in his neck as his voice ran up into a high whistle. The
room shook with his fetor and vigor.

Suddenly he stopped, his body contorted in a fist of tense
muscle. She winced, pulling her arms to her face. Slowly, he
relaxed into his previous self.

"Put your arms down, you filthy bitch," he said, laughing.
"It's over now. There's nothing you can do, so put down your
arms. You're fucked forever, man. The hex is strong. I saved
that hex my whole life. This is an evil place now. There's nothing you can do, no one can help you—the evil rock this home
silly, man." He turned away from her and ran out of the apartment in a belly laugh. "The evil *rock* this place." Still sitting
on the toilet, she could hear him laughing as he ran down the
hall. *"The hex rip you in half, man. Rock this place forever—
blow up that shit and rock that silly bitch to hell..."*

The light in the hall went bad the instant he left. The following day her kitchen was covered with blood. Two weeks
later the city was knocking on her door to steal her children
away. It didn't make a shit's bit of difference if I believed in
hexes or not. I wasn't gonna tell her they weren't real.

8

"THIS IS A POWERFUL MAN, I SWEAR," Delia said. "He sent
me so much evil the past two weeks. He comes to me—he can
come from nowhere and you don't see it. He puts devils in the
air. He could be here now even. In the next room or behind
that couch. It's so bad, I swear. I thought he sent you. That's
why I was...I'm so sorry. It's just, I thought for sure when
I saw you both at the door—he could do it, he can send
people...*Anyways*...You see how this apartment looks?
Look what I had to do. I don't know where to start."

"So you believe your husband's here right now?" I asked.

"Look, I told you already I'm not going crazy. If you're gonna ask me a question like that, we might as well not even get started 'cause it only goes down from here. Of course I don't think he's here right now. If he was here right now there'd be no mistake about it, believe me. He's a powerful man. No offense, but you should be glad he's not here now. What I said was that he comes from nowhere—not like he's knocking at the door and walking in, this man comes some other way, but don't ask me how 'cause I couldn't tell you. When he's here, he's standing right in front of me like the two of you are. He came to me like that several times in the past week."

"So you're saying you believe he can walk through the walls?" I asked.

"Now what would the two of you think if I told you my ex-husband can walk through the walls? I'm not stupid and I know why you're here, okay? No offense. I don't know how he comes in. All I can say is that when he's here, he's *here*. All right? I never see how he gets here. He knows when I'm in and out. He knows what room to catch me in because he's got one of his devils watching. If you think that's crazy then just look out that window cause he's got one on us right now while we're talking."

My stomach flipped. "Which window?" Laura asked.

"This window to my right here," she said coolly, her eyes fixed on mine. "I won't look at him. It's across the way on the roof of the far building. I don't look at that thing in the face."

"—*Oh good God, Marc*," Laura said, springing suddenly to the window. "I see him. I see somebody. There he goes."

"Where?" I asked, joining Laura at the window.

"He's gone now. On the roof over there. He's gone. He just left."

"It will be back," Delia said calmly. "You stick around and you'll see it again."

"He was just standing there looking at us."

"Laura, c'mon," I said quietly at the window.

"C'mon what?" she snapped. "There was a guy on that far roof looking right in here. When he saw me look at him, he ducked away."

"Where was he?"

"Just over there," she said, pointing to a distant roof. "To the right of that big chimney thing there. He was just standing there."

I strained my eyes on the far rooftop. It was another project, about a block away. All was still and frozen looking. Heating ducts and vent structures dotted the top of the building. A typical roof. The sky had turned from brilliant blue to sheet-metal gray in the short time we'd been inside.

"Don't you think it was maybe just some guy on the roof looking around?" I whispered to Laura.

"Marc, you didn't see him. He was looking right over here."

"That's pretty far away, though," I said. "He could've been looking at anything in this direction."

"But the way he ducked away when I saw him"—her face was pale in the wash of gray light—"...that was weird," she said to herself.

"That thing will be back," Delia said from the couch. "I keep those shades closed because of it. And I don't let the boys look out. It's been there ever since the hex. That's a devil for sure. I don't want it looking at my kids."

"What did he look like?" I asked Laura.

"I don't know, Marc—he just looked like a guy. I only got a glimpse of him. He had a beard I think."

"That's the one," Delia said.

"He's been there awhile?" Laura asked, returning to the couch.

"Two weeks, only I stopped looking after the second day. It just stares at me and smiles and I got it tough enough as it is without watching that. Those windows are off limits now.

We don't go near them." She glanced out briefly and looked back to Laura. "It's back?" she asked.

Laura looked to the roof again. "I don't see him," she said.

"Wouldn't that be something if the two of you scared it off," Delia said.

Delia's five-year-old came running on little steps around the corner with a puppet on either hand. He came to a stop in front of me and stood silently.

"He wants to show you his puppets," his mother said. "Go ahead, Chucky. Show the man how they talk."

Chucky held the puppets limply at his chest. He stared into my eyes, smiling silently as the jaws of each puppet yapped aimlessly at the floor.

"C'mon, Chucky," Delia went on. "You know how to do it. Go ahead and make them talk."

"Hello," Chucky said in a soft low voice. The puppet heads remained limp at his chest, their jaws flapping rhythmically with his voice. "Hello hello hello hello hello..." He clutched them suddenly to his sides and peeled back around the corner.

"Whoop. There he goes!" I said. "That's a good little guy all right."

"They're good boys," she said.

"What've they had to eat today?" Laura asked. Delia smiled uncomfortably.

"Oh...they've had their breakfast," she said.

"What'd they have for breakfast?" Laura asked.

"Well...," Delia said, looking at her hands. "They didn't actually have too much for breakfast today."

"Why not?"

"Well, there's been a problem with that. The food has been a problem. It's no good so..." Tears came back to her eyes.

"What did they eat today?" Laura asked.

"Well, the bread was okay so I gave them a little. But I was worried about that, too."

"What else have they had today?" Laura asked. Delia clenched her lips and shook her head slowly. *"Nothing?"* Laura gave me an oh-shit look and turned back to Delia. "So they're hungry right now. Why aren't you feeding them? I mean, you have to feed them. They're hungry. Do you have food?"

"There's food in the refrigerator," Delia said.

"So you have to feed the kids, right?"

"I know it. You're right."

"They're hungry so you have to feed them. I mean—how can we leave and say everything's all right if you aren't feeding your children—you know?"

"It's true—I know it."

"What's wrong with the food?" I asked.

"I found glass in it. I swear," she said immediately, confiding to me. "It's not safe. There was little slivers of glass in everything. I threw it all out and bought new stuff and that stayed good for a few hours so we ate it, but by the next morning there was glass in all of it. It's a good thing I checked it—can you imagine? That was two days ago. I threw most of it out. I don't know why I'm telling you this. You'll just take my children away and say I'm crazy. I know how this sounds and I know that you're thinking that, but I swear to you there was glass in all of it. I couldn't feed them that food—no mother would feed that to her children. It was bad, I swear. It was the hex and it got in quick. I gave it to my boys and I told them, 'You boys eat this as fast as you can. You eat it quick before it changes.' I told them to stop eating and spit it out if they hit the glass. We ate as fast as we could and we made it, but that was two nights ago. The bread has been okay for some reason. We ate the bread today. There's a little left."

"There's food in the fridge?" I asked. Delia shook her head yes. "Well let's have a look at it," I said, getting up to go to the fridge. Delia peeked over my shoulder as I looked through the shelves. The two boys raced to their seats at the counter and waited anxiously to be fed. I spied some apple jelly at the back of one of the shelves and grabbed it.

"You got peanut butter?" I asked Delia, who nervously shook her head yes and pointed to the cupboards. "You boys want some PBJs?" I asked over my shoulder as I went into the cupboard. They cheered and Delia cracked a tiny smile. "Go get me what's left of that bread, Chucky," I said pulling the peanut butter out and setting it on the counter. Laura pulled out plates and set them in front of the boys along with paper towel napkins and glasses of milk, which Delia told us would be all right. I opened the pail of peanut butter and looked inside to find—surprise—peanut butter. Delia looked cautiously into the pail as if she was afraid something would jump out and attach to her face. When she saw it was fine, she relaxed into a grateful smile. I picked up the apple jelly and she stopped me.

"There's glass in the jelly for sure," she said.

"Well, let me take a good look here and see if I can find any. All right?" Delia nodded her head and stood back a little as I opened the jar. The lid came off easily. I set it on the counter. Inside the jar, the jelly looked as pure and good as any of the miles of apple jelly I'd put past my tongue since childhood. I took a fork from the counter and dragged it through the jar several times just to be sure. No glass. "Jelly's safe today!" I shouted, and the boys cheered, pounding their fists on the counter and chanting "P-B-J, P-B-J." Delia smiled again. I made the boys sandwiches and even got her to eat one. The three of them sat at the counter eating and looking more and more like an everyday mom and two kids. Laura and I excused ourselves and went into the other room to talk. Delia and the boys didn't seem to care much what we did, they were so happy to be eating, and so grateful to us—the two strangers who came from nowhere and, with a touch, turned shards of glass into sweet goopy sandwiches.

9

I FOLLOWED LAURA back into the living room. When we were out of earshot, she swiveled instantly and spoke in a low serious voice. "I don't wanna take these kids, Marc. I like this woman. I don't want to take her children away. She's a good person, she's scared, and she's getting it back together."

"They hadn't eaten for two days."

"I know. That's bad."

"And that business at the door?"

"Right."

"She's unstable."

"I like her, Marc. She's fighting to protect her kids—we can't punish her for that. Can you imagine these things happening to you? Her ex sounds scary as hell, hex or no hex—you know what I mean? He's making her crazy just like any other old man, only he's calling what he's doing a hex." Laura pulled my arm to bring us farther from the family in the kitchen. "There's something in her that's strong. She's making it despite all of this. She's behaving like any mother would—she's protecting her kids from danger."

"She's protecting them from *eating*, Laura. I mean, what if there's something else, you know? What if she figures the air has turned evil so she has to protect them from *breathing*, for God's sake?"

"This is a good woman. She's not a bad person and she's getting better. I think we're helping her. She likes us—I don't wanna take her boys from her."

"That would be terrible, I know."

"You're right too, though—that case you had with Yvette last year?"

"Exactly."

"The woman throws her kids out the window so they don't burn in the Armageddon."

"That mother wasn't a bad person, either—a psycho, a lunatic, not evil—but who gives a shit when it gets to that. It doesn't matter after a certain point, you know? If the kids don't eat for two days when there's food right there in the fridge—right?—who cares what she's thinking?"

"All right, listen, here's what we do: We stay here awhile, I mean as long as we need to—really watch how things go. We give her every chance to be normal and we don't leave until she gets there; until she's completely confident that she's got whatever it takes to lick this thing—which I have to say would freak me right out, too, if it were happening in my apartment, and I saw that man looking at us, I don't care what you say. We're both agreed that she's better since we got here and that she's getting better by the minute, right?" I nodded. Laura went on. "So let's just tip her back upright and see if she stays that way. Maybe we can get her back together enough to leave the kids at least until the field office follows up in a few days." The field office would follow up with the family regardless of what we did—our decisions weren't as final as theirs. On the other hand, if the boys were in trouble, there was no telling when someone would actually get out to the home, and when they did, there was always the issue of the quality of the people assigned to the case. Those were things we had no control of, so we were usually wary about depending on them—especially in a situation like this, where we'd started to become personally invested in the well-being of the family.

"At any rate," I said, "we haven't been here long enough to decide—I mean, look at this place. It's been turned upside down—there's still a lot more to talk about."

Laura agreed. She left the room to call the office and give them the update. I went back to the kitchen where the Gammons were still eating. Delia smiled at me when I walked in.

"Laura's calling our office to let them know we're still

here," I said to her. "We'd like to stay for a bit and just make sure everything's all right."

"That would be wonderful," Delia said. "I really have to say I'm grateful to you for not just writing me off as some kind of a nut. That would've been the easy thing to do. I know how this all sounds."

I nodded. "So how would you feel about me hooking the lights back up? See if I can get them to work." She stopped eating midbite and stared at me with big eyes. "If anything weird happens, I'll just disconnect them and leave it alone." I said. She put her sandwich down to think about it.

"My brother put up the one in the hallway last week," she said. "It went bad as soon as he put it in."

"No kidding?" I asked.

"For real," she said.

I couldn't even go there. The light in the hall gave me the willies plain and simple, and Delia was a convincing nut if she was a nut at all. The slightest indulgence in that direction would send me in a fat panic right out the building and into the old canoe on a hightail back home and under my covers.

"Well there was glass in your jelly this morning, too," I said. I went the straight path—it was that or a ride straight out the door. Delia shrugged her shoulders. "I'll just give them a try," I said.

I went back to the living room and to an end table covered with all the lightbulbs for the apartment. They looked good. I gave each one a shake to see if their filaments were intact. None of them made the quiet jingle of a busted bulb so I held my breath and screwed them in. A minute later the apartment was filled with clean, bright light. Delia walked out of the kitchen in awe. We didn't speak at first, just looking from each other to every glowing light.

"This is how it starts," Delia said finally. "And then they go bad. They don't just go out, either. They start buzzing and then—*wham*—they flash out." We watched quietly for a moment. I was certain the lights would continue to glow, but I was also certain that if they went out I'd have to hold back on a major panic attack.

Laura had just gotten off the phone and joined Delia and me in the room. She looked with trepidation at the glowing lights. "How's it going here?" she asked us quietly.

"Good," I said, still looking at the lights. Waiting. "How's the office?"

"It's there," Laura said, looking slowly toward the lamp at her right.

"So far so good," Delia said softly. We waited another moment.

"Does it usually happen by this time?" I asked.

"I think maybe," she said, but they remained bright—as plain and good as the apple jelly in the fridge. Delia began to smile. "This would be so great if they stayed on. I can't believe it," she said.

"Well they look good to me," Laura said as she pulled the remaining cushions onto the couch and sat down. Delia slowly came over to join her. Still looking at the lights and beginning to fill with delight, she relaxed into the couch. I pulled cushions onto the other couch, pushed it back flush against the wall, and took a seat.

"This is incredible," Delia said, lifting her palms to the lights. "There hasn't been a light in here for seven days." She looked over to Laura. "Is the thing back yet?" Laura stood up and went to the window to check. After a quick look, she turned around with a smile.

"Why don't you come over here and take a look yourself," she said. Delia recoiled a little.

"Is it there?" she asked.

"Would I tell you to come to the window if he was? Get over here and take a look. He's gone. There's no one there." Delia stood up, walked slowly to the window, and peered out. The glass fogged with her breath as she leaned in. A smile that was becoming familiar returned to her face. She stepped back from the glass and flashed it at us.

"I can't say I'm surprised," she said with tears welling in her eyes. "That thing has been watching us for two weeks. Now it's gone and I really think this is because of the two of you. It ran away when you looked at it—you saw it happen. It doesn't want anybody to catch sight of it but me and my kids. I know it's a devil. It stopped watching us and look what's happening—everything's turning right now."

"Well, whoever he was, he seems to have found someplace better to be than up on that roof," I said. "It's too cold for anyone out there, I don't care what they are." Laura and Delia returned to the couch and the three of us talked for some time. Delia placed complete trust in us and went into detail about the days and nights since the hex was thrown. She told us how a hex needed to be *fed* to remain strong. She told us about the blood in the kitchen and about strange phone calls—some with her ex chanting on the other end and others with nothing more than the chilling sounds of an animal being tortured in her honor, for the hex and for her terror. She hadn't answered the phone in the past eight days, and—hex or no hex—can you blame her? She told us, without the slightest tinge of mania or delusion, about the wide paths she and the boys took around the windows even when the shades were closed—about the bulge she felt on her skin from the thing on the roof and the press of its glare, a feeling that stayed with her even when she slept. We heard about every quick bite of food before it turned rotten or sour or poisoned in some way or another. She spoke as plain and true as a roadside mechanic giving directions to the interstate.

Throughout all of it, Delia focused on protecting her boys. Regardless of what calamity set upon them, she would not be shaken from her role as chisel-tooth guard dog. We quizzed her repeatedly on her resolve and judgment regarding the safety of the boys, and she remained solid. About an hour later Laura and I had become quite convinced that the boys would be safe at home at least until the daytime office came for its follow-up visit in a day or two. And we felt like friends—something that never happens. Typical home visits last no more than a half hour or so—just enough time to say hello, lift a few shirts and lower a few shorts in a quick scan for bruises, check the cupboards for food, and leave. We'd already been with Delia over an hour and most of the time was spent simply talking. Once the kids have shown you their action figures and hand puppets, once you've cleaned the dishes and put them away, you're stuck. You can't remain at arm's length while your hands dry tears and caress shoulders. The more useful you become, the more fondness you feel. Feeling useful to someone is an affirmation. It makes you like them. The friendship comes as a package deal with hope for the friend to triumph through whatever winds are blowing against them. We liked Delia. We liked the boys. We liked the way they were with each other. We didn't want to mess with that.

The more we talked, the more normal Delia became. It looked as though we'd be able to go the long ride back to Manhattan without two sad faces in the backseat. We began to discuss the city's follow-up procedures and described to Delia what she should expect in the way of visits and contacts from the agency in the next few days and weeks. The boys had been running back and forth through our conversation, roughhousing and rabble-rousing like the two young pups they were. At some point toward the end of our discussion, Rick, the seven-year-old, interrupted us to ask me to make him and his brother another sandwich.

"Why don't you let their mom make them, Marc?" Laura suggested.

"Without a doubt." Delia popped up from the couch. "Their mom will make them one," she said on her way to the kitchen, and looked over her shoulder to me with a grin. "And Mom's PBJs taste better than *anybody's* PBJs—no offense." In a few moments, Rick was waltzing in front of us with a sand-wich in his hand and a smiling mouth full of apple jelly on his face. Laura and I gave each other a thumbs-up. Rick leaned in to the both of us with a giggle and gave a thumbs-up just to play along. Delia was just finishing Chucky's sandwich and it was feeling very much like we'd be leaving soon—now that everything was back to normal, now that everything was right as rain, now that everything was fine and dandy as maple candy.

Right.

10

FROM THE KITCHEN—I can't remember which came first or if they came at the same time—the smashing of glass and a shriek of horror. Delia came bolting around the corner with her eyes on fire. She swooped onto Rick, slapping the sandwich from his hand and squeezing his cheeks to expel the mouthful.

"SPIT IT OUT, RICKY—OOHHH GOD—THERE'S BLOOD IN IT! GET RID OF IT—GET IT OUT OF YOUR MOUTH, GET IT ALL OUT!" she screamed, shaking Ricky by the back of the neck. Chucky came out of the kitchen with eyes wide, startled by his mother's outburst. "*You* look at that damn jelly!" she shouted at Laura and me as she began to rake at Ricky's mouth. "You look at it and *you* tell me there's not something wrong with it." Laura pried Delia off of Ricky and got her to sit on the couch. She was hysterical.

"You go in there and you look at the BLOOD IN THAT JELLY!" she screamed. "Look close at it—look at the blood in it and then tell me it's good to eat. *Spit it all out, Ricky—* oh God help us—*and wash your mouth in the sink.* HURRY!"

Ricky sprinted to the bathroom as I headed for the kitchen on legs stiff with adrenaline. The glass and jelly were smashed low against the far wall and down into the corner of the room.

I saw it the second I stepped into the kitchen: a streak of red twirled through the yellow jelly heaving sluggishly down the wall. There it was, by God—a red spook in the jelly. It didn't strike me definitively as blood, but it was red and it was evil looking, spiraled like a small twister through the yellow blob. If I'd lived through her past two weeks, I can't say I wouldn't have thrown the same fit at the sight of it. And Delia was a real convincer. I didn't know what the hell was in the jelly, but if she would've been screaming about a buffalo, I might've seen that, too.

I leaned in for a good look. Delia was crying in the next room and still hysterical. The sound of her lungs straining against the tight knot of her vocal cords was mood music that would've made a newborn puppy a frightening sight. Chucky joined me to examine the jelly spirit—he didn't care. *Blood in the jelly? Cool—let's eat it!* A red smear in a little jelly is nothing to a five-year-old. It's nothing and no more than nothing—who cares if it sends your mom dancing barefoot on invisible embers? Chucky leaned in front of me for an extra close look at the jelly. After a brief inspection he turned back. "That looks *nasty,*" he said with a devilish grin and a wrinkle in his nose. *Cool—let's eat it.*

"YOU STAY AWAY FROM THAT, CHUCKY!" Delia shouted from the living room. "COME OUT OF THERE. YOU COME OUT OF THERE AND COME BY ME. I DON'T WANT YOU LOOKING AT THAT."

"Back up a bit, Chucky," I said, caught with the momentum of the jitters. Chucky moved behind me and I leaned in.

"So what is it, Marc?" Laura shouted from the living room.

"Hang on," I said. "I'm not exactly sure."

"*What do you mean, you're not sure?*" Laura yelled back.

"Just hang on a minute," I shouted. "Chucky, get me a knife from the drawer over there." His eyes lit up.

"You gonna touch it?" he asked.

"Yeah, I'm gonna touch it." Chucky was amazed. I was an

action hero now. He ran to the cupboards and retrieved a large knife, which he brought gingerly back to me. I took the knife by the handle and leaned tip first back to the jelly.

"You gonna stab it?" Chucky whispered behind me.

"I'm just gonna look at it, Chucky. See what it is."

"It's a devil. You should stab it."

"I don't think it's a devil, Chuck." I was right with him on that one, but somebody had to be the voice of reason.

"What are you gonna do with it?"

"Just lean back a little, Chuck." Slowly, I pushed the tip of the knife into the jelly. Then with the same slow movement, I dragged the sharp point up through the smear.

"*Oooo*, he stabbed it," Chucky squealed.

"*Marc—*" Laura called out.

"I didn't stab it," I shouted back.

"What are you doing with it?" Laura asked.

"I'm just looking at it."

"What is it?" she asked.

"It looks nasty, right?" Chucky whispered.

"Marc?" Laura called again.

"I don't know yet, Laura."

"What's the knife for, Marc?"

"I'm just looking at it," I said.

"What are you looking at a knife for?"

"No—I'm looking at the thing in the jelly here."

"You're looking at the thing in the jelly with a knife?"

"I'm just touching it, Laura."

"Well, what is it?"

"I don't know, it looks like a red smear," I said.

"I think it's a devil," Chuck said simply.

"Back up a little, Chuck," I said, dragging the tip of the knife through the redness again.

"I think you should put the knife away, Marc," Laura called out.

"*I don't want you in there, Chucky,*" Delia cried. Chucky and I didn't move, hanging like two dogs on an old dead frog while our owners tugged at the leashes.

"What do you think would cause that?" I asked Chuck, pulling the knife through the blob another time. "What would make a red smear like that?"

"Marc?" Laura called again.

"Okay, Laura."

"Put the knife away, Marc."

"Here, Chuck," I said, handing him the knife. "Throw it in the sink."

"Okay, Marc?" she asked.

"It's gone, Laura."

"So what's in the jelly?"

"Come here and take a look—I don't know what it is." Laura came around the corner with eyes wide and serious.

"Are you going to listen to your mother, Chuck?" Laura asked as she entered. "She's been telling you to come to her— so why are you still in here?" Chuck ran out of the kitchen without an argument. Laura looked at me for a moment and then mouthed a silent "*What??*" I pointed to the corner where the jar was smashed. Laura didn't move. "Where?" she asked quietly.

"Go look," I said. "Right over there—near the corner. You can't miss it." Laura inched her way to where I was pointing, leaning down as she approached the mess of glass and jelly—all sugary and razor-sharp; the devil himself cloaked in yellow apple sweetness. The soles of her shoes crackled and snapped against small shards of glass covering the tile floor. As she neared the corner, she began a slow crouch to get a better look. She moved with the caution of a wild animal, ready to jump and flee at the slightest provocation. Her shoulders were tight with fear, fear that clenches the stomach and squeezes at the back of the eyeballs. Suddenly a scream from Delia rocked through both of us. The shock crossed Laura like a revivalist struck by the hand of God. She rolled around to me in one jerk; her face drawn long and moon colored.

This scream was harder than the others—more urgent. Too shrill for a wail, but lower than shrieking. A scream with a bottom—and it wouldn't stop. Laura's moon face blurred; panic and hysteria are the authors of haze and slow motion. I *think* we rounded out of the kitchen in short order but we could've played a game of Twister first for all I know. Delia was on the couch convulsing with terror, shouting something about colors arcing across the floor and the appearance of a face. She was shouting at the face and pointing. She was screaming at Ricky to stay in the bathroom. She was clutching Chucky to her breast and pledging her protection. Somehow, she was doing it all at the same time. Laura and I, at either side, begged her to return to the planet. With a fair amount of effort she gathered focus, and shaking with tears, reached her index finger forward until her arm was fully extended and pointing to a pile of clothing about four feet high and directly in front of us against the adjacent wall.

"... *you see him?* ...," she asked in a controlled growl, never taking her eyes from the pile of clothes. Her arm trembled in front of her. We fell silent. "... right in front of us, the bastard...," she said slowly. "... you see his face? ..."

Just as I was about to conclude Delia was totally losing it, I saw it. Right in front of us and very clear—a face. Now before you conclude that I was losing it, too, take a good look at a pile of clothes yourself, or crumple up a piece of paper and examine it with an open mind: look at the clouds, the cream swirling in your coffee, tree bark, a pile of leaves, oh gosh— the *moon* perhaps. A multitude of faces lie in our midst. They're everywhere, whether we acknowledge them or not. The evil grimace in a heap of towels may tempt us to pull it out of shape, but when we do, we give birth to six smaller ones and the more we look away, the more hideous they become. The faces play best in peripheral vision—as we look away, they multiply. The more we avoid them, the more we see. So who's losing it now? The difference between us and the crazies is perspective—the part of us that goes, "Yeah, there's a face in every rock and shadow, but hey, the kids gotta be picked up from school and the car's due for a lube job—I know the universe holds untold fathoms of mystery, but in the meantime, the litter needs changing and I could sure go for a coffee about now."

Delia had stopped drinking coffee and changing the litter two weeks ago. During her stroll through a few of the fathoms, she'd neglected to feed her boys and had stopped using the lights, among other things. Hex or no hex, Delia had taken a trip, so to speak, and left the boys without a sitter. That's why we were there.

"All right, I see it," I said instantly.

"*Where—*," Laura said, reaching over Delia and grabbing my arm.

"No, no, no, no—it's nothing, it's—"

"*That's nothing??*" Delia interrupted.

"Where, Marc?" Laura pleaded.

"Right there? Okay—wait," I said, holding Delia with one hand and pointing with the other. "Relax, Delia, it's nothing, I swear to you. Right there, Laura, right there—it's nothing. Look...see? It's just the way the clothes are sitting. See?... Right down there."

"Right down where?"

"All right—there's the mouth," I said, pointing. "And the eyes...the nose goes like that—see? The chin sorta hangs down pretty low—"

"I got it," Laura said.

"You see it?"

"I see it," she said. "It looks weird, Delia, I can see it—I see what you're seeing." We were still trying to convince ourselves that she was within the outskirts of normal. "You see it,

Chucky?" Laura asked. He was at the far end of the couch. Rick peeked around the corner from the bathroom. "Right there—see?...It kinda looks like a face in there from this angle, it's okay though. C'mon out, Rick."

"Take a look, Rick," I said. "C'mere, look...see it?" Rick nodded his head. Both the boys seemed more shaken by Delia's outburst than by anything in the clothes. There's nothing that makes a kid crazy like the sound of his mother on the break.

"There were colors first," Delia said slowly. "Then the face, but first colors—all over the floor. They started in the crack over there," she said, indicating the far corner to our right. "And they shot over to me and then to the clothes. Red and some blue, but mostly red...more red than the blue. First them, then the face—"

"I can find a face in practically anything, Delia. I got a pile of clothes at home with a whole family and a couple zoo animals in it," I said. Delia listened respectfully but was not convinced. "And that red spot in the jelly there? I think that's probably just a little raspberry mixed in, you know?—when you make a sandwich with raspberry jam, or maybe strawberry, and then switch to the apple without rinsing the knife off? So a little raspberry gets with the apple—I must not have seen it in there when I made the first sandwiches. That's gotta be it, though. It's not blood anyways, 'cause a jar of jelly doesn't bleed, I don't care how hard you hit it—right, Rick?" Rick nodded his head for my benefit.

"The hex uses what's there," Delia said calmly. "It uses what's in the home to show itself. That's how it works, that's how the evil comes. You don't have to come all the way out here and into my house to tell me what a jar of jelly don't do— no offense. You don't have to tell me if a pile of clothes is all right or not. I know what I'm seeing and I'm not stupid. If you think y—"

She broke off suddenly with a look of shock on her face as the pile of clothing slumped toward us and then toppled over like something inside had pushed it. Delia fell back into the couch in tears, swinging her head from side to side and pedaling her legs as the heap rolled out around our feet. Rick darted his head back, disappearing around the corner. Chucky moved away from his mother, lines of distress crisscrossing his face. It would've been easier on him to watch the clothes jump up and samba than to have to witness his mother slowly disintegrating. He barely even noticed the clothes as he watched his mother wipe her face with awkward quickness and lean forward, shouting at the pile on the floor.

"*I'm not even scared of you anymore,*" she snapped. "*—And that's why I'm gonna beat you. I'm gonna fight you and I'm gonna drive you out, you bastard—filthy thing.*" She looked at Laura and me. "You've both seen it. You've seen *him*. I know you feel the same thing, too—you feel the evil in here. What made those clothes jump up then? What was it—something else that's *just normal* to you?—We got so many things around here that are 'just normal'—Everything's so *just normal* that it's *not* just normal. You feel the hex on this home. We are all feeling it. The bastard's here and you can feel him just like me—don't tell me you can't."

Fine then.

Hexes are real. Delia was under a hex. The hex was strong. The home was cursed. The clothes move. The food is evil. Blood appears in strange places. The face is everywhere. It's all true. So what does the hex make *you* do, Delia? We switched our focus to this in a final attempt to leave without removing the children. It didn't matter if all the toys in the apartment suddenly started playing football, and who cares if Cool Whip sprays out of the shower and the toilet starts laughing. We wanted to make sure Delia wouldn't suddenly lose control of her arms and start swinging kitchen knives at the boys. It didn't matter to us if the fruit bowl gave birth to a litter of kittens. What we cared about was whether or not Delia would wake up the next morning thinking the boys had turned into giant bugs that needed squashing—or maybe that they needed to chug a bottle of Drano to kill the little men from outer space living in their stomachs.

We calmed Delia down again—no problem with that; we were getting good at it. I lifted the clothes and put them back as they were while Laura poured a steady flow of reassurances in her ear. Delia relaxed again after a while and we quizzed her again at length on her resolve to protect her children and to keep them from physical harm. When we heard all the promises we could stand, we once more entertained the idea of leaving. Laura took Delia's hand in hers.

"We're going to leave soon, Delia," she said. "But we can't go until we feel that your boys are safe here. Okay? That's why we came out. I know you love them more than anyone and you want the same thing. You want them to be safe as much as we do."

"You're gonna take my boys," she said, breaking into quiet tears.

"No, no, Delia. We don't have to take them. We don't want to take them. Delia. We don't have to take them if they're safe with you, see?—if you can really take care of them even with all you're going through."

"I know, I know..."

"I mean—the three of you hadn't eaten in two days—"

"We had bread. The bread was fine—"

"Still though. I mean—"

"You're right, you're right."

"How can we leave—"

"I'm gonna feed them. Whatever it takes. I know I have to feed them."

"I'm being straight with you—"

"And I'm being straight with you."

"I know you are. I know."

"I'd do anything for those boys—"

"Listen, the truth of it is—I believe in you, Delia. I really do. I think you're strong. I can't believe what you've been going through. It's weird. It's disturbing. It's scary. It's all that. I don't have an explanation for any of it. I'm not even gonna try to tackle that. But I will say one thing: I think you're being manipulated by your ex-husband. I think he knows how to make you crazy and he's doing the best he can. He calls it a hex, but it doesn't matter what it's called—he's controlling you; he's trying to use your fear against you. Whatever he's doing doesn't matter. You can't let anything that happens between you and him get between you and your kids. That's the bottom line."

"You're right, I know."

"We're gonna leave, but there's going to be people coming back to check up on you. If you're not taking care of your boys, they'll take them. They don't care what's going on with you or what troubles you're having. If there's anything wrong with the boys—they're gone."

"I've never hurt my children. I've taken care of them all these years..."

"Well you've obviously done a lot of things right—they're such good guys. But listen, you're going through something huge here. You're in a bad space and you're scared as hell, right? You are. I can't blame you. But you gotta put Rick and Chucky first. No matter what happens, you gotta make sure they're okay. You can make it, Delia. You have to, right?"

"I have to, I know. I will."

"What can you tell us so that we know your boys will be safe with you?" I asked. "If you could say one thing to us as we walk out that door, what would it be?"

Delia thought for a moment with her head down, and then looked to my eyes with calm focus.

"I'm their mother," she said.

11

WE SPENT ABOUT ANOTHER twenty minutes with her before gathering up our things to finally go. I didn't know what Laura was thinking at the moment regarding removal or not. I didn't even really know what I was thinking. We would need to have a discussion in chilly #603 parked outside to come up with a decision. If I had to make a call, though, I'd have to say at that moment, we were both feeling like the kids would be safe at least until the daytime office's follow-up, which would be the next morning if we really put a red flag on it. We might be able to get away with leaving because of the assurance of a swift morning visit, though the follow-up workers always hated it because it read like "the children will remain in the home where they are presently safe, however because this situation may deteriorate rapidly, an immediate follow-up by the field office is necessary." The folks would go out the next day grumbling about if the kids needed removing in the morning, they needed it the night before, too.

We said good-bye to the guys and began to walk to the door when the phone rang. Delia went off like a concussion. "DON'T ANSWER IT—COVER YOUR EARS! LEAVE IT GO, RICKY, DON'T TOUCH IT! CHUCKY—YOU LOOK AWAY FROM IT! DON'T ANYONE GO NEAR IT!" She covered her ears. Her body flexed with each ring. When the ringing stopped, she uncovered her ears and said sheepishly, "It's been a problem with the phone. Like I was telling you when you first got here?—*anyways*..." She jerked her head around for a quick look out the window. "Still no devil," she said with a tight smile and her fingers crossed. "*Anyways*... well, I can't thank you enough for coming out. I'm actually really sorry to see you go—"

The phone rang again. Delia tried for a moment to control

herself but quickly gave in to a shriek as she covered her ears again and squinted her eyes shut. The boys, standing behind their mother, covered their ears and looked at us plainly as Delia ran in place with her head down and her hands on her head. When it stopped, she uncovered her ears and looked back at us. "*Anyways . . . ,*" she said with her eyebrows crawling over the top of her forehead. "Thank you again for everything. I just wish you weren't leaving."

"Someone will be out again soon," Laura said as I opened the door. Cherry glow of Kool-Aid worm rolled at our shoulders. "You just have to make it through tonight."

"It's gonna feel like a long time until tomorrow—especially if that phone keeps ringing. I'd rip it off the wall but I'm afraid it would ring just the same. I just couldn't take that . . . *anyways . . .*" Delia's tears were coming back.

"Just until tomorrow," Laura said, pulling a piece of paper from her bag and scribbling on it. "Here's my number at the office. You can call as soon as you need to—or I'll call you when I get back to see if you're okay—"

"*Don't call me—*"

"Right, right, right—sorry. You call me though. If you need to. We'll be back in the city in about an hour if the traffic's okay. You'll call me?" Delia shook her head yes and tossed us a nervous smile.

"Are you okay, Delia?" I asked. She looked at me, distracted, and then glanced quickly over her shoulder to the window where the man had previously been. "Delia?—"

"What?"

"What's wrong?"

"I'll make it."

"Call me," Laura said—the consolation prize. "Call me in one hour, all right?"

Suddenly Delia bonked herself on the forehead. "Oh my gosh, I almost forgot! I never told you why the place was turned upside down like it is—you know, why we had to pull all the drawers out and turn the sofa cushions on the floor— stay put one second." She left us and ran to her bedroom. We stood half in and half out of the apartment exchanging poker faces and not even close to imagining what Delia was about to bring to us. It was true, we had neglected to ask why everything was pulled away from the walls and either taken apart or turned over. We'd been slowly putting things back to normal without asking why.

Delia came back with her hands clutched to her chest and a smile on her face. "I can't believe I was going to let you leave without telling you about these," she said, opening each hand to reveal about twenty sharp objects: several nail files, a small screwdriver, some paper clips that had been straightened out, a couple long splinters of wood, a ballpoint pen refill, some pins, a pencil, a few needles, a broken hair clip, a couple nails, scissors.

"These are all we could find, but we're still looking," she said. "He sticks these in my vagina. He comes here, and anything he can find—he pushes it in. God it's painful, I mean look," she said, raising her open palms to us, "—*can you imagine?* I know you can't—as a man. But *you,*" she said to Laura. "I mean *look* at some of this stuff. Can you imagine someone sticking your vagina with some of these? Don't worry I've washed everything off so...He just comes from nowhere and...well. We've been getting rid of anything he might be able to use. I ripped these off the frame of the couch," she said, indicating the splinters of wood. "I mean—if he can't find anything to push in me, he'll just have to stop. Right? So," she said with a smile as she laid the items neatly on a chair beside her, "that's the story. That's why everything's turned over."

The items, lit with pulsing orange light, looked like props taken straight out of an old voodoo movie—crude objects of torture and conjure to summon everything from a crick in the neck to Beelzebub himself. Urchin spirits that rattle backbones and push the continents. Face paint and poltergeist, animal hide and hobgoblin, puka shells and werefolk, skullcaps, carved masks—all of it drenched in a hellkite rhythm under the savage stars. And scissors. I mean, *scissors,* good Christ. Maybe I can't imagine—as a man and all—but I can get close enough, you know?

"You had the boys help you find this stuff?" I asked.

"Oh my gosh—they don't want to see him hurt me any more than I do. Absolutely they help me. I never would've found the nails without Rick's sharp eyes—some of them were all the way back in the cupboards."

Laura and I stammered in an awkward pause.

"*Anyways . . . ,*" Delia continued, "I appreciate you coming out. Thanks again for listening to all this—I know how it sounds." She darted her head over her shoulder toward the window and turned back to us, raising crossed fingers. "Nothing yet. I wonder if it can tell you're leaving. Hope not. *Anyways . . .*"

"Good-bye, Delia," Laura said; more a test than a bidding. Delia pulled the door until it was almost shut and waved goodbye, watching us from the crack as we turned to walk away. We moved down the hall at a bridled pace, trying not to awaken the part of the mind that's as dumb as a chicken and prone to hysterical flight at the least provocation. We were almost to the elevator when Delia split her throat open one last time. The sound bounced and echoed down the empty hallway.

"Jesus—," Laura choked to herself as we chased back toward the worm with the clamor rising. We sprinted around the corner and down the hall to where Delia was hopping in the doorway. She looked at us through a flood of panic and pointed frantically at the wall in front of her. Directly beneath the bad light, a red stain curled rudely across the wall. Spread out over the length of several bricks, it was hard to miss, yet I didn't remember seeing it when we first arrived. It looked like paint, ink maybe—hard to tell in the bumping dimness. Delia went on and on about red spots and smears and blood—she reminded us about the red swirl she'd seen just before the blood volcano in the kitchen. Crying and shaking, she continued without stopping about the lights and the devil and the food and the faces and now *this* red stain and why was it there, and why was it red, and where would the next one appear, and what would it mean, and what should she do, and where could she go, and how should she stop it, and what would *we* do, and on and on.

It was just one more thing—either so normal it's just plain stupid, or utterly evil and proof positive of an entire realm lying just beyond our humble senses: milk and cookies or Armageddon; a splinter in the pinkie or all hell breaking loose. One or the other and nothing in between. Poor Delia worsened with every step we took away from her. I think if we could've moved in she'd have been just fine, but since that wasn't going to happen, we had to get the kids the hell out of there—clear the room of breakables so Mom could rumble with Lucifer, 'cause it didn't matter if he came out of the darkest realms of hell or from the depths of Delia and Delia alone. It didn't matter where the evil came from or what the evil was. It only mattered that it *would* come, and that Delia was in for the fight of her life.

12

THE COPS CAME QUICKLY. It was too cold outside for criminal activity. They arrived within two minutes after the call to 911—two lady cops, all bulked out in bulletproof vests and belts carrying every less-than-lethal defense known to man. I was always a little leery of lady cops, but not for chauvinistic reasons—quite the opposite. Some of the roughest, hardest-nosed, ass-kicking cops I ever worked with were women. The typical hulk of male cop brandishes his intimidation in his appearance, but beware of the lady cop whose only hope of controlling her adversaries is to beat them to the punch. A lady cop is quick on the mean and heavy on the holler; not all of them, of course, but enough to draw you to the conclusion.

After introducing ourselves, the four of us hustled into the building to get out of the cold. I warned the officers the lobby wasn't much warmer than the outside, but it didn't seem to make an impression on their stride. We got inside quickly. The lobby was still empty. One of the officers commented on it; we all agreed it was strange. We exchanged shield numbers and worker numbers, each scratching on pads of paper, getting the numbers down to please the paperwork.

"This should be a straight removal," Laura said to the cops after hitting the call for the elevator. "We shouldn't be in the apartment long. We've already spent practically the whole afternoon in there."

"The lady beat on the kids?" one of the cops asked.

"She hasn't beaten the children," Laura answered.

"Who's beating on the kids?"

"Nobody's beating on them. They haven't been beaten on."

"You two check for marks and bruises? 'Cause we gotta arrest the mother if they got marks and bruises on them," the cop went on.

"It's not that kind of a case," Laura said kindly. "It's not a—"

"Hey—," the cop interrupted. "But you can never be too sure though, right? 'Cause we gotta arrest the mother if those kids are beat up."

"I don't think you'll have to arrest anyone," I said. "We just need—"

"Well that's something we'll have to decide," the cop said, sharply courteous. "I'm sure you understand that, don't you?"

"All I'm saying is this lady hasn't done anything wrong, so there shouldn't be a need to—"

"If the lady hasn't done anything wrong—then why are we taking her kids? You see how that doesn't make any sense, right?"

The elevator door rolled slowly open and we stepped inside. By the time we reached the sixteenth floor, Laura was able to give the cops a full account of our visit with Delia, as well as talk them out of strip-searching the boys for bruises. Laura told them about the hex and we waited like bad comedians for a reaction, but we never got one. It made me feel like a big baby. They didn't flinch at the mention of the hex—I mean not even the slightest jiggle in the face. Cops have seen it all, I guess. It's what you always hear, but that's because it's true. I felt like making up a few details just to see if I could get a rise out of them *(Hey by the way—the mother has a complete wardrobe made of pancakes),* but I didn't.

When we reached apartment 1606, Delia swung the door open almost before we could knock. The first thing I noticed as we walked inside was the window that looked out to the roof where the man had been watching. The shades were drawn tight. He was back, at least for Delia. Several lightbulbs, removed from their sockets, sat neatly on the counter in the kitchen. It was sad and chilling at the same time. Delia walked immediately over to the couch where she sat quietly and stared at us. We were back, too, but the shades wouldn't keep us out. The cops stood at the far wall and were quiet except for an occasional squeak from their radios.

It felt like a cheap shot—bringing cops into Delia's living room after spending the whole afternoon with her. The cops were a cold reminder of the true nature of our relationship. Like the farmer who has a hard time at the slaughter of an animal he's become fond of, Laura and I had made the mistake of giving names to our cattle. Now that it was time for market, we were paying for the affection.

Laura sat on the couch next to Delia, who stared at her wide-eyed and totally without expression. She knew why we were back. The bulky cops in the corner left little room for hope against what we were there to do. "Only until you can get things back together," Laura said after a moment. Delia didn't speak and she didn't move. Laura took her hand. "Until things return to normal...I am so sorry, Delia. I didn't think we were going to have to do this." Delia's face remained barren of any emotion—she watched us without comment and without missing a lick. The boys came out of their room and stood in front of us. They, too, knew why we were back. They knew we were back for them.

"You boys have some good coats to go outside? It's cold as heck out there," I said. They glanced at their mother. She stared blankly back. They turned and went to their rooms, coming out shortly with their coats on. I helped Chucky with his gloves. He had put them on himself but they were backward. He looked at my face, more bewildered than sad or frightened, as I wrestled them onto his tiny hands. Rick was all set to go and standing quietly at the wall with the cops. Laura remained with Delia on the couch. She whispered to her quietly as Delia watched the boys get ready to leave. I couldn't hear what Laura was saying, but it didn't matter—I knew she was offering whatever comfort she could scrape together. I led the now bundled Chucky to his brother where he stood watching as I returned to Laura and Delia. Laura had just handed her the 701-b removal form. Delia looked several times between Laura and me and back to the boys standing patiently with the cops. She didn't say a word.

"I'm so sorry, Delia," I said, crouching down in front of her. "I can't tell you how bad I feel about this. I think it's the only thing to do though, I mean, with what's been going on. It's not safe for them here while you're battling this thing... whatever it is."

"These are your boys, Delia," Laura said. "Nothing can ever change that. They are your boys and they belong with you. They're going to be safe with us while you beat this thing...-

You are going to beat this thing, Delia... I believe in you. When things get right again, the boys will come home to their mother. You can count on it. You're going to make it, Delia. You can do it."

Delia shook her head yes. Her face remained expressionless but she nodded on Laura's last words—an earnest, determined nod.

We got up to leave and Delia walked us to the door. She didn't kiss the boys good-bye. They were down the hall with the cops in tow as we were stepping out the door.

"Good-bye, Delia," I said.

"Good luck, Delia," Laura said. "Take care of yourself. Those boys need their mother."

Delia nodded one more time as she looked out at us from the crack in the door. I looked back several times to see her watching us until we rounded the corner and were out of sight.

Back in the freezing silence of the lobby, the cops said they would be staying to wait for the ambulance they called. They were going to see to it that Delia was psychiatrically cleared before leaving her to battle her demons alone. It was a relief to know that Delia had touched their hearts in the short time they had been with her, and that now they were going to make their best effort to ensure her safety. We would take the boys to emergency foster care and the cops would escort Delia in an ambulance to the emergency room—no ordinary Sunday afternoon for the Gammons. Call it a hex or call it whatever you will; *something*, by God, shot a bolt of fire through the very center of that family—something like I've never seen before and don't hope to see again.

The boys got into the back of #603 neither frightened nor sad. Nothing that we could show them would upstage the drama of the past two weeks. We stopped for a Wendy's just before leaving Staten Island. The boys had burgers and Cokes. They split a medium Frosty for the car ride back to the office.

Laura got her fries and had the cashier pour some hot coffee into a large cup of ice with milk. I had my favorite, a double with cheese. We hopped into the canoe when we finished eating and paddled over the icy Verrazano Narrows Bridge. Ricky caught the first glimpse of Manhattan in the distance and his jaw went slack. He hit Chucky on the shoulder and told him to look. Strapped into the enormous backseat of #603, Chucky stretched his little neck as long as it would go.

"We're goin' *there?*" he asked, his eyes shining. Laura told them that's where we were headed.

"Wait," Ricky said, putting the spoon back into the Frosty. "Is that Manhattan?"

"Sure is," Laura said. The boys grabbed each other and squealed with delight.

"All right!!!!"—Ricky cheered over Chucky's laughter—"*We never been to the city!!!!*"

Laura and I exchanged a sigh of relief, the boys' laughter soothing across our brows. I filled with emotion at the thought of Delia alone in the dark with her demons and wished there was something more I could offer her than to remove her children. Our actions seemed to play perfectly into the hands of Delia's ex. Even as I relished the opportunity to cut a path to safety for the boys, I despised playing the role of a pawn in an old lover's dark design.

That night, back in my apartment waiting for sleep to come, the piranha man looked cow-eyed. His face was as contorted and terror filled as it ever was, but his eyes were wide and calm. Light from the street filtered through thin pieces of fabric hung in the windows as makeshift shades. The shadowy dappling of light on the piranha man plunged the scene underwater, leaving him to a fate worse than before: still being devoured by toothy jaws, but no longer afloat. The man seemed more doomed than ever—unable to breathe, and in watery silence, unable to call for help. The contradiction of his wide calm eyes in the midst of such doom shone through; the scene's only hope.

Wind blows against the shades and the water ripples. The man lets out a watery scream as his flesh is consumed. It's freezing outside but the air cools the room perfectly. The heater is stuck on so a crack in the window is just right. The fish continue eating, blindly vicious; tearing at the legs of the man and taking large neat chunks from his abdomen. A string of identical gouges festoons the man's arms, each one leaving a perfect outline of teeth like the bites out of a cartoon hamburger. The fish might be winning over the man on this night. The water ripples again, the breeze is cool and fresh on my cheeks. My eyes are calm like the man's. Flecks of light fade and appear around my blanket and I dare not touch my shoulders as I fall asleep for the gouges I might find there.

6

Nobody Nothing

QUARTER AFTER THREE; forty-five minutes before the *thunk-whump* on the four-to-midnight shift. I had plenty of time to catch the subway from the 110th Street station and ride it down to where I got off. After dropping the token and passing through the turnstile, I headed left and descended a dirty set of stairs to track level on the downtown side. The platform was nearly deserted—not so unusual as it was still winter with the temperature stuck well below zero. I scanned one of the thick wooden benches for gum or spilled soda or worse before sitting down to wait for the train. It could be long sometimes. Twice a day, five days a week, the wait had become a time to relax into the gray emptiness of the station, aware only of the distant rumble of the tracks that signals the coming ride. You see it with most everyone as they wait for the train. They look like dead people with their eyes open until the distant groan of metal wheels shoots them to life and to the edge of the platform.

With my shoulders humped up around my neck for warmth, I sat still so as not to invite the cold air in through the spaces of my leather jacket. I closed my eyes—an old trick from the ski lifts in chilly Wisconsin; you feel warmer when you close your eyes, for some reason. I was just about to float out of myself on my daily meditation when the sound of a voice invited me to stay. Across the tracks on the uptown-side platform, a young man bundled in a thick jacket with a stocking hat pulled low on his face sang a melody that had the unmistakable sound of an opera. A paper cup for spare change sat on the cement at his feet. The man's voice was smooth and surprisingly refined. His high notes were uncluttered and pure—deeply rich but without a trace of flash or bravado. The sound echoed majestically through the cold emptiness of the station. Then another sound—the click and swish of a station janitor sweeping up small bits of trash into his dust catch. He made his way slowly from one wrapper to the next with the peaceful ease of the singer's voice. The two of them performed for me—*The Janitor's Broom,* I imagined for a moment, an opera about the tranquillity of satisfaction. In the city, you take tranquillity where you find it, and so I did; closing my eyes after watching the janitor for a moment, to focus on the music.

The opera wasn't English—Italian, maybe. I had a friend who went to Juilliard for opera and he often invited me and the rest of the riffraff from 108th to the shows and recitals there. He was big on Italian opera so that's what I was most familiar with. I was almost certain *The Janitor's Broom* was being sung in Italian. With my eyes closed, I could feel the janitor's grace without even watching him—drawing on the click and swish alone to make his image. An occasional jingle from the keys against his thigh completed the picture. I watched him on the backs of my eyelids. The soft echo of his implements was as right and good in the station as the crackling sound of a rain shower in the forest. The singer's voice filled my head with anonymous sounds that I could assign any meaning to and so I did. They told a story of a working man who devotes his entire life to cleaning the filth from the enormous labyrinth of underground tracks, battling water-main breaks and electrical fires while people on the platforms above him scurry about on luxuries of love and jealousy. Just before the worker dies, he cashes in a sore back and a handful of calluses for the tranquillity of a satisfied mind—his reward for a life of hard work. When he dies, he is tired, but because his work was good and true, he is satisfied. I sat with my eyes closed for warmth and a smile pressed across my cheeks.

The janitor got close to me as he swept and suddenly knocked a wine bottle from where it sat on a ledge to my right. It fell to the cement in a violent crash of glass. My eyes flashed open. The singer stopped. A cop appeared from around the corner with his head low and his eyes suspicious. A cold wind blew in from the tunnel followed by the roar of an arriving train. It thundered in on the local track and set off its brakes with a deafening scream. I stood up in a kind of shock and walked to the doors of the train. They opened and I stepped inside, sitting on the nearest seat.

The whole sequence struck me, and I thought about it for most of the ride down; how quickly, with a simple twist of the dial, the deepest calm can turn to chaos—how stealthy the chaos is and what a convincing costume of serenity it wears. My frequent exposure to chaos on the job was having a cumulative affect on me. It was reaching a point where I was constantly on the lookout for it no matter where I was—preparing myself for its inevitable appearance.

I never knew what I was headed for at the start of a workday, so I wouldn't find out until later how perfectly the lesson I'd just taken in would be illustrated in a girl named Melissa who I'd be meeting in a few short hours—a little girl whose innocent look was a thin cloak for a horrible secret; whose sweet voice smashes a wine bottle against your ear just as you lean in to adore it. Hidden for the time being, the secret waits patiently to be discovered in a shudder. They wait—all atrocities do. They wait to be revealed. This one waits in Melissa for its time to blossom. It waits for the coming spring of discovery like the furious swollen bud of a new rose.

2

I HOPPED INTO THE OFFICE with my shoulders still at my ears, and bing-banged the time clock. Before getting off my coat, I'd put in an order for two coffees with Laura, who was on her way out the door with a few other orders. I got to the back of the office and sat at my desk after high-fiving Jesse and the boys.

"Yo, yo, yo, Money-Money," Jesse yipped as I passed him.

"Yo, yo, yo, yo, yo," I returned, tongue lolling back and forth in my mouth with the artless vigor of a drunken sailor in a foreign port.

Willie was hunched into his cubicle on the phone. He was speaking low and serious. Without looking at me, he held his fist out for a bump. I gave it a hit as I took off my jacket and threw it on the back of my chair.

"You put in your order with Laura?" Jesse asked me. "She's goin' to the Square, she just stepped out."

"Got her at the last second, thanks."

"If you ordered those nasty mashed potatoes again I'm calling your parents," Dana shouted over from her desk.

"What's wrong with the mashed potatoes at the Square?" Jesse asked, ready to defend them like his own mother's cooking.

"You mean besides the fact that they come in a coffee cup?" Dana replied.

"What'dja get, Jesse?" I asked.

"Masta Cheese on a double boiga wid friggidy-fries," he said, rubbing his chin and smacking his lips. *"An appetizer."* He let out his high giggle and high-fived the guys to his right and left. Jesse would high-five anything. His tiny quick giggle was like a child stuck in the mouth of a monster. They all began a rap—*boigeddy-boigeddy-boiga and friggidy-friggidy-fries*—pounding on the desks and against their jeans.

Fernando Perez looked up from the gun magazine he was reading, flashing me a quick smile and rolling his eyes at the ruckus Jesse and the boys were kicking up. The front of the magazine blazed with big orange letters: ".357 Magnum Shoot-out—*America's Favorite Man-Stoppers."* Fernando wasn't alone in his gun-mag interest, more than a few of us had one or two tucked into our drawers. I don't think anyone carried a gun into the field for protection—if anyone did, they didn't talk about it. Many of us carried knives, though.

A bit of a knife craze swept through the office around my third year there. Switchblades mostly. I carried one myself. We didn't carry them for people—you gotta be a Navy Seal to use a knife on an aggressor without cutting your own body into ribbons. The knives we carried were for dogs. The only time I ever saw police unholster their guns was when there was a dog barking on the other side of a door. Word was that the pit bulls owned by so many of the dealers in the buildings we visited were trained to do all sorts of clever things. The trick that really gave me the spooks was that most of them were trained to go straight for the crotch—when you'd knock on the door, the owner would simply open up, let the dog do its job, and ask questions later. The whole thing that sets a pit bull apart from other dogs—what makes them so terrifying—is their unlimited threshold for pain. They either don't feel pain, or they don't pay attention to pain, but any way you cut it up, the idea that you can *hurt* one of these dogs to get them off you is a myth. They gotta be killed to be stopped if they're after you. I didn't like the idea of carrying a knife with me— not because of the knife itself so much, but more because of what was causing the need for the knife. You look at your life and you ask yourself why you need to carry a knife and then you try to eliminate that thing. I went to places where it was needed; that's what bothered me.

The thing that really decided it for me and many others in the office was a story in the paper about a pit bull that clamped its jaws on a guy's wrist in a hallway on the sixth floor of a housing project we'd all been to a number of times. The dog bit first onto the leg of the guy's buddy. When the guy pulled on the back legs of the dog to get it off, it came off all right— it came off and clamped right into the guy's wrist. The two struggle to get the dog off—they gouge at its eyes, they kick its stomach, they kick its genitals. When they tire of that, they drag the dog, who is still attached to the guy's wrist, down *six flights of stairs* and out to the street where they flag down a cop. The cop gets out of his car and all three men start kicking the animal. The pit remains wholly unimpressed and so the cop starts bashing it on the head with his nightstick. After a few of those, the cop uses the end of the stick to jam the ribs of the animal but it looks like the guy is stuck with a permanent fashion accessory. The cop unholsters his gun and tells people to stand back. The guy extends his arm and the cop lets fly with a bullet. It has no effect. The cop shoots the dog again. The dog's jaws loosen but it's still hanging on. He shoots a third bullet into the dog and it falls from the guy's wrist. It lies on the ground for a second before *jumping up to come at the guy a final time.* The cop puts a *fourth bullet* into the animal and it goes down dead just as they were thinking about praying to it rather than killing it.

So.

The story circulated through the office and made an impression. It happened in a building we all go to. I said that already, I know. It bears repeating. Many of us got knives after that—switchblades mostly, 'cause you're not gonna open a Swiss Army with one hand pressed against a set of dog tonsils. I figured if it happened to me, I'd just whittle the dog's head off at the neck and bash it against the bricks until it falls apart. I could do that in the time it'd take me to drag the fucker down six flights of stairs anyways. Willie Samuels's dance with the pit a few years back wasn't enough to convince me, but the story of a dog who ate four bullets before going down was.

Laura came back with the orders and gave me mine—two large coffees, regular, no sugar. Jesse got his boigeddy-boiga with friggidy-fries. She threw Willie a can of mackerel in oil and an orange soda and returned to her desk with a gigantic iced coffee. Jesse started in on the burger immediately. He ate with his eyes closed—listening to the scratch of his headphones. Willie was still on the phone talking quietly as he cracked open his can of fish and got to it with a plastic spoon. It had to be some serious business with the way he was cupped into his desk. Willie was usually the ringleader of the circus at the start of the shift. Jesse took note and three bites into his burger, gave Will a tap, and put his hands out in a what's-up? gesture. Willie put his arm out in a wait-a-minute.

"...all right, all right, my brother," Willie said, as he finished the phone call. "Have a happy, stay tight, my man...all right—you, too. Peace." He hung up the phone and pressed his fingers into his eyes. He gave them a good rub and leaned back in his seat, looking around at all of us who'd become curious. "Sal resigned," he announced. "He's up for sexual abuse charges on his girlfriend's little daughter."

Sal was one of the gang in the back of the office, one of the boys. He'd been out on sick time for the past week, but we all figured he wasn't really sick. Since he'd been with the agency for years, we all assumed he was just bleeding off some extra sick days. If someone was out for more than a week, one of us would call to see if they were all right. That's what Willie was doing when he called and found out the real reason for Sal's absence.

Sal was the first person to take me to the field and show me the ropes. My second night at ECS, Sal took his three cases and me in a car and we headed out to the streets. We drove around the Bronx for the night and talked about everything from crack head to Cuban deli. After two more nights with him, I was given my own cases to handle. Three years later and the cop becomes criminal. Alleged, anyway—cases of sexual abuse are so tricky. They were some of the toughest cases I handled, for obvious and not-so-obvious reasons.

We were constantly assured that the cases that came into ECS were assigned randomly to prevent overworking those in the office who were known to do exceptional work. The bosses had also begun to avoid the practice of sending good workers out with bad ones. It made sense for running a fair office but was a real heartbreaker when Tweedle-Dee and Tweedle-Dum were sent out on a case requiring any amount of judgment, especially sex-abuse cases. It doesn't take long to imagine a worst-case scenario with two bozos from the office and a couple of male cops around a cowering eight-year-old girl asking questions like "Duh,...where did you say he touched you again?" In no other situation is there more opportunity to do harm in the investigation than with sexual abuse cases. Consequently, the bosses of the office ultimately initiated a unit whose specific purpose was to handle all the sex-abuse cases that passed through the waters of ECS. It was an all-volunteer unit and it became the Wisconsin unit. In all fairness, there were two caseworkers from Brooklyn and the supervisor was from Manhattan, but the unit was still considered badger country for the most part. I was a member of the unit for the next couple of years. I handled the same plethora of cases as before, only when it came to Uncle Chester getting a little sloppy when playing horsy with the nieces, it was up to me and the others to make it right.

3

THE CASE CAME IN MIDWAY through the shift. It was Alexandra's. She lofted it to my desk. "Marc, I just know you're dyin' to go to the Bronx. You just been sitting there goin'— 'Damn, if only I could go to the Bronx with Alex tonight.' " She flashed me an irresistible smile and cupped her hands in prayer, nails clacking against one another.

Alexandra was the Brooklynite in the unit. Born and raised in a housing project, her childhood summers were spent in the white blast of open fire hydrants. Playground jungle gyms and cement chips were her climbing trees and skipping stones. The distant sound of car stereos was her wind through the fields. Pigeons were her wildlife. We grew up on different sides of the planet, but at ECS we had become friends.

I was sent to the field with her several times before she was officially hired for ECS from one of the daytime offices during my second year. She needed a little tutoring, when she began, on some of the differences between the field offices and ECS— meaning mostly that instead of asking parents for their children's immunization cards, we skip straight to lifting shirts and pulling down drawers.

Alex was a knockout—the kind of good looks that walk right up to you to say hello. She told us she was taking classes during the day to become a mortician so she could quit the agency and open her own funeral parlor. Listening to this beautiful woman talk about cutting up dead bodies was something too strange for words. And Alex was a dresser. I never saw her looking anything but fabulous the entire time I knew her. She clearly spent most of her paycheck on wardrobe, hair, and makeup. Her outfits were always tasteful, but not without a bit of flash—not so much to make her cheap, but just enough to keep things interesting. And they were *outfits,* if you know what I mean; the pants went with the shoes went with the jacket went with the hair clip went with the lipstick went with the toenail polish. It worked somehow with Alex. She was around thirty-two, but I'm guessing with that—age was an off-limits subject with her.

She had a collection of fingernails the likes of which I've never seen. Painted bright red with rhinestones at the tips, they were no less than five inches long. When her hands rested on her desk, they yahoo'd from her fingertips like the red scribble of a child's crayon. When she raised her hands, they scrolled and glittered like streamers on the Fourth. The index finger of her right hand was short in comparison to the rest—only an inch and a half or so. She kept it that way so she could dial the phone or rub her eyes without popping them onto her lap. Short as it was, it was still impressive. For Alex, the nail was a canvas, the finger a gallery wall, with a new installation every week. Every so often I'd request a viewing. Alex would put a hand in front of me and continue whatever else she was doing. Sometimes the finger was a flagpole flying meticulously rendered flags from various nations. I remember a nature scene, complete with a rippling waterfall and birds flying into the sunset. There were cartoon characters, flowers, initials on occasion, and always the sparkling tangle of the other nine nails. Children Alex removed used to sit in the backseat completely mesmerized by her amazing claws.

That same tangle of claws was now sitting in front of her face and leading down to hands cupped neatly together, pleading to me. "I'm sure you owe me," she said, pulling her hands apart. "Don't you even get me thinking about how much you owe me—I believe I can recall a few nights that would have you carrying me to the Bronx on your back. C'mon now, brother, don't hold out on me—let's go do it."

"I don't know, Alex."

Her eyes got wide and she hissed with quiet urgency, "Marc—they're talkin' about sending me out with *Giles,* now *come on.*" Giles was sent out every couple of weeks when the bosses got sick of watching him stare at the phone, or his pen, or his index finger. Going out with Giles was a hell no one deserved.

"Is it a bad one?" I asked.

"It's a sex abuse."

"How many kids?"

"Four," she said. "Only one of them's been messed with. They're already at the hospital. I spoke to the doctor who did the exams."

"The other three are fine?"

She put her hands on her hips and cocked her head forward. "Well, why don't you stop acting like a damn supervisor and read the case."

"Okay, Alex, okay."

"Then go get a car." She walked away flashing another smile. "I'll be at my desk. I owe you one."

The report read like a slap in the face.

> Mother brought Melissa (8 yrs) to the ER after child's complaints of a painful vagina and odorous discharge. Melissa's preliminary diagnosis is gonorrhea. Physical exam shows indication of repeated vaginal penetration over a period of time. Two of the three other children in family have been examined and show no signs of sexual contact. Third child will be examined shortly. Melissa interviewed by hospital staff and denies sexual contact of any kind.

This job really does a number on any kind of romantic view of the world. The curly fax paper reports, over the past few years, had begun to wear a couple extra grooves in my forehead. I was dying to believe in a world where eight-year-old girls didn't contract gonorrhea, but I was dying to believe in a world without a lot of the things I'd come across in the past three years. I wasn't totally naive when I joined ECS as to how bad the world can get—it's almost impossible for anyone to remain sheltered in this day of instant media. But it's one thing to read about a little girl with gonorrhea, and it's another thing entirely to look into her face, listen to her voice, or feel her breath on your cheek as she speaks to you. As you learn about the story, there are tears instead of newsprint on your fingers, because you haven't been turning a page, you've been wiping a cheek.

I'd be lying if I didn't say that my first thoughts when I came across a report like this were usually along the lines of *Let's find the guy who did this and cut his dick off*—bright red and slippery, an uncontrollable flash of outrage shot through my head before I could do anything about it. It's the kind of outrage at injustice you indulge when you're a child, before you adopt an adult's complacency. There were nights when we were waiting for the time clock to hit the end of the shift when the older folks would squawk to us greener ones, "Hey you can't let this stuff get to you, and whatever you do, don't take it home with you. If you haven't figured it already, let me tell you: Life ain't fair, baby. It's hard and it just ain't too fair sometimes." That's complacency pure and simple with a bit of heartless thrown in to round off the kettle. It's called being knocked around for so long you can't even tell when the bat hits your face. It's called getting old, and I'm not talking about the piling on of years. I fought it tooth and nail.

Hey—I don't care if life ain't fair—see if you keep talking that bull when I go to the little girl with gonorrhea tonight and tell her that she won't be bothered again because I got the guy's dick in my pocket and a switchblade with a story to tell.

I know how this sounds, but a little inappropriate thinking in the midst of such inappropriate acts can't hurt, and didn't hurt, as a matter of fact. The most seasoned pro gets the same taste of blood on the back of his tongue every time—if he's still doing a good job, that is. If he's doing a good job, it's because it still makes him sick to his stomach. The ones who don't think about it, the ones who aren't taking at least a little of it home with them, the ones who don't get just a little crazy from it all—those are the ones who are just walking the bases. Show me a person who can do a good job without putting their heart into it. Then find me someone who doesn't get a little wild when they give that heart to a young girl with venereal disease, and I think you'll see what I mean. The people who tell you a real professional doesn't think in italics once in a while are the same ones who think a pit bull on the charge doesn't need a bullet. I guarantee there's no dirt under those nails. Leave them to the high road and we'll get the work done.

Alex and I put on our coats and headed outside. We got into old #603, cranked her over, and paddled her north up the FDR on our way to the Bronx.

4

DR. SHELLY HAD JUST FINISHED examining Melissa's third sibling by the time we arrived. As with the other two, she found no evidence of sexual contact on the third child. Rape kits were done on everybody just the same, but lab results wouldn't be in until two o'clock the following day. Dr. Shelly pointed out the mother of the children, Lucia Pagan, who was sitting in a row of chairs against a far wall with the three kids, who were playing with a surgical glove blown up like a balloon. Melissa was in a separate room where she was being interviewed by investigators from Bronx Detectives Sex Crimes Special Unit. The emergency room was a sizzling fry pan of activity—doctors and nurses in a cha-cha with heart-lung machines and blood-stained stretchers. Patients lay propped up on every available flat surface. Relatives stood at the elbows of most of them—their long faces growing bright when a doctor would approach, and then quickly falling like dogs at the pound, as they were passed. Like everyone else, Dr. Shelly seemed entirely overextended in her duties. She flipped us Melissa's chart as she ran by.

"Here. Read this," she said over her shoulder. "It's the girl's chart. My notes are on the bottom and extend to the back sheet. I'll be right back." Alex held the chart in one hand and her purse in the other. We stared at each other for a moment amid the mayhem, and then began to search for a place to sit down. In one corner, a guy spread out across three seats. His face was swollen tight and colored various shades of blue and red. He held a bloody piece of gauze against his left eye. I asked him to scoot over so we could sit down.

"Are you a doctor?" he asked, straining to see me through his puffed-up right eye.

"No I'm not, I'm sorry."

"Well can you *please* . . . get one for me? . . ." He was drunk.

"Well they're all over the place," I said as the man shuffled over to make room for us.

"*I know they're all over the place*—it's an emergency room. They're doctors—they're s'pose di be doctors all over the place inna emergency room."

"Have you been seen yet?" I asked. "Who gave you the gauze?"

"I got dis gauze off the tray over there—self-service. My face is killin' me."

"What happened to you?"

"God bead up by a couple a fugginassholes."

"Marc?" Alex asked politely. "Can we focus on the task at hand here?"

"Guy . . . *guy*—you gotta get a doctor over here, c'mon, all right?—this fuckin' place. My face is killin' me."

"Just a second, Alex," I said. She rolled her eyes and sat back in the chair to read Melissa's chart.

"This fuckin' place—what if I was *dyin'*? They call dis an emergency room. I got 'ere at five o'clock—I didn't even want to come. I hate this hospital, the cops made me get in the ambulance—*what if I died here?* this fuckin' place."

"I'll see if I can get somebody to see you," I said.

"Please, guy—I can't hardly see out of this eye no more, you gotta get—my face is killin' me, please—"

"I just said I'm gonna try to get somebody, all right? Just sit back a little."

"All right—*please...*"

I went to the nursing station and leaned in, shouting to no one in particular, "Who's the doctor for this guy over here?" Nothing. "Hello?...Hello—can somebody tell me who the doctor is for this guy over here?...Anybody?" The unit secretary looked up from his computer.

"What do you need?" he barked over the clamor of telephones and voices.

"There's a guy over here that needs a doctor," I shouted back. The guy looked at me like I had asked him to wag his bare butt in the air. "It's the guy over there on the chair," I continued. "He says he was brought in at five o'clock and it's nine now, so...that guy right over there on the chair."

The secretary stared at me blankly and called out over the loudspeaker, "Please, charge nurse to the front desk, please." His eyes never left mine. A woman in green scrubs bustled up to him and he pointed at me.

"The guy over on the chair over there needs to see a doctor," I said to the nurse.

"Are you a relative?" she asked briskly.

"No ma'am."

"Then you'll have to wait in the waiting room, this area is for patients and their immediate family only. You can see we're extremely crowded here so I'll have to ask you to please—"

"I'm with Emergency Children's Services," I interrupted.

"That's fine, sir, but I'll have to ask you to clear this area all the same—"

"I'm here on a case, I can't clear the area—I belong here right now. I was just sitting next to that guy on the chair over there and he told me his face was hurting him and he hasn't seen a doctor since he got here four hours ago so I was just wondering if someone could at least tell him when he'll be seen."

"Well, thank you for bringing this to our attention. You can tell the man that a doctor will be with him as soon as possible." With that she turned and was gone. I began to make my way back to Alex as the secretary shouted behind my back, "You're welcome."

When I got back to the chairs, Alex was gone. "Where's the woman that was just here?" I asked the guy.

"Did you get a doctor?"

"They said they'd send one. Where did the woman that was just here go to?"

"She went around that corner," he mumbled as he sank back into the chair. "This hospital sucks."

I followed around the corner where the man pointed, and sure enough, there was Alex with Dr. Shelly at the end of a hallway. As I jogged over to them, Alex looked at me with a smirk on her lips.

"All done with your new friend over there?" she asked. "Anyone else you want to help before getting started here?"

Alex introduced me to Dr. Shelly, a handsome woman in her early thirties. She wore a white lab coat with pockets bulging from medical gear and pharmaceutical manuals. A bright blue Cookie Monster puppet peeked out of her right breast pocket. A set of keys, a pen, and a small Superman figure hung from a chain around her neck.

"Busy tonight," I said as I shook Dr. Shelly's hand.

"Oh, this isn't so bad, actually."

"You're kidding. Holy cow."

"Stop by on a Saturday night around eleven o'clock if you want to see doctors on Rollerblades." We stepped aside to make room for several nurses and an old man on a stretcher that whipped by.

"So what've I missed?" I asked.

"We were just getting started," Alex said.

"Right, we were just getting started—" Her beeper went off. She pulled it from the waist of her pants and cocked her head to read the page. "It's okay—hang on," she said, scratching the number out on a notepad. "One of the floors I just sent a patient up to—I can get it in a second...all right, so—" We stepped aside again as a group of four cops squeezed by. "Hey, I know—let's use the room over there," she said, pointing. "I think it's free. This isn't gonna work here." We zigzagged through a maze of people, equipment, and staff, to a small examination room a few doors down from where Melissa was being interviewed by Sex Crimes. I closed the door behind us as we stepped in. "This should work until the charge nurse kicks us out, anyways. I just don't want the mother or the other children to hear us talking. The mother knows everything, I mean about me calling you and your involvement. She's appropriately upset at the findings on Melissa and she's going to cooperate fully with whatever you need to do. All right, so here's what we've got:

"Ms. Pagan comes in to have Melissa examined because of the girl's complaints of a sore vagina. She claims Melissa has been complaining about it for the past several days, but that it's been really bad today. So they're watching television after supper and Ms. Pagan 'smells something rotten' or 'smells a rotten smell' or something or other. She checks around and quickly discovers the smell is coming from Melissa. She brings the child here immediately. As the girl is being triaged, there's instant suspicion for sexual abuse so they call me to spare the child a dozen examinations by every resident in the ER."

The sound of a man screaming distracted me for a moment. I glanced at him through the small window in the door as he was wheeled by on a stretcher. He was restrained in messy coils of canvas straps from the waist up. The sheet had fallen away from his lower body and he was naked. His legs and head flapped wildly as he passed. The people tending to him wore rubber gloves and respiratory masks. Dr. Shelly paused for a moment before continuing without comment.

"So I get Melissa—who is a total sweetheart by the way— I get her alone in an examination room and I'm talking to her about what I'm going to do and she's just fine with every-thing—very pleasant little girl. I begin the exam. She's clean— by that I mean she's well looked after; bathed, groomed, etc. There's not a mark or scar or bruise on her. She's like every other little girl except for the odor coming from her panties that's more suited to a junkie/hooker than an eight-year-old. The smell alone is a dead giveaway for any of a number of venereal diseases."

More screaming from outside. More staff in gloves and masks passed the window.

"I have Melissa lay back and I remove her panties—I doc-umented in the chart what I found. Have you looked at it?" Alexandra nodded and handed me the chart. I looked it over as Dr. Shelly continued. There were two drawings in blue ball-point of Melissa's vagina illustrating a series of rips and abra-sions. "The hymen's been broken—there's not a trace of it intact. The overall muscle tone of the vagina is poor. There are several tears in the labia that I've indicated in the drawings there. They're at different stages of healing so that indicates to me they were caused over a period of anywhere from three months to...up to a year. Maybe more, it's hard to say ex-actly. Some of the trauma is recent, there's a slight bit of bruis-ing on the outside of the vagina that would have to have been caused within the last couple of days, which is hard to even imagine because the smell and discharge would've been present since at least then—so you have to imagine a perpetrator who not only doesn't mind having sex with an eight-year-old, but also doesn't care that he's playing around with a vagina that's quite sick.

"Here's something else that bothered me—Melissa cooperated through the entire exam. A typical girl her age should've been flinching every time I touched her. Melissa laid still staring calmly at the ceiling while I did some very intrusive procedures. She should've been all over the table. A normal eight-year-old would be trying to close her knees every chance she gets, but that was hardly the case here. Melissa is used to lying on her back and having her vagina touched. And I'll tell you—that's more disturbing to me than the discharge or the bruises and tears or anything else. All that's going to heal, but the look on her face... the way she just allowed me inside of her, you'd think I was only tying the laces of her shoes..."

"It's sick," I said.

"The girl's a wreck from the waist down—there's no other way to put it. She's in bad shape. Someone's raping her—she's being raped on a regular basis."

Dr. Shelly's beeper went off again. She picked it off her waist and gave it a look. "Damn," she said, tossing it into her pocket. "That's the floor again, they probably think I've abandoned ship. I'm gonna have to answer it. Well, anyway, I'm around all night. I can get most anything you might need here so don't hesitate to give me a shout."

She was about to step out when Alex stopped her. "In the report you say Melissa denies any sexual contact."

"That's right. I asked her point-blank who's been touching her vagina—not *if* someone's touching it—I asked her *who* is touching it. She looked at me like I was crazy and I didn't press it. I'm here to tell you this girl's having regular sex with someone infected by a venereal disease. I hope that between you people and Sex Crimes, somebody can tell me who that person is. I have to go answer this page. Keep me posted."

We followed Dr. Shelly out of the room and she disappeared behind the nursing station. My friend on the chair with the puffed-up face was still there. The gauze he held on his face was clean so he must've helped himself to another wad from the self-service cart. The naked man in restraints was in a side room covered with a sheet and either sleeping or passed out or sedated. The examination room with Melissa and the Sex Crimes people was still closed. I peered through the small window in the door but could only see the back of one of the detectives' suits.

Alex and I were actually supposed to be in there talking to Melissa with them. The city had just instated a mandated protocol in sex abuse investigations called "Joint Response." In a Joint Response, the child was interviewed one time only by a cooperative gathering of interested agencies. The protocol was set up to avoid the problem of a child having to explain the details of a sexual assault in numerous separate interviews with police, doctors, detectives, and Child Welfare authorities. It was generally a good idea, but sometimes there could be quite a crowd of adults huddled around a very frightened child, asking questions that you and I would have a hard time answering to a closest friend.

Sex Crimes would always get to the hospital before us because there were a couple units in every borough of the city. Their drive to the hospital was ten to twenty minutes, compared to our one or two hours in some instances. Detectives don't generally like to wait on anybody and they didn't generally wait for us. Alex and I didn't want to barge in on them and introduce ourselves just as Melissa was naming a perpetrator, so we decided to wait until they were done to see what they came up with. In the meantime we decided to speak with Melissa's mother. Dr. Shelly had already described her as appropriately concerned and cooperative, although we weren't about to rule out anybody as far as wrongdoing was concerned.

Abuse over a long period of time might point to neglect on the mother's part at the very least. I had seen enough cases where the sobbing mother ends up being thrown in jail along with the husband/brother/father/boyfriend for trying to protect him. I'd even seen mothers who'd exchanged the services of their young daughters for discounts from the local pusher, so until we bagged the monster, everybody was a suspect—life ain't fair, baby, to quote the geezers at the time clock. Life's hard and it just ain't too fair sometimes.

"What do you say, Alex?"

"Are you just dying to meet a mother whose eight-year-old is having regular sex and she doesn't know anything about it?"

I smiled. Alex had a great way about her in a charged situation like this. Rather than get crazed with outrage or be intimidated by the shock of a bad case, Alex would get testy. It was her way of sharpening her senses.

"Are you dying to meet a woman like this?" she asked again, with a crooked eyebrow. "Because I am." I nodded. "Hold this room, Marc. I'll get Ms. Pagan. We'll talk to her in there."

Alexandra shimmied up to the mother and the three children, introduced herself with a smile and a handshake, and then guided them over toward me. She took the mother into the room while I talked a nurse into staying with the kids until we were done. I stepped back into the exam room just as Alex was reading off the ECS report. She stopped while I introduced myself to Ms. Pagan and then sat on a chair against the wall. Ms. Pagan was sitting on the exam table with a bewildered look in her eyes. Alex and I looked square into those eyes for a moment before saying anything further. This woman had just heard maybe the worst thing a mother can hear. Was she grieving, in shock, crazed? The first moments were important. If the mother was guilty of anything, she'd usually tip you off right at the start. When the interview was in high gear and all the defenses were hoisted and full of wind, it was almost impossible to detect the wolf in sheep's clothing.

Ms. Pagan shifted her bottom and the paper on the exam table rustled loudly in the quiet between the three of us. She may have been in her late thirties and was on the shorter end of five feet, with a set of thick glasses and some pretty heavy lipstick. Alexandra returned to the report and continued reading where she had left off. Ms. Pagan already knew much more than what was contained in the report, having heard all the gory details from Dr. Shelly. Going over the report was more of a so-you-know-that-we-know kind of thing. I watched her closely as Alex read. When Alex finished, she looked up at Ms. Pagan. "Dr. Shelly tells us she's examined your other three children and that they are fine, but the exam of Melissa indicates the child is being raped on a regular basis."

Ms. Pagan dropped her head and shook it lightly from side to side. "It can't be true," she said, starting to cry. "I don't see how it could happen. There's no way."

The beginning of tears was another crucial moment in determining whether Mom was friend or foe to the investigation. It's easy in a heightened situation to manufacture some tears for effect and by the time the sobbing reaches cruising speed, there's little to distinguish it from the real thing. I could usually tell when someone was working up a head of steam as they tried to get it going.

"The doctor, she told me the same thing, but I can't believe it. When? . . . When could this happen? And why don't Melissa tell me if it's really true? And who is doing this?—there is no one who would do this to her. How could it be true?" Ms. Pagan looked at Alexandra and me with eyes wide in disbelief.

"You don't believe your daughter is being molested?" Alex asked.

"I don't know who it could be—I ask Melissa after the doctor tell me and she say, 'Nothing, Mommy, nobody did nothing to me.' I say, 'The doctors say it gotta be somebody' —but she don't say nothing. I can't believe this." Tears dripped from her eyes and they were the real thing.

Alexandra pulled a tissue from her purse and offered it to her. As Ms. Pagan dried her eyes, Alex gave her shoulder a rub. "Look, it happened. It's been happening. You have to believe it. Your daughter's in trouble but that's why we're here—the detectives, the doctors, everybody—we all want to find out who's been doing this to Melissa."

"She don't say nobody," Ms. Pagan said, looking up from the tissue as she shook it in her lap. "I keep asking her—"

"All right, all right," Alex said. "She says nothing happened, but it's important for you to understand that something did happen. Nobody knows your situation at home as well as you do—that's why it's important that you face the fact that your daughter is in trouble, so that you can help all of us discover who's doing the damage. Whoever's doing this has to be stopped. That's what we're here to do, okay? But we have to have your help. You gotta help us."

"But how, how, how? This is impossible—"

"Ms. Pagan," I interrupted, "your daughter has gonorrhea. Someone infected with gonorrhea is having sex with her— that's why she has it. It would be impossible for her *not* to have had sex, and that's taking into account the gonorrhea alone. There's plenty of other physical evidence to indicate she's being penetrated but the fact that she has a venereal disease makes it definitive. She's been raped—she's being raped, as recently as a couple of days ago, as a matter of fact, according to Dr. Shelly's findings. I can't imagine the shock if I had a daughter and somebody told me what we're telling you—but I don't have to imagine that. I have to identify a perpetrator— and I only have tonight to do it so I don't want to spend any more time discussing whether or not Melissa's been violated because she *has* been violated and somebody's gonna pay for it. Are you gonna help us or not? If you help us, there's a good chance we'll get the person tonight. If you help us, you have to face the awful truth that poor Melissa has been hurt terribly—the first step you have to take is to admit that. If you're not going to help us then you can just have a seat outside...I want to find this guy...I hope you help us."

Ms. Pagan had dropped her head to her chest about half-way through all that. She was silent. "Do you understand that your daughter has gonorrhea?" I asked after a moment. She nodded with her head down. "And do you understand what that means?" She nodded again, but very slightly. None of us spoke for a moment. I crouched down to see Ms. Pagan crying silently into her lap. When I touched her arm she burst into mournful sobbing. Alexandra gave her a fresh tissue, which she put quickly to work, mopping at her eyes under the bulging magnification of her glasses.

"Is there anyone I can call to come be with you? A familiar face around here might be just what you need right now," I offered. "A sister? A friend?"

"There's no one," she said, folding the tissue to a clean side. "It's okay, thank you. I have no one."

"Well, all right," I said. "If you think of anyone as the night goes on, just let me know if I can call to have them come down." She nodded her head as Alex flipped to a fresh sheet of notepaper.

"All right, Lucia, ready to answer some questions?" Alex asked.

She looked up and nodded. Her glasses magnified every tear-soaked eyelash. "Could I have a drink of water, please?" she asked.

"I'll get it," I said. "You two get started." I headed out the door as Alex began with the obvious. "Let's start with who's in the home. Anybody besides you and the children?"

In the ER I found a nurse and ran alongside of her as I asked where to get a cup. She pointed me to the cart where my puff-faced buddy was getting his gauze. Cups were in the top drawer. Self-service. I slid it open and took one out. When the drawer screeched closed, puff-face's good eye flashed open. He jerked forward and began digging into me for not getting him a doctor. After I explained that I'd done all I could for him, he asked for a drink of water. I grabbed another cup, quickly filling it before everyone in the place was screaming for some. On my way back to Ms. Pagan and Alex, I saw the Sex Crimes detectives leaving Melissa's room. As they stepped out, Melissa's brother and two younger sisters rushed in to join her. The nurse watching them followed everybody in and closed the door behind her.

Just before the door closed, I got my first glimpse of Melissa—a little girl who was probably told at some time or another that there are no such things as monsters. She was the picture of health and loveliness as she sat there, but with the bottom of a junkie/hooker, as Dr. Shelly so bluntly put it. I felt my eyes clench with disgust as my mind took a quick journey to the sun and back, the way minds do sometimes. I could barely stand the sight of her. The beauty of her face made it worse somehow. It shouldn't have, but it did. You'd see her at a playground all sugar and spice and looking just like the child on the next swing. She had a smile on her face and a giggle in her chest, even as the dark secret threatened to leak down her legs and put its stain on everything. I couldn't see a trace of it even though it lay just behind the little-girl charm—a secret as gruesome as anything in the world, riding between her thighs like a hot ember about to explode. I realized that I had expected her to look extraordinary for some reason, but she didn't. She looked like a kid—an eight-year-old kid. She was just like the child that fell in a well or that got hit by a car or maybe just like the kids on a floor above us dying of leukemia—all of them nothing more than children who've succumbed to a terrible fate—the fate being more extraordinary than the young lives touched by it.

I sidled up to the detectives as they approached the nursing station, a man and woman in their early thirties, both in very nice suits, and introduced myself. We exchanged hellos and the man looked down at my cup of water. "For me?" he joked.

"Hey, sure," I said. "It's all yours."

"Actually, I could use it—dry in here. You mind?"

"Not at all," I said, handing the cup to him. "It was for Ms. Pagan but I can get another one."

"You're going now?" the woman asked. I nodded. "Would you mind getting me one too while you're at it?"

"No problem," I said, heading back to the cart. I filled two cups and gave a refill to puff-face before returning. I stepped in on Alex and Ms. Pagan to drop off the water and told them I'd be out talking with the detectives. Alex's expression told me she hadn't uncovered any buried treasure since I left her. I returned to the detectives and gave the woman her water. The man was just finishing his and I thought if he asked me for a refill I'd have to do something serious about my informal exterior. He didn't so I didn't, and with everybody properly watered, we got to the problem at hand.

"So how's Melissa?" I asked.

"Could be better," the woman said.

"Very sweet girl," the man followed.

"So who's doing it to her?"

"The hundred-thousand-dollar question," he said.

"We don't know," she said.

"What do you mean you don't know? What did the girl say?"

"The girl says nothing happened to her—"

"Whoever this perp is—," the woman cut in.

"She says nothing happened," the man cut back. "That nothing happened so nobody did it, and that she would like to go home with her mother now, thank you very much."

"Whoever he is," the woman continued, "he's got some kind of control over her—he's threatened to kill her or the mother or siblings if he's found out. See a lot of that. Or worse, he says that if he's found out he'll start doing little sister—so she keeps her mouth shut to protect the family."

"Maybe the guy's promised to kill the family cat if she squeals—see a lot of them, too," the man said.

"Okay, but that doesn't do anything for us right now. What else did the girl say?"

"Hey, be my guest," the man said, holding out a hand toward Melissa's exam room. "If you can get something out of her tonight, we'd be much obliged. In the meantime, we're gonna ask that the mother get tested for gonorrhea. She says she isn't married and doesn't have a boyfriend, but it might be interesting to have her checked out just the same. I'd put pretty good odds on the chance that the same nobody is doing nothing to her as well."

"Well, we'll take a crack at Melissa," I said. "Will you two be around in case we discover anything?"

"We'll be here," the man said. "We gotta talk to the mother again as soon as your partner is through with her."

"Okay. We'll have a talk with Melissa while you do that. So let's keep each other informed, all right?"

"You got it, buddy—hey, where'd you get that water? I'm dyin' of thirst." I pointed the detectives to the fountain and went back to see Alex. When I opened the door, both Alex and Ms. Pagan stopped talking to watch me step inside. It was a bad sign.

"How we doing here?" I asked.

"I think we're done for now," Alex said, looking at Ms. Pagan. "We'll talk to Melissa and then we'll see you again. Okay?" Ms. Pagan nodded. "If you go on out and have a seat, I'll have a few words with Mr. Parent." She nodded again and stepped out. When the door closed behind her, Alex whirled around to me. Her notepad was blank.

"I hate this, Marc, I just can't stand this," she said, throwing the clipboard on the exam table. "You know when a little girl has been messed with by some piece of dirt, and when she tells you who it is and the mother tells you who it's gotta be and you get the cops and throw the nasty scum in jail—you know how good you feel when you see the cuffs on the guy's wrist and he looks at you with that sheepish stupid face as he ducks into the squad car? I'm getting a feeling that might not happen tonight and I can already tell by your face that the detectives didn't get much."

"I can't tell a lie."

"Damn it."

"What did you get from Ms. Pagan?"

"Oh—they don't live with anybody and they don't see anybody and she doesn't have any friends and the children never go out of the house and all the relatives live in Puerto Rico and they never come to visit."

"They don't see anybody? And the children never leave the house?"

"Right?"

"Well, that's not possible."

"Hello?"

"You told her that?"

"Of course I told her that."

"And what'd she say?"

"She sticks to her guns . . . You know I have to say, it's not really like she's protecting anyone. I can just about believe that all this has been going on under her nose without her knowledge. She's not the brightest star in the sky by any stretch of the imagination."

"Okay, Alex."

"So let's go to the source."

"Melissa."

"She knows who he is. She might be the only one who does."

"Let's go to Melissa."

5

WHO ON EARTH CAN IMAGINE what Melissa had been through? Too many people, I'm afraid. One of the more incredible things about being assigned to the sexual abuse unit at ECS was that it became a catalyst for disclosure of past abuses for a surprising number of my own female friends. At parties, it was, "No kidding, you work with sexually abused kids?" and then later in the night, or during a subsequent phone call, "Say, you know my mother's boyfriend..." or "Sometimes when we'd visit Granddad..." For a while it seemed like every woman I knew had lived through some episode of sexual abuse in any of its varying degrees. Nobody ever had a childhood case of gonorrhea as far as I knew, but thwarting the advances of the family friend or baby-sitter or neighbor or relative seemed to be a rite of passage for many more women than I would've ever imagined. They sink or swim through a torrent of advances and then spend the rest of their lives trying to redefine these initial experiences into a healthy regard for sex in adulthood. No one—male or female—can imagine the destruction this type of abuse produces unless they've experienced it. I couldn't imagine the horror Melissa had been through, but I'd learned through many Melissas that I didn't have to feel her pain to help her—as long as I respected the difference between the knowledge of sexual abuse and the experience of it.

She smiled and said hello the second we were through the door. She looked very much like her mother without the thick glasses and lipstick. I chased the siblings and the nurse out of the room so we could be alone with her. Alex set her things in the corner and pulled a chair up to the child. I sat directly in front of the door, blocking the small window as the detective had earlier. Different clothing, same questions—who the hell's been messin' with you, little girl? You gotta tell us 'cause we're gonna knock his block off. Melissa shuffled back on the table and the paper rustled as it had with her mother. As she moved back, she grasped the back of her hospital gown to keep her behind from sliding out. Alex introduced us. Melissa was less than amused at meeting yet another set of adults with a bucketful of nasty questions that she would have to respond to.

"After I talk with you guys, can I go home?" she pleaded politely.

"Sweetheart, we all want to get you home as soon as possible," Alex said. "More than anything else—that's what we all want." Melissa let out a sigh and leaned back against the wall. A simple yes was all she wanted. With her chin at her chest, she looked at her legs flat out on the table before her. She gave them a shuffle and the paper rattled again loudly. I glanced at Alex. She was looking for an opening, her eyes waited for Melissa's to meet them. Melissa sighed again and ruffled the paper.

"Melissa? . . ." Alex leaned forward. Melissa's eyes remained at her knees. "Melissa? . . . I know a lot of people have been asking you some pretty awful questions tonight, right?" Melissa blew her bangs out of her eyes and nodded. "Well you gotta be strong a little longer because we gotta do the same thing. We know that somebody's been bothering you and we want to make sure the person doesn't bother you anymore." Melissa huffed and rolled her eyes. "What is it, hon?"

"I don't know what anybody's talking about," she whined. "There's nobody bothering me. I told the people before, that man and that woman—I told them and the doctor, too. I don't know what anybody's talking about. Nobody's buggin' me—I keep saying it."

"Why are you in the hospital, darling? Why do you think we're all in the emergency room tonight?"

"I know why," Melissa said after a pause.

"Tell me why."

"Do you know why?" she asked Alex.

"I know why," Alex said.

"Does *he* know why?" she asked, pointing to me. Alex nodded and Melissa slapped her palm to her forehead. She looked at me with an embarrassed smile.

"It's okay, Melissa," I said, trying to be reassuring but sounding like a big idiot—there was nothing okay about anything in the room and the last thing an eight-year-old girl wants a twenty-six-year-old guy to know is that she even *has* a vagina, much less to know that hers was in such bad shape.

"Why are you in the emergency room tonight?" Alex pressed on. Melissa smiled. "You can tell us," Alex said. She looked to me and back to Alex. She slapped her forehead again and rolled her eyes.

"Here we go again," she said with slaphappy lightness.

"Go ahead, Melissa," Alex said, serious. "Tell us why." Melissa rolled her eyes again and let out an exaggerated how-silly-this-all-is exhale. She looked from me back to Alex and then, almost as if trying to be funny, pointed in a quick awkward gesture to her crotch. The humor came out of a bed of nerves—the mouth was smiling but the eyes were scared as hell. It made me sad like nothing else during the whole night. It was sad to see an eight-year-old point to her crotch with artificial levity in an exaggerated gesture. Alex's question was cruel, but kind and polite questions would get us nowhere.

"That's right," Alexandra said after Melissa's gesture. "And what about that? . . ."

"Something's wrong with it," Melissa said, suddenly serious. The understatement of the century.

"That's right," Alexandra said again. "What happened down there? . . . Do you know what happened to it? . . ." Melissa shrugged her shoulders. "Do you? . . . ," Alex asked again.

"I don't know," Melissa said, almost bewildered, ". . . it hurts . . ."

"The doctors will make it better," I said. Melissa stared at me. "They'll make it stop hurting..." Anger roiled at the back of my tongue.

"Who made it hurt?" Alex asked. The hundred-thousand-dollar question. Melissa looked straight into my eyes. Alex asked her again. I could practically see the perpetrator in her pupils. Suddenly he was there. She knew him better than she knew anybody. She knew his name. She knew where he was and she knew how to get there. Her eyes strained to reveal him as she looked at me, but her mouth betrayed her.

"Nobody...," she said. "Nobody made it hurt...it just hurts...that's all—nobody did nothing..."

"I don't even think you expect us to believe that, sweetheart," Alexandra said, putting a hand on her shoulder. "We know what happened to you. We want you to tell us who did it."

Melissa shrugged her shoulders. "I don't care if you believe it. I'm just telling you the truth anyways."

We pressed on gently for a few more minutes without progress. The perpetrator was safe and secure behind her eyes. After spinning our wheels a bit more, I stepped out to give the office an update on our progress, or lack of progress as it was turning out.

The detectives were waiting for me. I wove through a gridlock of stretchers to reach them at the nursing station. Ms. Pagan was sitting with Melissa's brother and two sisters several seats down from puff-face. The kids had a new surgical-glove balloon they were arguing over, but puff-face's gauze was the same old thing he'd had earlier. He was asleep or passed out...or dead—*What if I die in here, this fuckin' place*—though I doubted that. The detectives were getting ready to make an exit.

"So what's the perp's address?" the woman asked as she slipped on her coat.

"Where are you going?" I asked, ignoring the sarcasm.

"Pagan don't know anything. So'd the girl crack open?" the man asked.

"Well she hasn't yet, but we've only just started."

"That's no surprise. She's not gonna tell you guys anything. I hate to break it to you," the man said, putting on his jacket. As he lifted his arm, a large silver gun peeked out from the side of his suit.

"The perp's got his hands on her mouth—says he's gonna kill her mother or her brother if he's found out—something like that. You see it—pretty common," the woman said.

"Melissa knows who the perp is," I said. "And I think she'll tell us if we can convince her she'll be protected. We've just started to talk with her—it's gonna take a while to get her naming names. You have to leave this second?"

"We'd love to stay, but there's nothing else here," the man said. "Hate to break it to you. Besides, we just got a call on another case at Bronx Municipal—it's sickos' night out."

"Dr. Shelly's gonna admit the kid, so she'll be all right for tonight," the woman said. "We'll pick this up tomorrow A.M. Where do we reach you?"

"We're only on this tonight," I said. "It goes to the field office at eight."

"Well if you two get anything out of the girl tonight, give us a call," the man said, handing me his card. "We'll pick the guy up and book him—just tell us where he is. Personally, I think the only thing left to do right now is pray that the mother's got gonorrhea. If the perp left his fingerprints on her and they look the same as the ones on the kid, we got it made. If Pagan's got VD, then it's a family thing and we beat the floorboards till the rat comes out. Anyways, it was a pleasure," he said as he closed the last button on his jacket. "Seriously, give us a call if you get a name and we're all over him—we'll take him out, I don't care what time it is. If we don't hear from you tonight, we'll be on it first thing tomorrow. We'll get this guy. He's sleeping like a baby tonight, but we'll get him sooner or later."

"He's either sleeping like a baby or sleeping with one," I said. "Perp like this doesn't put all his eggs in one basket. See a lot of that."

"See a lot of that, too. Guy like this has got more than one date for the prom. You're probably right." He shook my hand. "Been a pleasure—hope to hear from you." The woman reached over and we shook hands. Her gun was blue, just as big. The two of them turned to leave and I watched them go. I found a phone and called the office.

Riiiiing... ninety-nine... *riiiiing*... one hundred... *riiiiing* ... one hundred-one...

"Emergency Children's Services—"

"It's Marc. I'm at Jacobi on the Pagan case—"

"Hold on, Marc, I'll get you a manager."

The managers were higher up the line than supervisors. They usually liked to be involved with fatality and sex abuse cases. All the managers at ECS were a small gathering of folks who hadn't been to the field or to an emergency room like the one I was swimming in since Babe Ruth and trolley cars. Their role in cases like this one was no different than that of a regular supervisor except that they were paid more to recite the same agency doctrines.

She came to the phone after several minutes and I began to tell her about the case. She stopped me.

"Hang on, hang on, Marc..." Shuffling paper. "I just reviewed that case with your supervisor—here it is, okay, hang on a minute..." Reading the report. Crunching sound—egg roll from Ho's Wok, I'm thinking, dipped in mustard sauce. "Child's been examined?"

"Yeah, they found—"

"Hang on, Marc, hang on." Paper shuffling; the second

page. Another crunch. A sip. Green tea, I'm thinking, very hot. "Mom and sibs at hospital?"

"Yup. Everybody's been examined and—"

"Marc, will you just hold on one second—lemme just read what I got here, okay? One second." Another sip and a crunch. Chewing. "Mmmm... all right... hang on." More chewing. Loud crunch. Fortune cookie for sure. Another sip. "Now Marc, has everyone been examined?"

"Yup. They didn't find—"

"Hang on, Marc, I'm writing. Okay. What did the exams on the other children show?"

"No evidence of sexual contact. No indications for venereal disease."

"Cultures done?"

"Yup."

"Rape kit?"

"Uh-huh."

"And the eight-year-old has definitely been abused."

"No question."

"Sex Crimes gonna arrest the perp?"

"Not unless we find out who it is."

"No perp yet?"

"Still working on it. Melissa denies sexual contact but we're still talking to her. Alex's with her now. Sex Crimes left on another case, but they'll do an arrest as soon as we call them with an ID. Melissa's gonna be admitted."

"The perp is still at large."

"That's right."

"Then you have to do a removal on the three sibs," she said flatly.

"Wait—they're fine. There's not a thing wrong with them."

"That doesn't matter—if the perp's at large, we remove all the children. Period."

"Wait, wait," I pleaded. "Let's just go a little further—the sibs are perfectly fine, the mother is appropriately upset, there are no other adults in the home, the mother—"

"I don't have time, Marc," she crunched. "C'mon now, don't play this with me—you know the procedure we follow here. If we can't identify a perp, I want to see you and Alexandra coming back to the office with three children in tow. Period."

If we can't *identify the perp—like sitting on your rear end eating mustard-soaked egg rolls constitutes an investigation.*

"Just indulge me one second," I said, barreling headfirst into her crunching oil pan. "This would be a disaster—to remove the other children. Really. I mean—"

"Marc, there's really nothing complicated here. I appreciate your concerns for the feelings of the family, but you should really be thinking about the danger that an unidentified perpetrator presents to the other children—"

"I am—"

"—not to mention the fact that the mother has demonstrated she's not capable of protecting her children from this perpetrator—"

"She didn't know it was happening—hard as that is to believe. You have to look at her to understand it—to believe it," I said, and then lowered my voice, "Listen, I don't think she's very bright to tell you the truth—the mother. She has a hard time of it, you know? At any rate, she knows what's happened, she's devastated, she wants to find the bastard, and she's going to do everything to make sure the other kids remain safe. I mean *everything*—she's gonna watch them like a crazy person. They're not gonna leave her sight. We're gonna hammer her into a watchdog before she leaves here—she won't let the kids stay with their own grandmother when we're done."

"Sex Crimes has left, the case is over for you. You're going to remove those children and leave the rest for the follow-up. You have to understand, Marc, this is a perpetrator that's threatened the child in some way or another—he's told her that he'll have the family killed if he's found out—that he'll kill the mother or the brother, maybe one of the sisters."

"You see a lot of that."

"We *do* see a lot of that. He may have threatened to kill the family cat..."

"...uh-huh."

"We don't know what we may be up against here"—muffled crunch—"what dynamics may be coming into play."

"...okay."

"All right...so it's the perpetrator or the kids then."

"...right."

"You gonna be okay on this one, Marc?"

"Yes, I will be...So we don't give any credit to a parent who's going to do everything in her power to protect her children as opposed to someone who's just a dumb animal and doesn't give a shit. We don't acknowledge the difference between these two people. The perp's out so we take the kids."

"There may be other dynamics that generally come into play—"

"But that's what it boils down to."

"Not in every situation—"

"Tonight that's what it boils down to."

"With the dynamics as they present themselves here, I'd have to say yes, that's what it boils down to."

We ended our conversation shortly after that. When you're sinking in the stinky and someone starts talking dynamics, you know it's over. This particular manager was always looking for a chance to get academic. I saw it coming so I bailed out to escape an intellectual conversation that would get us nowhere. I used to go back and forth with her forever, even picking up in the office where we'd left off in phone conversations. The discussions never amounted to anything—just her giving me one thousand reasons why she was right and I was wrong. There was usually a glint in her eye as we'd tie up a packageful of this way and that—like she'd really given me a lesson on life, packed my ear full of wisdom and food for thought. She'd glare at most of the people in the office for just about any reason, but me, I'd get the glint and a oh-you'll-learn-someday-and-then-you'll-thank-me at just about every turn. Made me wanna yell into a pillow.

As I left the phone and returned to Alex I bumped into the on-call social worker, who was making her way to Melissa's exam room with two large cloth dolls clutched under her right arm. These dolls weren't in the same class as toys pulled from the bottom drawers to distract young patients from dreadful procedures—they weren't dirty or ripped up, but clean and neat; a man and a woman, and in the arms of a social worker that could mean only one thing. Under the innocent clothing of each doll would be hairy adult-looking genitals rendered in blunt detail of yarn and peach-colored fabric. Nothing is as it seems in an emergency room—like Disneyland but in the other direction. Only in an emergency room would you find smiling dolls with X-rated crotches.

The social worker stopped me in front of Melissa's room. She said she'd been called by staff on a sex abuse and brought the dolls in case we wanted to use them. Leave it to a social worker to have a doll to illustrate just about any of the most undoll-like situations. Manipulatives, they called them: dolls with broken arms and black eyes, paraplegic dolls, dolls that give birth to other dolls, smoking dolls and drinking dolls with dark stains on their removable lungs and livers, bald chemo-therapy dolls, dolls that smoke marijuana and shoot heroin, and these—dolls that molest each other. I was willing to try anything to avoid a removal of the siblings so I took the social worker up on her offer and grasped a doll in either hand. As she handed them over, she tugged on the pants of the man doll to reveal a penis the size of which would make any guy proud.

"Make sure they get back to me," the social worker said before she left. "These things cost a fortune, for some reason."

"You gotta pay for that kind of detail, I guess."

"Oh—the woman doll has breasts in case you need them," the social worker said. Sure enough—I peeked down the shirt and there they were. They might be big goofy eyes anywhere else, but in the ER, the big goofy eyes on a doll were breasts. They sat oddly on the cloth chest waiting for the next young child to reveal unspeakable horrors in a pantomime of fondling and sucking. I released the blouse from my pinch and the collar snapped modestly back around the neck. The man doll had a loose mustache of brown yarn covering the mouth, which I initially thought was smiling, but it wasn't. The eyes were smiling—squinted slightly with crow's-feet stitching at the corners—nice touch. The mouth wasn't smiling. The mouths on the man and the woman were the same, as a matter of fact—both a conspicuously open O with room inside for whatever might fit in them. These dolls did it all. Meticulously stitched lips rounded their overall freakish presentation. When a doll is called a manipulative, user beware. It's not the type of thing a kid likes to find next to a birthday cake.

After losing myself momentarily to the strangeness of Mr. and Mrs. Genital, I glanced up to see the social worker walking away through a bramble of people and equipment, searching for the next calamity to throw a doll at. Looking to my right, I caught Alex's eye through the small window of the exam room. She smiled and pointed toward me. Melissa leaned into the window and waved. They'd been making friends. Alex was great at that. She was a good-looking, well-dressed woman with a quick mouth and a warm heart—little girls went nuts for her. I stepped into the room with the dolls in tow. Alex recognized them immediately. As she took them from me she gave Mr.'s crotch a subtle feel to make sure. She gave me a knowing look as she set them on her lap directly in front of Melissa.

6

ALEX GAVE MELISSA ABOUT A MINUTE with the dolls before getting right to it.

"These aren't ordinary dolls," she began. "They're not the kind of dolls you can get at a toy store." Melissa held them with sudden caution as if they might ignite if handled roughly. "Take a look at this one," she said, bringing the woman doll to Melissa's attention, setting aside the man and his jack-in-the-box for later. "Take her shirt off." Melissa looked at Alex with eyebrows up. Alex made the same surprise face back at her.

"All right...," Melissa said, shrugging her shoulders. She pulled the shirt up and the doll boobs popped out—red nipples like siren lights. "Ooo weeeeird...," Melissa crowed. "She's got boobies..."

"Just like you and me. Yours shouldn't look just like that yet, though," Alex said. "When you get older they'll look like that."

"I know that already—I've seen my mom's before."

"Every woman's got them—your mom, the nurses out there, even that lady detective you were talking with before."

"But I've never seen them on a doll before—Barbie dolls have the bumps, but they don't look real like these."

"That's not the only thing this doll has," Alex went on. "Take the pants off."

"No way," Melissa giggled, her face turning red. "She's got her thing down there, too?"

"Take a look and see," Alex said. Melissa peeked down the pants and then looked up, slapping her palm against her forehead. "Go ahead and take the pants off," Alex said again. Melissa tugged the pants off easily. These were pants that were designed to be peeled right off. The doll lay in its glory, naked on her lap, O mouth ready for anything. Melissa dropped the pants beside her, and the three of us stared at the doll's "thing down there" blooming out of the cloth crotch like an exotic saltwater creature.

"This doll is soooo weeeeeird...," Melissa squealed, staring at it. She had that right. It was a weird doll. No expense had been spared on the mouth, breasts, and genitals, but the rest of the body was quite plainly made. The same brown yarn as the man's mustache surrounded the thing's vagina. As with the man, the genitals were large and out of proportion to the rest of the body. The detail was striking—colors and intricate stitching, in sharp contrast to the rest of the body. Another O shape sat in the middle of the trimmings ready at any moment to welcome the star of the show.

"It is quite a doll," Alex said after Melissa's outburst. "I know I don't have to tell you what that is between her legs— you and me both got one of those." Melissa flashed her eyes at me. Yes, I was listening and yes, now I knew. There was no denying it. I knew Melissa had a vagina much like the one sewn onto the thing on her lap.

"This doll's thing is weird looking," Melissa said, bending in for a close look. Then she did something terrible. She gave herself away. Out of the blue, her middle finger went to the top of the vagina and gave it a wiggle. "Wooooooo...," she said, giggling to herself suddenly, and then—"uuh, uuh, uuh"—as she darted the same finger quickly into the hole. In an instant the creepy little doll was validated—it worked. The careful stitching and intricate detail of its crotch had coaxed Melissa into doing exactly what a sexually abused child is supposed to do. She might have learned it on her own, but the quickness of the behavior, almost like a reflex, made that doubtful. The first thing a typical child thinks of when looking at a vagina or a penis is peeing out of it. The gesture was a sudden reminder that we were dealing with a girl for whom there was little difference between a vaginal exam and tying her shoelaces.

After the quick touch with her finger, Melissa moved up to the doll's head and combed its hair with her hand. "This doll doesn't have very good hair," she said after a few strokes. "The eyes are pretty, though." Alex and I watched for any more giveaway behavior as she continued to comb the yellow yarn through her fingers. We lost her for a few seconds while she gazed into the eyes of the doll, as little girls sometimes do. After a few more strokes, Melissa took the doll's arm between her fingers and made it wave to us. She looked up from the doll and our smiles met hers.

"Can I have this doll?" she asked, softly hopeful.

"This doll belongs to the hospital," Alex said. "We'll have to leave it here." A small pout took to her face and looking back down to the doll, she began to stroke the hair again. The silence between us allowed the sounds from the other side of the door to come through. A woman on a stretcher whisked by, followed by a mob of panicked relatives. I watched them as they passed our small wired window. I wondered for a second if puff-face had seen his doctor yet or if he was still covering himself in a heap of rust-colored gauze.

"Don't you have any dolls at home?" Alex asked Melissa.

"Yeah, I have one, but only one though. And it's not as big as this one and it's made out of plastic, too—not cloth like this one."

"You just said this doll is weird," I said.

"I still think it's weird, but the eyes are pretty and the hair is nice now 'cause I combed it. Can I put her clothes on?" Melissa asked, still looking into the doll's face.

"Here, just give her to me," Alex said. "I want you to look at the man doll." Melissa exchanged dolls. Alex left the woman doll naked on the table and sat Mr. Man on the child's lap. Melissa looked down at the doll and then back to us without any of the levity or curiosity she had for the female counterpart.

"What's this one for?" she asked blankly.

"This one is the same as the other doll," Alex answered. "Only this one's a man, of course."

"I don't like this doll as much as the other one," she said. Alex asked her why. Melissa looked at the doll for a moment and then back to us. "I just don't like it as much," she said, with her hands resting on the table at her sides and showing no signs of moving to explore the doll. I picked it off her lap. Melissa was aware that the doll might have the same details under the pants as the other one, and she didn't seem interested in exploring the probability.

"This doll is just as weird as the other one," I said, pulling the shirt off first and then the pants. I held the doll in front of her, feeling just a few degrees shy of a flasher—*Lookie here, little girl—ever seen one of these???* The idea here was that the child might look at the penis and say something along the lines of "Hey that's not what they look like," opening up a discussion about the what they *do* look like and how they work and *whose she's seen.*

"What's that right there?" Alex asked, pointing to the penis.

"I know what that is," Melissa replied.

"What is it?"

"I know."

"Can you tell me?"

"It's his thing," she said.

"Have you ever seen one before?" Alex asked. A pause. Melissa nodded. "You've seen one of these?" Alex asked, pointing again. Melissa's eyes were deep and serious. She nodded again. Alex leaned into the child. "*Whose was it?*" Melissa looked from me to the penis and back to Alex. *Oh pleeease,* I thought. "Whose was it, honey?" Alex asked, giving Melissa's knee a soft shake. She looked back at the doll. "Tell me who it belonged to."

"My brother."

"You saw your little brother's penis?" Alex asked. Melissa nodded. "When did you see your brother's penis?"

"I saw it in the bathroom once," she said. "When he was going to the bathroom I saw it. He didn't know I saw it but I did."

"Did you get a good look at it?" Alex asked.

"Oh yeah," Melissa said with a small smile.

"Did it look like this one here?" Alex asked, pointing again to the doll. Melissa's face got stony as she stared at the doll. "Not really, huh," Alex said. Melissa looked at Alex and then back to the doll. "Your brother's penis didn't look like this one, did it." Melissa shook her head, still looking at the doll. "Your brother's penis was smaller than this one, right?" Melissa looked to Alex. "There wasn't any hair on your brother's, was there?" Melissa shook her head. Alex brought her hand to Melissa's shoulder and spoke softly, gently, "Have you ever seen a penis that looks like *this one* . . . right . . . here, Melissa? . . ." The perpetrator pushed again on the back of her eyes as she turned to stare at the cloth penis. He pushed harder this time, his identity straining to escape the darkness of her pupils. She was thinking about him, I saw it—she held him in her face; the way he looked, how he smelled, the sounds he made, the way he tasted. I felt as though I could just about reach him. He was with us in the room—so vivid in Melissa's mind—practically on the verge of materializing in a poof before us. A name was all we needed, just a first name, the start of a name. What on earth kept him inside? What was the combination that locked him in? Alex pulled in close to Melissa's ear as she tinkered with the dial—"Who did it, baby? . . . ," she whispered. "What's his name? . . . Tell us his name, sweetheart." Melissa looked forward, trancelike, on the doll. He passed in a rumble across her eyes like a face in a Christmas bulb. His laughing mouth. His forehead. A cheek. Hand.

Nostril. A worm twirling in the cocoon of her iris. Alex stroked the child's hair. So incredibly close.

The door burst open behind me.

"ARE YOU USING THIS ROOM??" a portly nurse decked out in light blue scrubs bellowed. I could only stare back at her as the blast of the ER flooded in around us. "THERE'S SOMEONE IN HERE ALREADY," the nurse shouted over her shoulder and then turned back to us. "IT SAYS THIS ROOM IS EMPTY ON THE BOARD," she said. Her right arm held the railing of a stretcher with a rotund woman barely covered by a single sheet. The woman was in pain.

"Could you go to the board and write down that we're in here?" I asked.

"DOES THE CHARGE NURSE KNOW YOU'RE IN HERE?"

"Yes she does," I said.

"WELL IT SHOULD BE ON THE BOARD THEN."

"Okay. Then could you put it on the board?"

"THE CHARGE NURSE PUTS IT ON THE BOARD," she said. "I GOTTA FIND A ROOM FOR THIS WOMAN SO I'M NOT SURE WHAT TO TELL YOU."

"Okay. Well we're busy right now...so...could you step out and close the door please?" She stared at me a moment and then stepped out.

"Does that door have a lock, Marc?" Alex asked. It didn't. Melissa had pushed herself back against the wall. She was looking at the woman doll to her left. I held the man doll at my side, penis dangling at my knee. Alex wiped her face in her hands and let out a long sigh. Melissa picked up the woman and pulled her hair into a ponytail.

"Can I put her clothes back on?" she asked, without looking up.

"Go ahead, baby," Alex said, looking up from her hands. We both watched in silence as Melissa carefully dressed the doll. When she finished she pulled the hair into a ponytail again.

"It would be great if we had a rubber band for a ponytail, 'cause her hair isn't so good. It looks better tied back..." She looked at me. "Do you have a rubber band?" I told her I didn't. Alex pulled her purse onto her lap and fished one out. She gave it to Melissa and the doll's hair was put up a moment later. We watched Melissa fuss with the band to get the hair just right and then move on to the clothes, trying to get them to fit a little better somehow, which was impossible with the fat vagina pulling everything out of line. Suddenly I couldn't hold back any longer. Alex was doing a fine job and I was leaving her to the nitty-gritty but now that I had held the dangling penis doll in front of the girl's face, I felt like I'd breached all sensitivity barriers and there was nothing left to watch out for. I was a man, but so what—I was a person first and a person who was dying to get my hands on a devil.

"Melissa," I said, crouching down to her level at the table. I'd thrown Mr. Doll on a chair in the corner. "Give me the doll," I said, taking it from her and handing it to Alex. "Honey, we're not here in the emergency room to play with dolls. We're here because you're sick. The dolls are here because other kids come here sick just like you are. Sometimes when kids play with these dolls it makes them think about what happened to make them sick. Now before we came to talk with you, we talked with Dr. Shelly—the doctor that examined your bottom. We were called to come here with the detectives because of what Dr. Shelly saw when she checked you out. Melissa, have you ever seen someone that's been beaten up?—someone who's been in a fight, maybe somebody that's lost a fight—have you ever seen a person like that?"

Melissa nodded. She was with me.

"What does a person that's been in a fight look like? What does their face look like?"

"Messed up," she said plainly.

"That's right. Their face looks messed up because it's been hit, and scraped, or maybe pulled on—right? It's got scratches on it and it's got some bruises maybe. There could be something puffed up because it's swelling. The person's face is sore—right? It hurts when they touch it or if they move it—right?"

"Uh-huh," she said, nodding.

"You see a person like that—you see the bruises and the scratches and you know they were in a fight. Right? You can tell 'cause their face is messed up—you can tell they've been in a fight. You say to yourself, 'Hey, that person got in a fight—they got messed up.' Right??"

"Yup, I saw a kid at school messed up once. I didn't see the fight though. I just saw him after, but he looked bad."

"Melissa, you got beat up just like the kid in school. We know you got beat up because of what Dr. Shelly saw when she examined you—just like you knew about the kid in school even though you didn't see the fight. You didn't see the fight but you knew that kid got beat up from the looks of his face. It's the same thing here with you. We know that you've been in a fight because of the scratches and the bruises Dr. Shelly found on you...the scratches and bruises on your vagina."

She started to cry.

"Someone's been messing with you for a long time, but this is the end of it. Tonight it stops. We came here because the person who made those scratches and bruises was wrong to do it. I don't care who it is or what they told you, whoever it is that hurt you is a bad person and we want to get him tonight so he can't ever hurt you or any other little girl again. You're the only person who knows who it is. You're the only person who can help us. The only way we're gonna get him is if you tell us his name."

"But I keep tellin' everybody," she said, her voice flying up and down through tears, "I keep tellin' everybody I don't know how it happened. I already said it and said it and said it—

nobody did nothing to me." Alex moved from her seat, jumping up on the exam table and putting her arm around Melissa's shoulders.

"You're telling us nobody ever touched you?" I pressed on.

"Nobody did, I swear . . . ," she bawled.

"Nobody ever touched your vagina?"

"I keep on saying it to everybody—"

"Then where did the scratches come from down there?"

"I don't know—"

"You have bruises down there—how did you get them?"

"They just got there—I don't know what happened—I just felt them hurting—"

"Something hit you or pressed against you—"

"*Nooooooo*—"

"*—What was it, Melissa*—"

"*—I don't know—they just came there—I didn't look*—I DON'T KNOW WHAT HAPPENED—" She was screaming.

"Hang on, hang on, Marc. Hang on a minute," Alex said, curling the sobbing Melissa into her side. I stood up from my crouch and leaned against the door. Melissa's shoulders bobbed up and down in Alex's arms. Alex and I stared expressionless at each other, listening to Melissa's sobbing. Five minutes later we were exchanging the same expression at the nursing station as I told her about the office manager's instructions to remove Melissa's brother and two sisters. Alex asked if we had to. I said yes. She wanted to know if the office knew that the mother would protect the children at all costs and did we really have to remove if the perp remained on the loose. I said yes and yes. Did I try to talk them out of the removal. Yes. Why did we have to do it, she wanted to know. Dynamics, I told her.

"I don't want to remove these kids, Marc. This is stupid," Alex said. "I can't believe we don't even have a suspect. I mean if this was a single incident, I could see it, maybe. But we can't even get a suspect when the girl's been done as many times as she has?"

"Doesn't make sense," I said.

"Somebody's spending enough time with this girl to get her into the shape she's in and 'nobody knows nothing'—right?"

"We should put more heat on the mother. There's gotta be something she's missing—I don't care if your scores are low on the SAT, you'd have to know *something* about your own daughter being raped repeatedly—you gotta know something about that—suspect something, somebody, anybody—"

"Might be all we need to get the office to leave the sibs out of it."

"Right. All they want is a head, who cares if it belongs to the perp or not."

"I don't have any problem removing kids when they're in trouble," Alex said.

"I'm with you—"

"But this preventative, cover-your-ass kind of thing—"

"Yup."

"*. . . damn . . .*"

"I gotta say one thing, Alex," I said. "There was something about the way Melissa was crying when I started to lean on her—"

"I think I know what you're gonna say—"

"She was crying out of her frustration with my persistence rather than out of some memory of being raped or anything like that. I was the one making her cry—I was the reason, you know? Not visions of the perp, but me. Not the questions themselves, but the fact that I kept asking them. Like if I asked you how your trip to St. Louis was, only you've never been to St. Louis, but I keep asking you just the same. Everyone you know is asking you about St. Louis—how's the food, who do you know there, where'd you stay, what'd you do—and all you can say is that you've never been there and you don't know what the hell everyone's talking about. You know?"

"All right, Marc—"

"—You asking me why I always wear a red shirt and I

don't even own a red shirt—'Sure,' you say, 'You got it on right now'—only the shirt I'm wearing is blue. I don't even have a red shirt. 'Why do you wear that red shirt all the time?' you ask again. A couple hours of that and I might be in tears myself."

"All right, all right already—only you're eight years old and I'm asking about your rear end."

"Exactly."

"Would drive any kid to tears whether or not someone's messing with them."

"And for Melissa, it's like it really didn't happen. To her, it didn't happen. 'Nobody did nothing'—she's never been to St. Louis; she doesn't have a red shirt."

"I've never seen a kid hold out like this."

"Well... *the perp may've threatened to kill the family cat if he's discovered—who knows what kind of dynamics we're up against.*"

"Please, Marc..."

Ms. Pagan watched Alexandra and me talk to each other from where she sat next to puff-face. There was no way she could hear what we were saying. Her two daughters sat on either side of her staring blankly forward. The boy slept. Puff-face gazed forward in a sort of conscious, voluntary coma. Then without any warning, he jumped up suddenly and started screaming and raving like a complete lunatic. Take note, one and all—he was seen by a doctor immediately.

Alex suggested we have another go at the mother. I agreed—just short of a brass-knuckles go at her. Alex told the charge nurse to call hospital security and instruct them to make sure none of the Pagan children were taken or moved from where they were in the ER. Pagan had no idea of the possibility of a removal. She would know in a few moments that it was a certainty unless we could get some kind of lead on a perp. If she couldn't help, we didn't want her to try a sprint on us.

Security came down like water and stood casually at all possible exits. We hauled Pagan to a side hallway and took turns shaking her up. We didn't hold back a thing—empathy and courtesy, thrown out the window. She would hate us, but unless she felt like going home alone—unless her kids were dying for bologna-and-mustard sandwiches—it was for the best. We told her it was impossible to believe she had no suspicions—impossible given the number of times Melissa'd been abused—given the severity of the abuse. We went into the severity of the abuse. We spoke from the chart and we got specific. We tried to get her as crazed to taste the perp as we were. We went on and we went on with her. She cried. We let her use her sleeve. We gave her nothing but questions—pounding her with them. Slamming her with them—stripping her bare and dressing her back up with them. She had to know *something*. You can't live in New York City and not encounter other people. We asked about her building, the school, the other buildings on her block, the men at the grocery store, the men on the corner, friends—friends of the friends—but nothing, nothing—just a pile of "how could it be"s and "there's nobody, I swear"s and "this is impossible"s.

"Where does your daughter Melissa *go*? Where are the places she goes when she's not with you?"

"It's impossible, oh my gosh—"

"What—what's impossible—"

"Melissa, she don't go nowhere, I swear, mister—I never take my eyes off my children—they don't go nowhere, it's too dangerous—"

"But you haven't seen anyone having sex with your daughter, have you?"

"No I swear—"

"So she's being molested *when you're not around*—someone's doing it to her—you don't see it—you're not around. *Where else does she go??"*

"It's impossible—there is no one, I swear—"

"I'm not asking a *who*—I'm asking a *where*. Where else does she g—"

"*She don't go nowhere, I swear*—I BELIEVE MY DAUGHTER—*she say nobody touch her and I believe her. She don't lie to me—how could this happen—*"

"*The doctor examined—*"

"That doctor, she lie. *That's the only thing. I don't believe her. I know my daughter—she don't lie to me. I ask and she say, 'No mommy, no mommy.' How can it be?—I watching all the time. The hospital lie sometimes. It's no good here, I think. The doctor, she's lying—my baby is just sick—that's the only thing. Nothing else, just sick.*"

"That's it for me, Alex," I said. "*I can't anymore...*"

Alex picked up where I tired and the two of them went back and forth for a good while until Alex dulled her ax into a club. Finally, with nothing left to try, nothing else to do, we held out the revolver—both of us, in a flurry and at the same time.

"*If we can't find the person who did this to Melissa—*"

"*If we can't find him—*"

"*If we can't find whoever* raped her—"

"*—just a name even—*"

"If we don't get a name—"

"*We're gonna* take the kids—"

"*We're going to have to take your children away from you—*"

"*—all of them—*"

"We have to take them away until he's found—"

"*—until we find him.*"

It was the truth, but I'm not sure what we thought it'd get us at that point. Maybe it was what would finally pull something out of her—knowing the stakes had just risen. Maybe that's what we thought, but we were wrong. For Lucia Pagan, it was the shout of "Fire" in a crowded theater.

"*Oh my gosh...,*" she said slowly, and then snapped her

mouth shut with her hand as if the world had turned against her. She walked past us as we talked to her, trying to explain further. She walked back to where she had spent the night sitting with her children and gathered them around her. I saw her speak to them but I couldn't hear what she said.

7

As I WRITE THIS, only now am I considering the chance that Melissa really didn't know who her abuser was—the possibility that Melissa might have actually been suffering some kind of trauma-induced amnesia; some survival mechanism where she could click out of herself when her body was being ravaged. In the two moments when I could practically see the perp in her eyes, she was a long throw from amnesia—but for the majority of the night, I think it's entirely possible that Melissa didn't have the slightest idea who her abuser might be. I wish I'd have considered the possibility that evening. Maybe then I wouldn't have gone in to see Melissa the final time. It seemed nothing short of insanity to take three unharmed children, remove them from their mother and their home, split them up from each other, and throw them into foster care—when one word out of Melissa's mouth would set it all right. A name. A name was all I needed and a name was all I went for. But what if she didn't know?

I did go in a final time to see Melissa. With Lucia Pagan clutching her three children's shoulders to her breast, I swooped into Melissa's room and did a five-minute hellfire interrogation. It was bad. Remember when I said that there was no other situation with greater opportunity to do harm in the investigation than with sex abuse? Well, by the time I was finished, Melissa was hysterical and I felt about as low as I could get because after all the shouting, we were still nowhere. The detectives with their swaggering confidence and the office manager with her detached remove were right all along.

The case was over. The perp would be left sleeping peacefully as the Pagans got ripped through the heart. It didn't always go like that, but on this night with this family, that's exactly how it went.

We walked over to Ms. Pagan after discussing the removal and asked to speak with her alone. She refused to leave the children. We tried explaining that her children would be better off if everything went peacefully, but she didn't respond; she avoided all eye contact and reserved her full attention for keeping the kids at her side. Alex went outside to bring #603 around to the ER entrance as I continued my attempts to talk Lucia out of a fireball finale. She spoke over me to her children in Spanish. One of the guards translated for me.

"She's telling them to hold on to her clothing," he said. "She's telling them no matter what—to hold on. She's told them you are going to try to take them away from her forever and that they'll never see her again."

Alex came back quickly. She left #603 with its engine running at the ER entrance. Everybody in the room but the most severely injured and the staff tending them had stopped their activities to watch the fireworks. You know it's bad if the ER staff stops to watch.

Security closed in on the family, and as they did, Lucia screamed something in Spanish and the four of them bolted to the far wall, knocking through trays, stretchers, and equipment. Alex and I followed them quickly along with security and cornered them together where the children crouched down to the floor, rolling themselves into a tight ball around their mother. Additional security personnel came raining in to help. Lucia ran a torrent of commands over the children—all in Spanish. Several of the guards shouted back at her—also in Spanish. I had no idea what was going on at this point but I didn't need to—the task at hand had been reduced to brute physical labor:

load the wood into the truck, watch for splinters, and you'll break your toe if you drop one. The ball grew tighter as we closed in; each of the kids wrapping their fists around whatever clothing on their mother they could find. It was like watching a team get ready for the tug-of-war finals—gripping and re-gripping at their best holds to achieve the ultimate grasp. Their hands and arms worked in a flurry as they coiled themselves to one another in every conceivable fashion.

It took every single guard to split it apart.

Alex and I stepped back as the blue shirts of the guards descended onto the family, almost completely obscuring them from view. Their shoulders jumped and swayed with the awkward quickness of a fight. Lucia moaned terribly over the squeals of her children. Many of the nurses looked away. You know it's bad when the ER staff looks away. One by one the screaming children were birthed from the rumbling pile, each one emerging with a burly-armed escort. Alex and I ran out the door and into #603 to secure them in the backseat as they were brought out by the men. With everyone strapped down, we rolled out like thunder. Two blocks from the hospital might as well have been two hundred miles away—gone from it all and with three crying children terrified and holding each other—tears and sweat pouring from their faces and fistfuls of their own mother's hair wrapped around their fingers.

Alex and I didn't speak a word over the sobbing in the back. The eldest girl stopped crying quickly and began to focus a hate at me through the rearview mirror, the likes of which I hadn't seen since Gruff Robby. She held each arm around her brother and sister, stroking their shoulders and glowing with disgust. I wondered what on earth Lucia might've told her children about us to make them so terrified. I did my best to assure the eldest girl. I asked her to try to calm her younger brother and sister, promising that they'd see their mother soon and that they would be safe with us no matter what she may have told them. Alex tried to help, explaining that we had to protect them from whoever hurt Melissa, and that they would be returned to their mother when he was found.

They cried through it all.

Alex begged them to stop, promising we wouldn't hurt them. She waved me off as I tried to stop her and continued spinning her wheels in the slick mud of their contempt, until finally reaching the same conclusion that I had—that there was no use, that the case was over, and that you don't talk to wood, you haul it. We rounded the ramp off the Willis Avenue Bridge and entered the electric slide of the FDR Drive running down along the East Side—three of the tightest, fastest lanes in the city. Suddenly the youngest boy, through his tears, suggested to his sisters that they pray.

So they did. Hail Marys for most of the way back and then simple cries of "*Please God, oh please God help us,*" their voices wet and shaking with fear. The boy's shirt was soaked with tears. The youngest girl's hair stuck to her cheeks and across her forehead. It looked as though she'd long forgotten what she was crying about but was too weak to break from the rhythm of it all. I glanced over at Alex. She was crying too. She tried to hide the tears at first, but then gave in to them, soaking through several handfuls of tissue. I felt close to breaking myself; listening to the tearful prayers and knowing that I was the evil they were pleading deliverance from. By the time we got to the front steps of ECS, my head was throbbing like a bastard.

We opened the back doors of the car and reached in to help the children out. They jumped back from our extended arms as if from flaming hooks. We grabbed on to their arms to keep them from running into the street. They were taken from us as soon as we stepped inside by the nursery staff at the command of our dear Ms. Attacking-Animal-Purse. Alex rushed to the bathroom for what I guessed would be a good splash of water and a brisk makeover. I dragged to the back of the office and let my head fall to an empty desk.

Alex walked out of the bathroom after a bit and went to a desk to begin the case write-up. I asked her if she was all right. She said she was fine—wanted to write everything down and get the hell out of the office, she said. Did she need help with the write-up, I asked, did she need anything? I could get her a coffee or a soda at the deli...No thanks, she said. I told her it was late. She said she knew that already. I put my hand on her shoulder. Her eyes filled with tears. She told me not to get her crying again—that she was seeing a man tonight and was enough of a wreck already. I told her I felt terrible. We did what we had to do, she said. That was true. This job is too hard sometimes, I said. Alex agreed. I told her I was going home. See you tomorrow, she said.

"You think they're ever gonna find the person that hurt Melissa?" I asked as I rose to leave.

"If she ever says who it was," Alex said. "I'm pretty sure she's the only one who knows."

"You think she'll tell someone?"

"I wonder," she said, gazing at the wall behind me. Her eyes welled with tears again. "...maybe not, I think," she said, and then snapped her eyes to mine. "We did what we had to do, bro, now stop it. How you been working here this long thinking like that? Put it down already—the case is over, go home."

"You're right, Alex."

"The sun *will* rise on a new day," she said, wiping the bottom of her eyes quickly. "Don't you make me have to put my face back together," she said. "This beautiful face don't come easy—"

"I know that's not true, Alex," I said. "I don't believe you've had a bad-looking day in your life."

"Don't think you can make me cry and then try to kiss up—it ain't like that so don't even try it—I got plenty of men to do that one on me. Go home, brother." She leaned in and gave me a kiss—not a typical move on her part but about the nicest thing that could've ever happened. It was just what I needed before leaving.

I walked to the time clock and threw my card at the slot. The machine took a bite and left its blue-and-red imprint. I glanced at the mark before returning the card to its place on the wall with the others. As I did so, I noticed a large hand-written sign posted just above the cards in a place that made it hard to miss. The word "ATTENTION" was written in red Magic Marker and underlined three times. The notice read:

OUR BELOVED SAL HAS BEEN CHARGED WITH THE SEX-UAL ABUSE OF HIS GIRLFRIEND'S DAUGHTER AND IS IN NEED OF FUNDS $$$ FOR THE LEGAL BATTLE AHEAD OF HIM—ANY AMOUNT WILL BE APPRECIATED—LEAVE DO-NATIONS IN CAN MARKED "SAL" BELOW, OR YOU CAN GIVE YOUR MONEY DIRECTLY TO ONE OF US AND WE WILL MAKE SURE HE GETS IT—C'MON Y'ALL, DON'T HOLD OUT ON ONE OF OUR OWN—GIVE WHAT YOU CAN—HE WOULD DO THE SAME FOR YOU!!!

Jesse lumbered over as I was reading the sign. When I finished, he picked up the can with a little smile and gave it a jingle in my direction.

"Have you given your share today?" he asked, his voice high and silly to cover his embarrassment at the solicitation. "Have you given at the office?" I didn't know what to say. "C'mon, Money," Jesse said, a little more serious. "Don't hold out on the Sal."

"Did he do it?" I asked. Jesse's face went slack.

"What do you mean—did he do it?"

"I mean—did he do it? Did he hurt that woman's little girl—did he do it?" Jesse stared back at me cold.

"That's low, Money," he said finally. "That's a low blow, brother." He put the can back where it sat beneath the sign. "Ain't about—did he do it, Money," he said, walking back to his desk. "It's about—he'd do it for you, my man. He'd do it for you."

On the train ride home I thought about Melissa lying on a stretcher in the ER with an IV in her arm waiting for a room to open up on the floor above. I thought about the perpetrator lying cozy in his bed and secure behind her eyes. I shuddered as I thought of an eight-year-old with the bottom of a junkie/hooker—who allows a vaginal exam like someone tying the laces of her shoes—

Life ain't fair, baby. It's hard and it just ain't too fair sometimes.

—and I thought about Sal.

I thought about some of the first times out with him—when he was training me. I remembered him pointing out a little girl once, walking just ahead of us as we went down the street. She might have been about eight herself—dressed in a short black shirt with her belly showing and black tights cut off at the ankles with new high-top sneakers.

"It's wrong for that girl's mother to dress her in an outfit like that," Sal said, pointing to the girl. *"People don't realize there's a lot of perverts around. They don't realize the danger—what an outfit like that will do to some guys."*

I remember looking at the girl and thinking she looked like any other kid in the world. At the time I thought the comment was strange and the way it came out of the blue, the way he stared at the girl and the look in his eyes, all of it was a little beyond me on my first week at the job, so I let it ride and soon forgot about it—or so I thought. The news of Sal's troubles made me think again about the look on his face as the girl, holding her mother's hand, skipped merrily ahead of us. Thinking back on it with the perspective of three years on the job, I saw Sal's face again as he looked at her. I saw the concern that was there that night, but I saw something else, something that passed way over my head at the time. There might have been hunger in his gaze, sitting right next to his concern for the girl's safety and his disgust at a man who might hurt her. Sal knew the mind of a perpetrator, sometimes it takes one to know one. Just as the train stopped at 110th Street, I concluded that it might really be true—Sal might've done it. And if it were true, some little girl sits with his image locked behind her eyes—a new member in a sisterhood of girls with the face of a perpetrator peeping out from the dark edges of their pupils, and a mouth that betrays them with quiet utterances of nobody, nothing.

The apartment was quiet when I walked in. Everyone sleeping. I dropped down to my underwear right at the bedroom door and stepped inside, quietly maneuvering around James in the dimness. It never got dark in that room—the streetlights and the neon cross from a church across the street. I didn't notice until I was lying on my back, and then, only after rubbing my face and jockeying my head around on the pillow to find The Spot—the wall with piranha man was peppered with holes ranging from two to five inches in diameter. Holes busted right through the plaster. I would find out later that morning around coffee and hot cheese blintzes at the Hungarian Cafe that it was because of the rats, or because of the hammer, really—because of the noise of the chewing and the scraping and the crawling, because of the crazies that take over after a certain point, but mostly because of the hammer—because it was there and they were there and James had had enough and because it probably felt amazing to bash the living shit out of the walls and send the dirty devils running. I would hear all about it later on, but now there were only the holes and my drowning piranha man.

Headless.

Gobbled mindlessly by razor-sharp jaws. Beheaded—bashed in the face with a hammer while struggling for a last breath—the holes in the wall pretty much obliterating everything above the neck. A sloppy decapitation of a drowning man. And the fish don't seem to care either way—they gnash on, head or no head.

A good wind comes in through the crack in the window, setting the curtain to a brisk flap. The man's body fights headlessly on, slapping fist to jaw-teeth and scissor-kicking to beat the devil. Wind blows again, cold through my hair this time as it thrashes the water to a shimmering boil. As I contemplate the headless man, I'm suddenly grateful for my own, silly as that seems. The wind blows hard again and it's too cold outside for that. I think about closing the window but feel too comfortable to get up. The day fades on the horizon like the man pulled out to sea. I fall asleep with my hand at my neck.

7

The Slam

This isn't a dance. This is
a fight. You get bloody in
a fight—you lose rounds.

—Andrew Vachss
November 13, 1995,
New York City

IT'S SO HARD TO DETECT your own deterioration. Like falling asleep at the wheel of a car—it's nearly impossible to pinpoint the moment it happens. We never see the gates of sleep opening before us even though we hear them slam shut with a flash of the eyes and a sudden jerk of the head. Waking up is sleep's only confirmation—the only proof of purchase. The slam is its affidavit—the thing that tells us where we've been and what we've been up to. If you don't wake up, you weren't sleeping. The slam is everything. If you don't hear it, the show's over.

So it goes when we deteriorate as apathy creeps in and we begin to fall apart. I thought I was still doing a good job. I acknowledged it was tough to keep up the quality control in the face of the endless grind, but I thought I was doing well all the same. I'm not sure when, but somewhere along the line I'd stopped doing a good job. I'd fallen asleep. So, how long do things stay nice and cozy when you're asleep at the wheel? A lesson in physics comes quickly and turns everything upside down. You wake to the slam and the noise of ripping metal, realizing what's happened about a half second before it doesn't really matter. It happened to me. I don't know how I got there, but I can tell you how I got out. The fall into sleep is slippery; it's the waking up I remember. The fall is a haze, but the slam is still vivid.

I was feeling low in my fourth year at ECS but things were tough all over. The reports flew in like they always did—they flew in like they did yesterday and the day before yesterday— like they would tomorrow and the day after tomorrow. Multiply these four, from a typical night, by a couple hundred, and you begin to see what I'm talking about—

Called in by a relative on her five-year-old nephew:

> Child has bruises on both eyes, nose bridge, legs and head. Child has never been free of marks. Mother stated that child fell out of bed. The next day she said that child ran into the couch. When child was asked, child became nervous and refused to talk.

An anonymous caller:

> Mother is on crack. Her eight-month-old is not fed adequately, he receives one bottle a day. He is very weak and hardly moves. Mother takes infant out in bad weather when she buys/uses drugs, with no shoes, hat, or other appropriate clothing. He frequently falls or is dropped by her out of carelessness. Mother rarely changes child's diaper and he is very raw from this. Child is dirty.

Sex abuse report from Brooklyn Hospital:

> On numerous occasions Mother's boyfriend sexually abused her son. Mother's boyfriend put his penis in the child's mouth and rectum. Boyfriend also put the boy's penis in his mouth. Boyfriend gave the child money for these acts. Mother is now fearful of boyfriend. He is known to be violent. She and her son currently hiding out at a friend's home.

From the 103rd Precinct Detectives Unit:

> FATALITY FATALITY   Child was born today. Mother gave birth while on the toilet bowl. Child ended up in the bowl. It is unknown if child fell, was dropped, or was placed in the bowl. Father proceeded to flush the toilet with the child in it. Child died. Child's death is suspicious.

My last year at ECS began like the three previous—with a hot-down-summer-in-the-city into a brisk beautiful fall swirl of golden leaves and McDonald's bags. New people came in and old veterans were retired. People were promoted, transferred in, and transferred out. No one was fired. The Union. Giles, the phone-sex junkie, was ferreted off to one of the field offices in Brooklyn where he would become someone else's problem. Sal, our own alleged child sex offender, was cleared of all charges. He was rehired by the city but not for ECS. He came by several times to thank everyone for the generous donations gathered on his behalf. Our dear Yvette—the office hard body in the short skirt—was hired by Parole. She came back to visit several times during my fourth year, in the same sexy outfits but accessorized with a bulletproof vest, which she wore like a corset, and a silver gun the size of her head. "You'd like Parole, Marc," she told me on her first visit after she was hired. "It's easier than this place. I could get you a job in my office if you want." Since parole officers were issued guns, I suggested, they might be in the position someday to shoot somebody's head off, and I was trying to minimize that sort of thing in my life. "They pay a lot more than this place," she said. "It's up to you, though—if you change your mind..."

In my fourth year at ECS, I turned down my second offer for a promotion and watched as people I trained became my supervisors. My thinking was that supervisors stay in the office and get fat on egg rolls. I wanted to stay in the field where the real battles were being lost and won. William Samuels was on a slow fade but was hanging in there. He slowly became less animated, in that fourth year, beginning an incremental withdrawal into himself. His hair started to sit flat against his skull. He wore the same clothes several days in a row. He got pretty haggard looking in the final weeks at the job. I remember him telling me how his son had developed a problem that required a steady flow of cash. He'd granted the boy numerous loans, but eventually the well ran dry. When it came to family, Willie was heavy into turn the other cheek, and in this case, he'd just kept turning until his head twisted off. Willie had watched other friends and family do the same old dance until the music stopped and they all fell down. Watching his son jump to the same moves was just a little more than a little too much. It began to take its toll. There were some in the office who said Will was doing a dance himself in the final days, but I can't say I know anything about that for sure. No one heard from him after he was gone except for a few of his friends on the late crew who said they'd met him after their shift on several occasions to lend him hundred-dollar bills. I don't know the official reason why William eventually resigned. I remember him going in for numerous meetings with agency bosses toward the end. The meetings were long and he used to look pretty worked over by the time he walked out. I imagine they were going back and forth about the double thunk-whump, among other things. He eventually caved in under the pressure and the magic he spun with broken children was cast no longer. He kept himself straight on the job, and his heart was in the right place. He cared about kids. He did right by every child he came in contact with, which is more than I can say for many people in the office. Several months after he'd left, I saw him looking very rough at three in the morning while I was on a field visit in Harlem. I crossed the street to avoid him.

Two of my favorite people left the job in my final year—first, Laura, my iced-coffee fiend, and then Dana, my sassy lesbian. The Wisconsinites in the office had been slowly trickling away for the past few years, and Laura was the last.

We were sent to the field together on her final night, going against all superstition—*how sad, killed on her last night of work* was the tune flying through her head, I'm sure. It was an anonymous report about a mother with her infant daughter in a crack house on 118th Street in Harlem. We cruised up to the address with Laura very nervous and anxious to be rid of the remaining hours of her last shift. The building where the infant was supposed to be was abandoned. By that, I mean every window on every floor was blown out, there were no lights inside, and the front doors were covered with sheet metal. We drove slowly past the building and did a U-turn at the end of the block to eye it up a bit and discuss our options. Laura was going mad. On her last night we would be going into what, to this day, was the worst building I'd ever been to. We decided instantly that if there was an infant in the building, we would remove without question. Trouble was, the report didn't say where in the building the child was supposed to be. As we sat there in the car discussing the problems, groups of men were going in and out of the building through a crack in the front where the sheet metal was ripped away from the door. The building, which looked dead on the outside, bustled with the activity of the local Kwik-Trip. The men were in groups of four to six. More of them went in than came out. Each group had several pit bulls in tow. No place for an infant. No place for a Marine, while you're at it. I left Laura in the car and ran out to call 911 for police escort. I told the operator that we had information there was an infant in the building but that we didn't know where in the building that might be and since we'd seen seventeen or twenty men as well as at least eight pit bulls slipping through the crack of sheet metal in the front door, one squad car with two cops would not be sufficient. When I got back to the car, Laura quickly asked if I'd requested more than two cops. I told her I had. After five minutes of waiting, one car with two cops pulled up to the front of the building. In that five minutes at least seven more guys went inside. Eleven-thirty at night.

"I'm sorry guys, this isn't gonna work," I said to the cops through the passenger-side window. "I requested more than two cops."

"We'll call more guys if we need 'em," the one closest to me chirped. He couldn't have been over twenty-five.

"We've been watching from our car on the corner over there," I said. "There's gotta be over twenty guys who walked in since we got here. I mean, look at this building—no offense, guys, but really, we can't go in there with just two of you."

"Hey—we know that. That's why they sent us. You got two right here," he said with a smile, indicating his partner. "And I'm good for three—so you got five cops on this job." I held firm, keeping my promise to Laura—*Marc, we can't go into that building with only two cops on my last night—please!!!* I told the cops if they couldn't get more guys, then we'd just go back to the office and have them send out someone else.

"There is supposed to be a baby in there," I said as a final appeal. "If it's true, it would be best to go in right now. If there's a baby in this place, we should get it out as quick as possible." The cops agreed and so we struck up a compromise.

"If we go in there, just the two of us," the cop began, "if

we go in there and secure the area—make sure it's safe—will you two come in?"

"You guys go in first?"

"Right, and then my partner steps out and tells you to come in if we got it secure—"

"What's the shortage—where the hell are all the cops tonight?" I interrupted.

"Guy—they're all over this place if I make a peep in this radio, all right? So let's just go in and get this baby."

I cleared the plan with Laura, who was waiting in the car with eyes as big as dishes. "They promised not to call us in if it's not safe," I said. Did I think we could trust them, she wanted to know. I told her I guessed we had to. "The poor baby, if it's in there," she said. I agreed. Laura began to fill out the 701-b removal form.

"If they tell us to come in and there's a baby in there," she said, "we just take it and run, okay?"

"Sounds good," I said.

"*This building*—right?"

"No place for a baby."

"My last night, can you believe it?"

I drove the car to the front of the building next to the squad car and told the guys it was a go. They raced up to the front, pulled back the sheet metal and slipped inside. Just before going in, the cop looked back and shouted to us, "We find a baby in here, you guys'll come in, right? I tell you it's okay and you come in?" I gave him a thumbs-up. Now the whole block knew what we were up to. Laura crouched into a ball on the floor of the car saying something about the certainty of being shot at in a situation like this—especially on the final night on the job. I tried to assure her by saying there was no way there was a baby in there—green fields on the moon before a baby in there, I said—we'd be going home any minute. Laura agreed, but as she did so, one of the cops came flying out of the crack in the door and waved us in. Laura cursed as we left the car and walked to the building—the both of us white-faced and sick to our stomachs with fear. I asked the cop if they found a baby, and he nodded his head quickly yes. He went back in first and held the metal open for Laura and me. Laura made some comment about not believing she was doing this. I agreed.

The inside of the building was the most depraved scene you could imagine—almost pitch dark, lit every seven to ten feet by a candle on the floor. The ceiling had caved in at several points down what used to be a hallway. The cop pointed out the clear path as he hopped quickly through collapsed drywall and sagging metal supports. We jumped and ducked like beetles through an old skeleton on the verge of collapse, Laura ahead of me chanting, "Oh God, oh God," more prayer than curse. We rounded a corner and quickly found ourselves in a large candlelit room—the center of activity. The place was lined with men—all standing, all looking very unhappy, all with their hands out in front of them. The other cop stood at the entrance with his gun drawn and pointing at the floor. A thick haze of cocaine smoke hovered at our chests. A low table in the middle of the room overflowed with works—needles, lighters, bent spoons, glass pipes, rubber tubing. A stroller with a baby was in the far corner.

"HEY," one of the men shouted the instant we walked in. My stomach lurched. *"What the fuck are these two for?"*—he started stepping toward us—"Get the fuck out of here—"

"Shut the fuck up—," the cop said, raising his gun to the man. *"Back against the wall—hands out. Hands out in front of you.* NOW. *Don't anybody fuckin' move."*

"C'mon, c'mon—," the other cop said, looking at me. The place was about to blow.

"Whose baby is that over there?" I yelled, barely catching my breath. A horribly thin woman stepped forward.

"Dhat'z ma baby so ooo d'fuck you thingk—"

"This is for you," I said, cutting her off and handing her the 701-b. *"Go ahead, Laura—go ahead!"* Laura on autopilot stepped in and scooped the baby out of the stroller, blankets and all. The shock of that gave us about three seconds to sprint out of the room before the eruption. We bumped and weaved as fast as we could, through intermittent candlelight and broken-down walls, dodging holes in the floor and snares of old electrical cords. Laura was first. I followed just behind her with one of the cops covering our backs while his partner did his best to hold the mob at bay. We flew out of the front of the building and toward our car.

Laura dropped the child's blanket as we raced down the steps. I ran over the blanket, Laura turned back to get it. We crashed into each other. For some reason, I took the baby, Laura grabbed the blanket, the cop yelled, "Hurry up, God-damn it!" or something or other. I ran ahead to the car, dove into the backseat with the child in my arms, and Laura poured into the front. She squealed the tires and ran two red lights on our getaway.

"The cops didn't get our names," I said as we entered the FDR South.

"I'll call them back at the office," Laura said. She looked like a ghost.

"You okay to drive?" I asked.

"I'm okay," she said. "How's the baby?"

"Baby's okay," I said. "Hey, Laura"—she looked at me through the rearview mirror—"You made it—*you made it...*" Her eyes wrinkled into a small smile and she let out a long breath of wind. "Slow down a bit," I said. "We're okay now. It's over, we made it." She heaved the car to the right lane and slowed down to seventy. The FDR is one quick river of steel. Laura leaned over, hit the radio, and left the volume up. The baby began to squirm in my arms so I offered my pinkie and she took to sucking my nail off. The East Side sky-line whizzed by the window at my right. Led Zeppelin screamed through the car. The little girl sucked at my hand the entire way back. Her eyes eventually closed, but she never stopped sucking.

Laura's last night.

We'd started at the same time, and she had really become my best friend at ECS. She didn't know what she was leaving to do—had a few ideas, but mostly wanted to take her life out of housing projects, welfare hotels, and abandoned buildings, I suspect. Though I never found out her exact reason for leaving—after that last night, it seemed like a stupid question. Like Laura, I felt the odd mixture of weariness and blood-red fear that came with doing the job night after night, but it wasn't yet time for me to go. I would go, I knew that, because, like Laura, I knew something better. I knew a life without the tears and screaming that currently filled my weeks. I had lived in an easier place just as real as the one I was currently in. Watching Laura go that night, I was overcome with the power we had to remove ourselves forever from the world we'd come to know so well. At the drop of a time card she would never again step foot in the grim neighborhoods and tragic homes so many were desperately trying to escape. The choice to never go back was so easy for us while at the same time being so entirely out of reach for the families we visited.

Dana was different. Where Laura switched from television to radio, Dana merely fidgeted with the dial. She became an arbitration specialist for the troubled New York City public schools. Her job, as I understood it, was to develop and implement a program to get rival gangs to work through their difficulties without shooting each other's faces off. Dana was the kind of person who liked to change things up as soon as they became predictable. She, too, had turned down promotions at ECS that would've taken her out of the field and left her safely holed up with an egg roll in the office. She, too, believed that the real job was in the streets and there was no way and no amount of money that could keep her from being where things really mattered. Both Laura and Dana kept in touch after they were gone, and the office was still filled with friendly faces and happy hellos, but it didn't matter. After they left I was as good as alone.

One of the better supervisors retired in my fourth year. She was only fifty or so, but I remember her saying something about needing the peaceful weekends more than the money. I sat on a bar stool with her after one of her last nights of work to have a few too many beers. She told me about how she started working for the city "just to give it a try" and how that was some twenty years ago—how it all passed by in a blink and how I'd better make sure I'm pursuing what I really want in life rather than spending my best years giving something a try. She stopped just short of the whatever-you-do-don't-end-up-like-me speech, talking about the things she might've done had she not become addicted to a steady paycheck—about her plans for the world. Big plans. Never realized. She talked about it all and the sharp consonants of the words put spit on my face. It's the same thing all over—go to a bar and find someone who's drunk. Not totally drunk. Loose. Ask them to tell you about something they started twenty years ago. When they tell you about it, see if the words don't leave spit on your face.

I wiped my cheek with my sleeve when she wouldn't notice. She went on and on, and I tried to make her feel better. Beer is like that—both of us hanging our heads, shaking them back and forth, talking about how sad it all is, and having a good time all the same.

She asked to be spared from the inevitable retirement party but a few stubborn folks got together to throw one anyway. I wasn't there but I saw the remains of it around her desk the next day and something about it hit me like a cold shower. After twenty years on the job, you get a few yellow ribbons tacked to your bulletin board, a small plant with a flower stuck in the dirt, some crumbs on the floor, and a silver helium "BEST WISHES!" balloon that loses its life as fast as the memory that you were ever there. I moved away quickly but couldn't get my mind to stop before it got through a few rounds of the bony fingers song. I felt like I was getting old faster than that helium balloon. I knew that I was working my tail to dust every night for more than a bulletin board to call my own—that there was more to rescuing children in peril than an old rose jammed at the base of a philodendron, but I was losing sight of it.

2

IT WAS LIKE ANY OTHER NIGHT. I was paired up with Kai for a visit to four cases in the Bronx—two for me and two for her. Kai was a petite Asian woman in her early thirties whose parents had immigrated to America when she was an infant. She was fluent in her native tongue, but because she grew up in a Queens housing project, the rhythm of her English was New York street, through and through. She could rap with the boys in the back of the office like the best of them, and she often did. Kai and I didn't have much contact with each other when she began, but now that Laura and Dana were gone, we did everything we could to go out on field visits together, and the supervisors generally tried to accommodate us. We were among the senior caseworkers of the office—me going on four years and Kai with two. The average caseworker didn't usually have more than two years on them before quitting or being promoted. Practically every caseworker was a rookie.

We handled my cases first and then went to one of Kai's before stopping to get a bite to eat. Kai had introduced this white boy to Asian cooking about a year earlier when she felt as though I'd earned the honor of being taken to her tucked-away sacred places. I was the only Caucasian for miles as we'd step into the restaurants, some of them nothing more than holes-in-the-wall. Kai was always in first. She'd fill two trays with food and I'd haul them to a table. We'd sit and eat, me asking, "What's this?" and "What's this?" every other bite. Kai would tell me to shut up and eat, that she didn't wanna hear from me unless I didn't like it. I always liked it. This was good food—so good it was practically ridiculous.

We guzzled it all down without much chitchat and headed back to the car to find the last case. It had gotten late. Kai had saved it for last because it was the only one that might cause some problems. The office managers would kill you if you handled the rough cases first because if they ended up taking all night, your easier cases would be left undone and have to be reassigned to the next shift. I picked up the case on the seat between us. I hadn't even looked at it yet.

> Mother lives alone with her five children—aged 2 yrs to 7 yrs. There is no furniture in the home. Children sleep on the floor and are frequently seen "running wild" in the hallways. The building is very run-down and there are drug dealers on every floor. The children are often seen naked and unsupervised. Unknown if there is food in the home now. Mother just had a baby and the infant appears to be thin and weak.

I set the case back on the seat between us without saying anything to Kai. She knew what I was thinking; I knew what she was thinking. There was nothing to say. We would find what we would find and do what we would do. We'd embarked on so many perilous evenings together, been in so many horrible buildings—whole blocks where it felt like a joke to check on the safety of one child or one family when the whole area wasn't safe for anybody, where the only decent thing to do would be to remove every human in sight, burn it all to the ground, and start over. We both knew the feelings rushing through each other's veins when reading a case like the one on the seat between us, but there was just nothing left to say that hadn't already been said.

As we drew nearer to the address, the landscape grew increasingly remote and desolate. Blocks were still defined by their dark cluster of buildings, but every other one was a shattered vacant hull: windows blown out, entrances boarded up, rooftops decorated with scrolling razor wire. I dug my head into my trusty map of the city, all tattered and torn, with ink marks peppering years of previous visits. Kai drove carefully to my calls of left and right as we snaked deeper into a landscape all but forgotten by the world. The farther we drove, the worse it became. Another right and several more lefts, and whole blocks were decimated—trundled flat somehow and left open for rot and decay. Entire buildings had been crunched up and hauled away, leaving debris-filled craters surrounded with chain link. No businesses in sight—no deli, no supermarket, gas station, church, restaurant, travel agent, bank, no social club, not even a pawn shop. And no people, not on the streets, anyway. Good sense and a keen eye for survival kept everyone locked six and seven times behind the sturdiest thing in their lives—the door; metal, usually—three inches thick, without exception. And heavy, by God. Heavy as a mausoleum wall. Heavy as the hearts it locked inside. Take a drive up there if you don't believe it. Nothing but orange-lit empty streets and an occasional low-ride jammed to the rims with hooded homeys on the prowl for an unsuspecting skull to crack.

Kai and I didn't speak an unnecessary word. The space between us was as quiet as the streets ahead save for an occasional "left here" and "now another left" from me. I don't have to tell you we were scared—as many times as we'd been in bad waters and we were still scared. This was a place where the dark cracks between abandoned buildings hid junkies with nothing to lose except another minute without a high, desperate enough to slit your throat in half for the five dollars in your pocket. In the quiet air of the car I would actually daydream about a bullet piercing my side, the feeling of it rushing through my spleen and liver, slowing in my chest and shattering my lungs. I imagine a few wet gurgles of breath as I drown on my own blood while some smelly addict ravages my pockets with dirty fingers and runs off with a few loose bills. I'm gazing up into the orange spray of the streetlamp above me. It's the last thing I see and as it fades I can only think, *Damn it...* Then I'm back in the car suddenly, with Kai asking if she should go left, right, or straight. "Straight," I say, "two more blocks," but all I'm thinking is *Hope to God I got a few of my lucky stars out.*

3

WE ROUNDED THE LAST CORNER on spook path through desolation valley to find a behemoth of a building—our building. Pitch black against the pink haze of the sky, it was a real monster. Not a tall thing, but fat; a twin building, two identical halves connected at the center by the front door and a common elevator. Fencing and razor wire surrounded a massive hole that was once the neighbor to the left of it. The building on the right was abandoned; front doors and every ground-floor window bricked down and shut up tight. Several old cars, smashed to bits and stripped of everything remotely valuable, lurched sideways onto the sidewalks down the block. Not a soul in sight.

I stopped the car directly in front of the large dark thing and we stared at it silently before Kai let out a long breath. I knew what she was thinking, and she knew I was thinking the same thing—we should round up a couple cops for this one; we should wear a few of the boys in blue around our throats. Let their guns precede us and the fuzz of their radios scare off predatory denizens like cat claws scritching against wood floors that keep the mice at bay. Getting police was the thing to do, but the office had recently made that a difficult option. The bosses had just handed down a policy that denied us the con-

venience of dialing 911 at the corner phone. If we wanted a
police escort (and we should "always take police if any safety
issues arise"—thanks so much for caring), we were to go to
the local precinct and make our request to the desk sergeant,
who would assign personnel at his discretion. The process
could take several hours and shoot the shift straight into overtime. Kai and I were already riding on the cusp of a late night
so we decided, with our hearts in our throats, to go this one
alone.

Most of the lights in the building were dark. The walk up
to the front of the building was lined with huge trees that had
long outgrown their sidewalks. Gnarled trunks pulled themselves roughly from the cement that held their younger trunks.
Their roots heaved the slabs terribly askew—the slow-motion
battle, after decades of opposing forces, finally showing a win-
ner. Kai made her way up the walk. I'd fallen behind, looking
up to the dim windows through dark hailing limbs. The building seemed to be curling itself around us. Kai and I were still
speaking on a need-only basis and were both scared as hell to
be walking into the only standing structure on one of the most
chewed-up-and-spit-out pieces of real estate in the city. Kai got
to the door, heaved it open, and stood waiting for me to step
inside first. My turn. I did and she followed straight behind.

The lobby was huge—opulent almost—an instant reminder
of a thriving area and better days—men and women in fine
clothing sitting on marble benches running along the perimeter
of the entrance that were now only broken mementos of how
good it used to be. Ornate walls of curling wood and plaster,
once the pride of the building's tenants and a reflection of their
wealth and good taste, were now broken and peeling, covered
with graffiti's vigorous dark lines. The entire space was lit with
two small lightbulbs high and away at either corner. In the
center of the ceiling a large fixture hung directly above us,
stripped of the cascade of lights and crystal it must have certainly once held. Just ahead of us was the elevator. Someone

had spray-painted a crude sign on a piece of plywood hanging directly above the doors: WARNING ELEVATOR STOPS ON ALL FLOORS. Kai pressed the call and we waited for what seemed like forever while the cables and pulleys behind the doors moaned and popped with unnerving persistence. We couldn't help backing up a little when they finally wheeled open like the tired jaws of a hungry old crocodile. Inside, a fan on the ceiling of the car had one of its fins bent into the grill and with the doors fully open, the scraping sound that filled the lobby was unbearable. The far right corner was soaked with urine. The smell about knocked me flat. Kai and I decided against using it and let the doors slowly close without stepping inside.

Wide staircases led up from either side of the lobby. They were dark. We had to take the one to our right. Noises were coming from that one, from one of the floors above. We needed the eighth floor. Side by side, we took the first couple of steps up and paused to listen. The noise was talking—men's voices. *Could be nothing,* I thought. *Then again, could be anything, could be* everything. This seemed a perfect place for the pierce of a bullet, a perfect place to drown on your own blood. Don't think I wasn't practically feeling it all happen as I stood there. Jesse and Yvette had an Uzi pointed at them in a stairwell just like the one we were standing in about a year ago. They threw up their arms and screamed that they were only there to check on children. The Uzi lowered to let them pass, and they used a different exit on their way out.

I shook my head. Kai snickered but she didn't think anything was funny. She reached into her pocket, took out a switchblade, and snapped it open. It was the dagger kind; the long thin blade that's sharp on both sides. Jimmy Dean. She held the knife in her right hand and wrapped the report and some other papers around the blade to keep it hidden. I took mine out but left it closed, and we headed up, making as much noise as we could. Clomping our feet on the stairs, kicking loose cans across the floor, Kai sang and I dragged the metal grip of my knife on the railings. The last thing you wanted to do was surprise a dealer in the middle of a transaction. Each flight of stairs put us straight on the floor. We had to walk down the hall and past several apartments to get to the next flight. By the time we reached the third floor, the voices were gone. We did all eight and I'm still here to talk about it.

This was a building on its way out. On the eighth floor, every second apartment was abandoned and chained shut—two sloppy holes jackhammered straight through the door and the wall just above the knob with a fat chain snaked several times through them and padlocked loosely. Abandonment to a building is like a cancer and this one was going down. The hallway was dim. They were all dim, but the one on the eighth floor seemed especially so because we had to walk all the way down it. Kai muttered something about why did the damn apartment have to be at the end of the hall. Her switchblade was still open when we got to the door and she kept it wrapped in the report as she knocked. I had mine back in my pocket.

"*Who is it?*" The voice came quick, a woman's. Very hostile.

"It's Child Welfare," Kai returned. "Hello?..." Silence. "Could we speak with you please?..." Kai knocked again, "Hello?..."

"It's Child Welfare?" the voice came from the other side.

"That's right. We need to come in and speak with you..." About seven *click-clinks* went off around the perimeter of the door. A woman pulled it back and it banged against two chains that held it at a three-inch crack. She peered at Kai, who tried to assure her we were the real thing. The woman held a kitchen knife behind her back. She didn't know I could see it. The two of them spoke politely to each other with knives hidden at the ready. The knives were defensive. There were no killers here; the women on either side of the door were afraid and for good reason. Several moments later the door was open. The woman hopped quickly into the kitchen. Putting away the knife. Kai unwrapped hers and folded it away before the woman returned, and we stepped inside.

"I apologize about all that at the door," the woman said, pulling it shut behind us. "This building, you know. It's pretty bad."

"We noticed," Kai said.

"We never leave the apartment after nine."

"That's probably a good idea," I said. A mouse ran along the floor by the wall and behind Kai, who let out a shriek and grabbed me like she'd fall out of a tree house. Five children came racing around the corner from the next room. Some had shirts or socks on, but many wore bare bottoms. They were wild in the truest sense of the word, packlike, all running and falling and laughing together. Children pack if left to themselves. I'd seen it before. Several of them barreled up to me, took ahold of my arms and began pulling. One grabbed Kai's clipboard right out of her hand and dropped it as he ran back to the others. The woman made no effort to control them. There was a squeak from the other room and she quickly excused herself to check on the infant. While she was gone, the children had their way with us. Kai and I lost each other for a moment, engulfed in a downpour of tiny fingers pulling at every part of us. We hadn't been in the apartment thirty seconds and we were practically caring for the woman's children—pulling them out of each other's hair, keeping the big ones from falling on the little ones, and trying all the while to keep our things from being taken and thrown out the window. Several mice ran by our feet before the woman came back with the infant in her arms. Kai stiffened into a quiet hysteria. She said something about not being able to "take mice" as she held my shoulders and hopped from one foot to the other.

The woman chased the swarm of children to the next room and Kai read through the report, stopping several times to let out a muffled shriek as mice passed back and forth against the wall. The woman laughed and apologized each time Kai stopped.

"Them mice can't hurt you," she said when Kai finally finished reading. She flashed a warm grin with several teeth missing and put her hand on Kai's shoulder. "The *rats*. I'm just like you with them. This place don't have no *rats*, thank God for that—"

Another mouse darted by and sent Kai reeling. The pack came flying around the corner, some laughing, some in tears. The woman yelled at them to be quiet and stop running. They didn't. She chased them back to the other room. Another mouse. Kai rocked back, pedaling the floor.

"I can't take this, Marc," she whispered, practically climbing onto my shoulder. "I can't take mice." I told her to hang tight and that we'd make it quick. The woman came back, bouncing the infant in one arm and a crying two-year-old in the other.

"Why aren't the kids wearing any clothes?" I asked, getting right to it.

"They got their clothes," she said. "I can't keep up with them—they don't keep 'em on even though I tell 'em. You see how they are like this. This is all the time. Could you imagine me trying to get clothes on these kids with them going on like this all the time? They never stop. I tell 'em, 'Put them pants on' but they don't want 'em, they don't listen." The two-year-old twirled out of her arms and ran back to join the pack. The infant chirped and set his mother's arm bouncing.

"Brand-new baby," I said.

"That's right," the woman returned. "That's it for me."

"That's it for you?"

"No more babies," she said. "I'm gonna get fixed as soon as I can. The doctor says I gotta wait 'cause I just had this one, but as soon as he says it's okay, I'm gonna do it—tie them tubes up. No more kids for me, no way, I'm finished. This is the last one."

Another chirp, more bouncing. The pack came back, screaming through—half of them chasing, the other half being chased. The chased half whipped around behind me to block the chasers. I was pulled off balance, stepping quickly to avoid squashing tiny bare feet and to keep from falling. The woman hollered for the children to stop. They didn't. I told her it was okay. I held the pack's attention and Kai took the woman to her kitchen to check on the food supply. By the time they came back I felt like taking a shower. The children were dirty and I was covered with them. They hung at my neck and swung from my arms, playing on me like a human jungle gym.

"Where does everybody sleep?" Kai asked the woman as they emerged from the kitchen. The woman pointed to the corner and a beat-up mattress lying on the floor, covered with old coats. It was the only furniture in the room.

"The children sleep on the mattress," she said.

"All of them?" Kai asked.

"Oh they love it. It's no problem, they sleep. Them coats work just fine for the blanket. I sleep on a couch right in here," she said, bringing us to the other room. "The baby got the crib, the hospital gave me that." The crib was the only brand-new thing in the apartment—all white and lacy, a snowflake in the furnace. "The hospital gave me *all* this," she said, indicating the bedding, soft blue flannel with lace-covered bumpers and a few blankets. "I told them I was gonna take the baby to sleep on the couch with me and then they gave me all of this. I'm grateful for that—I did it with my other baby, I took him on the couch with me, but that crib is really the thing."

"How old's the baby?" I asked.

"He's one week old today," the woman said proudly. She pulled the blanket back from his face so we could look at him. "He's my skinny one," she said with a chuckle. "He's the skinniest of all my babies."

"You're breast-feeding him?" I asked, glancing at the little face in the blankets.

"I give him the bottle. He don't suck so good, but the hospital gave me a whole bunch of formula and I got vouchers to get free ones at the store until I can have them put him on my budget for welfare."

"He's been eating okay?" Kai asked. I glanced at him again.

"He eats okay," the woman said. "Not very much, but he does eat."

"He looks thin," Kai said. "How much has he eaten tonight?" More mice. Kai yelped and jogged out of the room. The woman laughed.

"Damn, Marc," Kai said, peeking back into the room. "Three of them. There were three of them."

"There were only two, Kai."

"I saw three. Where'd they go? Are they still there?—I'm sorry, miss."

"I don't mind," the woman said with another kindly chuckle. "I got a sister that's just like you are. She don't come here to visit, we gotta go to see her. She don't go anywhere near them mice."

"*God...*," Kai said, still peeking around the corner. "There were three of them." A crash and sudden tears from the next room. The woman and I whipped around Kai to where the pack had converged on itself like one body tending its wound. The group scattered as I approached, revealing one of the younger girls, who was already dabbing away tears and getting up to join the pack that had reconverged behind me. She was all right, just a bump on the head. I turned around to see Kai, who was looking again at the infant in the woman's arms.

"When is the next doctor appointment for the baby?" she asked.

"I got a clinic appointment next Thursday. It's the two-week appointment. They gave me the number to call to get a time. I didn't call it yet—we don't got a phone and the one on the corner on the street just got ripped out. They don't put a phone on that corner for two weeks and it gets busted. People around here need a phone on the street—they ain't got none in they homes. I'm gonna call when I go shopping for groceries tomorrow."

"So do the kids run in the hall like it says in the report?" I asked.

"Now, you see how they are and you're gonna ask me a question like that?" The woman asked with a smile. "I only got one more lock on that door they haven't figured out yet, so I only use it after nine o'clock when the hallways get bad with them junkies. If I used that lock all the time, they'd figure it out, and I'd never be able to keep 'em in."

Made sense.

Suddenly the pack flew in and around me, grabbing my shirt and pants to slow their momentum. I made a conscious effort to keep my body calm through the onslaught of limbs. The woman yelled at the pack—told them to "stop touching the man." They didn't. I said it was okay. They ran back to the other room. Another mouse ran along the floor, jumping frantically at the bare wall and racing into the kitchen. Kai jumped at the opposite wall. The woman laughed, but she didn't think anything was funny. One of the children hit the floor. I ran into the other room to see if anyone was hurt but couldn't tell which one of them fell. I was almost tackled as I returned to Kai, who was looking at the infant in the mother's arms a final time and explaining to the woman that the field office would follow up soon. The woman seemed grateful.

Shortly after that, Kai and I left and didn't come back.

4

TWO WEEKS PASSED. I'm sure the day was like any other—a *thunk-whump* at six minutes after four o'clock, two coffees, a mountain of memos, and—without Dana there to give me hell about it—a paper cup of mashed potatoes from the Square.

Early in the shift, before the onslaught of cases, a supervisor called Kai into her office. Kai rolled her eyes as she got up and walked away, disappearing behind a carpeted partition. Office meetings called before cases came in were usually to address housekeeping annoyances—"There have been complaints about your handwriting from the field office" or "Car 495 had a pizza crust on the floor after you used it." That kind of thing. They took no more than five minutes. Kai was gone for almost an hour. When she came back around the partition, she didn't look annoyed anymore. Her eyes weren't rolling, they were falling out of her face.

"*Damn, Marc,*" she whispered intensely. I pushed out a chair next to my desk and she fell into it. *"That kid we visited died..."* We stared at each other for a moment. I didn't know what she was talking about, but the look on her face was beyond bad. The words on her lips spoke my greatest fear. I couldn't say a word. *"That kid—,"* she went on, *"That baby—with the woman in the bad building?... C'mon*—two weeks ago. The case with the mice everywhere and the kids all jumping on us and everything... with the baby and the woman with the new crib? *Marc,...* the baby died..." Her eyes begged mine for a reaction. "He *died,* Marc—," she said again, near tears. "That little boy died after we left him there."

For a split second, I couldn't have moved if my shirt were on fire. The sounds filled me completely—*after we left him there.* I knew what she was saying but I waited for her to take it back. She didn't. She couldn't. Nobody could—ever.

"They said he died from emaciation—he was a failure-to-thrive kid. *Oh God...*" Kai's head swayed and dipped. She began to cry. "Think of how that baby looked—you remember? *He was too skinny, Marc...*"

And then I saw him—really saw him—for the first time. The night of our visit, I only glanced at him, but there at my desk, I *saw* him. His face was awful—a baby about to die, grimacing—clinging to blessed life even as it slipped away from him. He *was* too thin. And too thin on a baby is really strange.

"Remember his face??...all wrinkled and shrunk up like an old man's? I said it, remember? I said he looked too skinny. I was wondering about taking him to the hospital 'cause he didn't look right, remember? Can you believe this?—*I didn't think he would die, Marc...oh God, he died—that little baby...*" She tilted her head back to catch tears and then leaned forward, very serious. "They're gonna send me downtown. I gotta see the Inspector General—*they're gonna put me before the board, Marc...* they wanna know why we didn't take him. They might need to see you, too. We could be in big trouble. They told me to call the union. Can you believe it?? They want me to call the union—*I gotta call the union...*"

My face fell into my hands. I looked through the dark shadows of my fingers at my desk. A voice took shape in my head, the beginning of a voice—cruel and furious. Calculating. Destructive. Rumbling deeper than any sound and radiating like a heat that nothing can cool. The initial welts came buffeting through as I held my face like it would fall off.

...you're the worst kind, my man. You are. You're the worst—and you wanna know why? I'm gonna tell you why. You're the worst because you been thinking you're the finest worker in the office, the one who cares about kids, who's doing the job for "The Cause." For almost four years you been thinking you're the best thing to happen to the inner city since Goya Foods. You jump up and down on the soapbox, getting all high and holy about "saving children" but you're no better than any other boarded-up, sleep-walking, pay-me-and-leave-me-alone-cause-the-shift's-over-and-I-need-a-beer, piece-of-shit civil servant. You are. You're no better and you're worse, my man. Take it like a big boy now, 'cause the truth hurts, don't it? Kick back and welcome to the cesspool, buddy. Everybody falls in sooner or later—all a matter of time...

"When did he die?" I asked through my fingers.

"He died before the field office people could follow up. We were the last ones from Human Resources to see him."

"But when was that—how long did they wait to follow up? They're mandated to follow up within forty-eight hours."

"And I wrote for them to go out sooner—"

"So when did he die?"

"He died on Sunday. We went to see him on Thursday—"

"Three days—"

"They didn't make it."

"It was three days. They would've had to see the family the next day to make the mandate—they would've had to see him that Friday."

"Right, because of the weekend."

"So they didn't do the visit on Friday, and because of the weekend, they missed the mandate."

"Plus, I wrote down they had to see him sooner."

"...right..."

"...they blew it," Kai said, but the words rang between us false as a hooker's affection.

"...we should've taken that little boy to the hospital, Kai—"

"Oh c'mon, Marc," she snapped. "Don't you think I know that? We could be in big trouble here. They're sending me to see the board. If they don't like what they hear from me, you'll be next, and then we'll both be on the front of the papers. *Of course* we should've taken him to the hospital—it's easy to see that now. So go tell it to your girlfriend. We're in some serious shit, brother. If the field office would've done the right thing— if they would've gone to see him on that Friday, he might still be here. I wrote it down—told them the child was thin and to get out to check on him ASAP and that's what I'm gonna say when I go downtown—not gonna say, *we should'a taken him to the hospital* and get strung up on a pole for everybody to throw shit at my face."

Kai felt as bad as I did except she was the one who was

going downtown. She had to keep her focus. The possibility of a front-page flogging on a slow news day was very real. Sure, the field office messed it, too, but that fact gave me exactly three minutes of relief. We could've done something to save the life of a child who needed us and we didn't. That was the bottom line and that's what began to dig a big hole in my head.

Kai went off to the bathroom and I put my head on the desk to get acquainted with the voice that would stay with me for some time to come, growing larger and playing deeper as it pummeled me, over time, into a despair like I've never known.

*Yeah he's dead, all right. Cold in the ground as the desk on your cheek. Should we begin the list of should-haves now, or do you want to look forward to it—wait'll you get home? Oh hell, there's so many, might as well get started. How 'bout the big one—*SHOULD'VE TAKEN HIM TO THE HOSPITAL... *There's plenty before that one:* SHOULD'VE LOOKED AT HIM, *should've taken him out of the blankets and given him the once-over. You looked at the mice longer than you did at the child. There's plenty of should-haves and we'll hit 'em all, but the big one is the hospital—when a one-week-old baby looks like a ninety-year-old man, when the skin around his face hangs down like an old pile of laundry, when his cry sounds more like a cheap whistle than a baby—*YOU TAKE HIM TO THE EMERGENCY ROOM. *Really should'a done that, my man, you really really should'a...*

Kai came out of the bathroom in her coat and walked straight to the clock and punched out. She didn't turn to say good-bye as she left. Her supervisor leaned out of a cubicle to watch her go. When Kai was gone, the supervisor turned to look at me for a moment and then disappeared behind the partition. I put my head back to the desk and lasted for about two minutes before throwing on my jacket and punching out early myself.

I hit the pavement with a stiff stride and skipped the subway—not a conscious decision. A half hour at a steady pace and I about froze my ass off with my legs bouncing numbly underneath me; past the sweating, past the fatigue, past itch and tingle, past it all, and just moving along dumbly. I turned in to a subway station around midtown in another unconscious impulse. The mindless walking did nothing to quiet my head. Everything around me blurred with the stain of tragedy. The voice took on clarity, twisting the sound of its relentless taunts like razor wire around my bones. I saw the dark place I was headed for, but there was no place to back up and turn around. I was going straight down, straight to the bottom. The voice played on, the whole way home.

... *so let me get this right, just make sure I got it down—that I'm not exaggerating anything. You're paid to go see children in their homes to make sure they're not in any kind of danger, right?—to make sure they* DON'T DIE, *or something. Your job, right? You're the one on the front line—the last hope for a kid in trouble? Do I have this correct? Okay. So you go out to check on a newborn, and you have information that this newborn is in some kind of trouble—he's "thin and weak," you're told. So you go out to see if this thin and weak baby is okay, make sure he doesn't* DIE *or something, right?—Not because you're a nice guy, because it's your job. And the way you accomplish this, your technique to ensure his safety, is to glance at him while he's mostly covered with a blanket. This is how it went, stop me if I get it wrong—you look at the baby's face for—how long?—three seconds? Let's be generous—eight seconds? And in this glance, you assess his wellness? His viability? This is how a professional does it? These are the measures taken by a person who "cares about children," you piece of shit?* .... *convince me, you asshole... you fuck ...*

I didn't make it into work for the next three days.

5

"SO HOW'YA BEEN DOING, MARC?" Sam asked as he lit his pipe. I'd gone straight in to see him after reading a note in my box from the director of the office telling me to do so. Sam glanced up from his pipe after it was lit. The look on his face was what you give to someone in a hospital bed. I nodded as the smoke rose between us. The office was quiet. I had come in early in hopes of getting an easy field visit so I could slip back out before getting caught in a web of small talk, with everyone in the office trying to get a glimpse of my eyes to see if they were the same color. "You wanna sit down?" Sam asked. I looked at the chair on the other side of his desk. "Go ahead, Marc. Have a seat," he said, leaning back and sucking the pipe.

"Kai been back?" I asked after sitting down. Sam gave his head a quick shake.

"Kai's out, Marc," he said, and then thought for a moment. "I believe Kai told Ros she was gonna stay out until she goes before the board." I nodded. Ros was the director of the office. She drove a Porsche to work. "I believe that's the story there," he said. He took a puff and looked to the right wall like he was looking out a window.

"Ros left me a note to come see you," I said.

"Yes, she did," he said, turning from the wall and leaning forward on his elbows. "How do you feel, Marc? . . . You all right?"

"I think so." I knew Sam was checking on me to report to the office brass, but concern showed in his eyes as well, so I wasn't bothered.

"Been gone for three days."

"Yes I have," I said.

"Been sleeping okay?" he asked.

"Not very much."

"Look tired, Marc."

"I know."

"Eating?"

"A little bit."

"Oh you gotta eat, Marc." He gave me a long look over the top of his glasses. "You gotta keep your strength up."

"Anyone talk to Kai?" I asked.

"Think so."

"You talk to her?"

"I didn't talk to her, Marc." Sam set his pipe to the side. "It's good to take a few days off when you need it." I nodded. "You do good work here, Marc."

"...okay, Sam."

"Don't look so good though. Sure you're all right?"

"I haven't been sleeping."

"Oh, you gotta get your sleep, Marc. That can catch up with you. Gotta keep your strength up."

"You're right...," I said. We stared at each other a moment before I broke the ice. "We really should've taken him to the hospital, you know."

"Might've happened to anyone here, what happened to you two," he said, without missing a beat. "Might've. It's no picnic out there."

"It's true."

"You bet it's true... Listen, I'm sorry about what happened—everybody is. Very sad case. That's tough stuff out there. Tough to always know how it's gonna go." Sam looked back to the wall. He picked up the pipe and placed it in the corner of his mouth, taking a quiet sip of smoke.

"Why did Ros want me to come see you?"

"Well, Marc, we're concerned about you, about how you're taking all this," he said, still looking out the imaginary window. "Want to see that you're okay."

"Why else?" I asked plainly.

"Marc," he said, turning to me and setting the pipe again on his desk. "If you want to take some more days off, you go ahead and do so. Might be the best thing. Stay at home for a while if you'd like—don't worry about the time on your card, we'll take care of it...If you'd rather come in to work, well then you're more than welcome, of course, but we all think it might be a good idea if you'd handle in-house cases until you're feeling better. We'd like to keep you in the office here at least until this thing comes to some type of resolution. I'm not gonna play around with you, Marc—that's why you're here to see me. We all talked about it and think it's best. Don't think that means there aren't a lot of people that want to make sure you're all right, me included. It was an unfortunate thing out there. You're one of our good people, Marc. You know that. Why do you think we send you to the field with every rookie that comes through here? You've helped to train half the field-workers in this office. If it could happen with you, it could've happened with anyone else here just as well. We all agreed. Very unfortunate."

"So I stay in the office and handle bullshit cases."

"I wouldn't put it like that, Marc." I turned to look out the wall. "I understand the field office didn't get out on the follow-up visit as soon as they were supposed to..."

"Yeah. They left him over the weekend."

"Well there you go, Marc, it's a field office problem. If the field office had done their job, we wouldn't be here talking about any of this."

"One way of looking at it, I guess."

"This'll smooth out for you and Kai in no time. After she sees the board, we'll get the two of you back on track. In the meantime, just kick back and take it easy a little while. Nothing wrong with that, you could use it. I've seen you look better, Marc."

"Is there a question, in light of all this, about my ability to handle cases in the field?"

"I wouldn't put it like that, Marc . . ."

". . . okay, Sam."

"Until things smooth over a bit. Let me know if I can do anything for you, all right? I mean it, Marc. Try not to take this home with you."

I went back to my desk and thought about clocking out and leaving, but changed my mind quickly. There was no relief out of the office, the last three days had been complete hell.

Getting home that first evening after hearing the news, my body ached. I had the wrong shoes and jacket for walking fifty blocks to midtown. With feet soaked and legs numb and thumping, I headed for the bathroom as soon as I tumbled the locks to 108th Street open and shut. I kicked off my shoes, pulled off my shirt, and stepped out of my jeans in one movement. There was no shower at 108th. With one twist of my wrist, water came tumbling into the tub. It was the huge old-fashioned kind, lifted up off the floor on bird's feet. I stood naked, waiting for the water to heat up. Steam began to rise from the flow and I flicked the drain shut. The tub filled quickly. I eased in slowly until the water kissed my mouth and ears. The warmth sunk into me quickly as I lay still and tried to think of nothing. It worked for a few minutes until the sound of nothing became the sound of the voice—until the sound of nothing became the sound of everything.

. . . you ought to be arrested, you know. Really. If there was any justice in the world. What would we do with a cop who witnesses a brutal stabbing without ever unholstering his gun? Or how about a fireman who eats a sandwich while he watches a roomful of people go up in flames? The surgeon who neglects to stitch up his open-heart patient and sends him to recovery with his lungs dragging on the floor? You oughta be locked up, my man—you oughta be sent down. If fair was fair, you'd be history. What were you thinking? Try to articulate just what on earth you were thinking when you left that baby. What was

so bad and awful about the whole place that you had to bolt the hell out of there and leave him behind?

Wish I could say. Beads of sweat sprouted above my lips and eyebrows.

It wasn't the mice. You live with rats four times the size, so don't say it was the mice. That'd be too easy.

It was the mice for Kai. The mice sent her running from that place. I'd never seen her so skittish.

Hello? That's why there are two of you, why they send you out in pairs. The strong one picks up the other's weakness. You dropped the ball, my man. Nothing to do but face the music. Mind if I play on? 'Cause it's not so simple as a couple of mice on the floor. Lucky for you if it was, but it's not. It goes way deeper than that and it's more disturbing than a whole squirming pit of mice. Try this and see if it doesn't fit: That baby was just one more kid to a woman with too many already—one more kid in one more family like every other swarm of them in that whole pitiful building, just one more overgrown pack of fatherless offspring that roil through the whole tumbled-down area—the child wasn't worth more than a glance to you. "The last one," remember? "Then I'm gonna tie up them tubes." The woman was a slob, I'll give you that, at least. Never say it to anyone out loud, but c'mon, between you and me, she was a pig. Don't even try to say you would've made the same mistake with a better woman in a better neighborhood. Here's the bottom line—the kid wasn't worth it because the mother wasn't worth it, 'cause the family wasn't worth it, 'cause the building wasn't worth it, 'cause the whole damn ten-block area—all of it ain't worth more than a glance. After you've been in it for this long, after seeing the rotten side of everything more times than Bambi—it just ain't worth more than a glance anymore—don't matter what it is, don't matter if it's a baby about to knock off.

The child's only crime was that he was born in a bad neighborhood to a dim bulb who can't remember to get her tubes tied. Not his fault, poor one—but the crime committed and the execution carried out. It wasn't the mice that sent you flying out of there like an elephant on wings. Lucky for you if it was, but it goes way darker than that. You were running from the sucking despair of the whole God-forgotten place. You ran, and you left him to die, big man. Tragedy is a high-yield crop in the inner city, so what's one more little body to load on the hay wagon. Nothing to people like you. You'll go to hell for it—you'll go to hell, but I'm gonna give you a good taste of it in the meantime . . .

My body had quickly pulled the heat straight out of the water. I flipped the plug open until my knees appeared like twin islands and then flipped it back shut. I gave the hot-water knob a gentle twist until it released a thin silent stream of heat. My head was soaked with sweat. I plugged my nose and dunked back into the water. The groan of building supports ran amplified through the bath, followed by the low roar of a subway train. *If sounds were visible,* I thought, *the water wouldn't look so inviting.*

—Trying to think about something else. Anything else. I understand. Well whatever you do, try not to think about the face. Right? You know what I'm talking about—the child's face. Looked awful, didn't it? I mean now that you think back on it—at the time it looked like . . . Well, what DID it look like at the time? At the time, YOU COULDN'T HAVE SAID what the face looked like—just another one of Mom's chattel, at the time. You couldn't really say, but time does a number on a glance, doesn't it? You can see the face of that child perfectly now, and does it look terrible or does it look terrible? When they say not to take it home with you, that shrunken-up, awful-looking face is the kind of thing they're talking about . . .

I flipped the drain again and watched as the nubby twins emerged and turned into legs. When the tub was empty, I ran the cold water and pulled some at my face to stop the sweat. I got out of the tub, weak with heat and all the rest, stood on my pants, and used my shirt for a towel. The apartment was quiet and empty. I wrapped the shirt around my waist and made for the bedroom. It was early, but the bed seemed to be the best of my options. Sleep would be a sweet relief, I thought. I was wrong about that. Sweet relief was as available to me as a breath of fresh air for baby boy. With my eyes closed, the voice spoke louder and with more abandon—a wealth of taunts available now that pictures and images could be used as visual aids. The murk of sleep released the voice from the constraint of reality. Whole episodes could be played with a myriad of gruesome details tossed in for effect. And they were. Throughout the night, my average was about fifty percent on waking up just as a dream was getting the best of me or about to reach some gory climax.

I woke the following morning before the sun, feeling as though I'd slept through a night of shelling. Pulling on a shirt and pants as I walked into the kitchen, I looked inside the fridge for something to eat but found nothing to rouse my appetite from its hibernation. I sat for a moment at the kitchen table in a haze—too asleep to be awake and too awake to be asleep. The air was quiet, the voice tired for now from its all-night gala performance. It seemed as good a time as any to hike over to the east side of the city and watch the sun climb its way out of Brooklyn. There's a spot along the East River with a nice long stretch of benches right at the water's edge. A coffee and a sunrise, I thought, was just what I needed to put the world right again. So I bundled up and hit the street.

It was chilly at the water's edge, but I'm fine with chilly. With a piping hot we-are-happy-to-serve-you paper cup of coffee, chilly is just about right. I leaned back on the bench, cupping the coffee in both hands to my face. Brooklyn spread out before me like a dirty gray oyster about to give up its pearl sun. The first pierce of light appeared over the distant buildings in the horizon—the only fleck of color in sight. Thirty seconds later a shimmering path of light raced across the river and hit my face. The voice had been silent and remained so as I watched the day take shape. A wooden guardrail ran eye level along the horizon where I was sitting. I had to slouch on the bench and peer under it to see the sun come up. As it rose, I rose, too, until the rail blocked the sun from view. Raising myself up a bit, I could see it again. I lined up behind the rail to watch it peek over the wood, going from a pinprick to a bright wash of brilliance. When it became too bright, I sunk behind the rail a little more to watch it rise again. I watched the sun rise twelve times that morning. Twelve sunrises and I still felt like caving in. Twelve sunrises in one morning, a warm belly of coffee, and a light fresh wind from the water—

Nice try, but no dice, my man. You're a good one at making yourself feel better when you get wracked up. The sunrise trick is cute and you love that first cup of joe but don't think for one second that any of it's gonna put this fire down. Be serious—"the sun will rise," it's what they say, right? That's how it goes? Hey—so what. Watch it rise twelve times. The sun rose on Hiroshima. The sun rose on Auschwitz. Be serious—this is reality. The sun don't give a shit...

The day just beginning, sleep nowhere in sight, and the voice threatening to pick up where it left off, I felt drunk— sleep-deprived and no food since four in the afternoon the previous day. And then I thought, as the pearl grew whiter, drunk might be the only respite for the day. Might be just about right. The thought of a mild drunk never seemed more appealing. When I was younger I promised myself I'd never drink to ease a pain, but I made the promise never imagining I'd be blaming myself for the death of a little boy. I thought about the promise as I gazed out across gray Brooklyn oyster; about how growing up isn't really about birthdays or the piling on of years—how the events that hurl us from one age to the next aren't ushered in on victories and valor as much as on the losses we've had and the pain we've experienced. In the past fifteen hours, I had begun to feel like a man, not in the way you usually think of it when you hear the phrase, but in a real way, in the truest way. So I thought about the promise in the brightening sky and concluded that if I took a few swallows outside the confines of a good time, then so be it. A man will break a boy's promises. Kids drink to have fun; men drink to forget.

I hauled myself up and hopped the subway straight to Coney Island, the perfect place to bring a heavy heart and a head full of demons. Coney Island in the winter is nothing more than a fat gray boardwalk on the sea and a few beer joints filled with a smattering of men drinking to forget and other hard-luck stories. It's a great place to go and feel bad because you fit right in with the scenery. The short story on Coney is that it was a great thing that went to hell. I couldn't have felt more at home. I spent the day twisted on lukewarm Budweiser, staring out at the ocean and trying with a drunk's fury not to think about the face. I was successful for the most part—dousing it back with a shot of bartender's choice whenever it came into view. By late afternoon, with a belly full of beer and cheap whisky, it was either hit the train back home or head straight into the ocean. Given the temperature of the water, the train was a more comfortable option.

On the way back I had a flash memory about a guy in college named Bulldog who tried to drink an entire bottle of vodka on his birthday. Me and a few of his friends sat in a room playing cards while he chipped away at the bottle and told stories. He got about two-thirds of it put away before we had to throw a beanbag chair at his head to keep him from breaking his fists against the wall. The memory of Bulldog and the idiot look in his eye, swinging aimlessly as we held him down, did nothing to stop me as I got out of the train and headed straight for the nearest deli to pick up a couple Advil and a bottle of Sam Adams Triple Bock to wash them down.

There you go—pills and booze just like any other skid on the skid. Hey, might as well, why not? If you're gonna do the middling lowlife trip, at least go for some consistency—some purity of existence even if it's on the underside of things. You gonna succumb to mediocrity on an apathy play like the rest of the losers, might as well pill and booze with the best of them on your way down. Ya big baby. Just don't think this little display of self pity is gonna do anything to change the way things are. You can duck me between swallows, but I'll be back. There's more to this than what we've covered, my man. Keep it up and we'll have a nice chat over a thumping mother of a hangover. See you tomorrow, asshole, bright and early...

Back at the apartment, the boys were more than willing to catch up to my blood-alcohol level without asking any questions. Before too long, we busted out the guitars, as we sometimes did, and began to reel through a couple belters—music that's more fun to play than to listen to. I pushed up my volume to a nerve-deadening level and the boys followed gladly, though it wasn't a happy thing. We played a long time. We drank a lot more.

Not that it mattered.

What mattered is that I woke up at some point in the clothes from the previous morning. What mattered is it was day three with no sign of light and the crazies still looming on the horizon. What mattered is that the voice kept its word and was very much on time. I could move only my eyelids at first.

They pulled open on that third day and as I watched the room grow bright, the voice played crisp and clear as a mountain morning on a sunny deck with a bowl of Grape Nuts—really awful stuff, the worst; questions about how he really died came up—how he felt, if he was in pain. There was more on how he looked, more on the face. With all the arguments played out—all the angles used up—the voice resorted to cheap shots; throwing up gore and twisting it just enough to heighten things without making them unbelievable. The bottom line was that I was into my third day of thinking intensely about a baby whose death I felt responsible for, and it was getting to be too much. I hadn't eaten, hadn't gone to work, and had avoided my friends when sober—anything I could think of to find some relief, more than that, to find some piece of myself as I was before the death—but there was nothing.

I spent most of the third day roaming through the city. Back in Wisconsin, when I was feeling wracked up about something, I'd drive—just head straight out on a road with a full tank of gas, not knowing where I was going and finally stopping for a bite when I was hungry at whatever town I happened to be in. The third day of roaming was a city version of the Wisconsin road trip. The day passed like a dull ache. When it came to a close, I was still on the rack. It started to feel strange—the way it hung on. I'd tried everything I could think of. Time, the powerful healer, with three days to work on it wasn't able to put a dent in the misery that clung like humidity. Time off was time to think and thinking was nothing more than a series of blows to the face.

So on the fourth day, I returned to work.

6

I RETURNED TO MY DESK after the discussion with Sam to find four cases sitting by my phone with a note that read, "This is it for the night, take your time and drop them in the manager's basket at the end of the shift." I gave them a quick read and estimated they'd take about an hour and a half to complete. The suspicion code on two of them was for educational neglect. Both were called in by school psychologists who were long gone by the time I tried to reach them at their offices. I made calls to the homes and spoke with family on each one. Both offered an excuse for why their kids had been missing school. I told them they had to go to school. They said, okay then. The write-ups took less than a page. The third and fourth cases were positive tox—newborns on cocaine. On both of them, there were no other kids at home so all I had to do was call the hospital and tell the staff to hold on to the babies until the field office said what to do. Both mothers denied drug use. I asked them why the babies had cocaine in their blood. They said they didn't know why. They never knew why. I told them the field office would follow up. Those write-ups took about a page. I finished with most of the shift ahead of me and was told to "hang tight" in case anything else came in. Meanwhile, the rest of the office was flying back and forth on unicycles and spitting fire.

One week later, Kai and I were exonerated of all responsibility in the death of Baby Doe. Sam called me in at the start of the shift to break the news. He said he had expected no less. He smiled a lot and told me everything was okay now—a close call, but we had made it. You do good work, he said. Kai, too. You both do good work. He had spoken with Kai an hour earlier and she never sounded better—really gave it to the board, he said, really let 'em have it. How can the work of this office mean anything, he asked, if the field office doesn't do their job on the follow-up? We're no fortune-tellers, he said— can't predict the future—it's why the field office has a time-frame mandate on the follow-up. He said a few more things that included the words "follow-up" as he patted me on the shoulder. I had held out a small hope that exoneration might give some small relief. It didn't. I felt it as soon as the smile on Sam's face faded, all the pats and accolades in the world couldn't lift me from the gutter I'd fallen into.

When in the last four years have you ever paid attention to a disciplinary talk when you knew you were in the right? Why should it be any different with an exoneration when you know you're in the wrong? It doesn't matter if they found an excuse to hang around your neck—sure you get to keep the job, but it won't do anything much for a good night's rest. You know the truth and the bottom line and the whole story—you saw the face and heard the cries—braid it together and put a band around it; it reads: You Blew It. Always did . . . Always will . . .

It was still with me, its truths no less brutal, but with most of the mock and sarcasm drained from it. Over the past few days, the voice had become less of an enemy. I began to listen to it rather than fight it, answering its questions like you do with an old friend who doesn't cut you any slack when there's something you need to understand. Time, over the past week, had slowly taken care of the shock and grief, but it could do nothing about the hard questions ringing in my eardrums—questions that demanded answers. Interrogation reverberated through me—*my* voice this time; stretching me back over years of work and hundreds of children, searching for the truths that might shed light on my impossible lack of consciousness and its tragic outcome—Why did I leave that night? Where am I numb? What hope is there when the crack of children's bones fails to make me wince as I once did?

"—about you with all the top brass," Sam continued, unaware of my drift. He lifted his hand from my shoulder and swung around his desk to have a seat. "We're relieved to hear the word from the board," he said, "and feel that in light of their findings, we can return you to full and unrestricted duty—in the office *and* in the field . . . Congratulations, Marc."

"Thank you."

"Never doubted you." I nodded. "Never doubted either of you."

"Appreciate that, Sam."

"Of course, Marc, don't mention it." I nodded. "Anything else then?" I thought for a moment. Yeah, there was something else. I was off the hook but I still felt the pierce in my back. I couldn't imagine returning to "full and unrestricted duty" in the shape I was in.

"Sam, do you think it'd be okay if I stayed on in-house cases a bit longer?"

"Think you need that, Marc?"

"I just wondered if it'd be all right."

"Getting used to the cushy life, are ya?"

"Just gotta work a few things out, is all."

"No problem, Marc. You let us know when you're ready. Take your time."

"Thank you, Sam."

"Been getting your sleep?"

"Appreciate that."

"This oughta make things a little better, then."

"Okay, Sam. That's it I guess."

I walked back to my desk and stared at a case already waiting for me. Kai waltzed in suddenly, wall-to-wall smiles and looking like she'd been away on a cruise. She wheeled around the office with big hellos for everybody and hopped over to my desk as soon as our eyes met. The spring in her body was triumphant.

"Did you hear?" she asked, her eyes glittering.

"Sam just told me—"

"*Damn* . . . right?"

"Right—"

"I was shakin', I swear. There were all these people there —all lined up behind this long table—all gettin' ready to bust on me."

"When did you see them?"

"This morning—I saw them this morning and then Ros called me this afternoon at home. She goes, 'Kai, you must've told them what they needed to hear,' and I was like—'*Oh, damn*,' right?"

"They never doubted us."

"You know?—And I appreciate that."

"What else did Ros say?"

"They told her—they said, 'The issue would be dealt with in the field office.' She said it was a closed case for ECS."

"What did the board ask you?"

"*Everything*. They basically had me go over the whole visit."

"The mice?" She gave me a look like I asked her bra size.

"They don't wanna hear about mice, Marc—"

"So what did you tell them, then?"

"I told them everything—"

"So what'd you tell them?"

"*I told them about the case*—now what's your problem?"

"You tell them the kid was too skinny?"

"Of course I told them the kid was too skin—what kinda question is that? They knew the kid was too skinny—of course I told them that."

"So why didn't we take him?"

"That's what they asked me—"

"What did you tell them?"

"I told them the truth—"

"Good—tell me. I need to know what the truth is."

"What? . . ."

"What's the truth, Kai?"

"What are you talking about, what's the truth? What are you asking me for? You were there."

"I asked you why we didn't take him. You said the board asked you the same thing. What did you tell them? You said, 'The truth.' So what's the truth?"

"Why do you have to act like this, Marc? What's wrong with you?"

"Why didn't we take him, Kai?"

"Lighten up, brother—"

"What's the truth? Why didn't we take him, huh? Why did we leave him, Kai? What'd you say? How could we leave him there?—what's the truth, Kai? I need to know . . . *I'm dying to know . . .*"

"You don't gotta be all intense with me, Marc—"

"But I do, Kai. I have to be all intense. I can't help it—I've tried everything, it's no use. I've been all intense ever since you told me it happened."

"So why do I have to tell you about what the truth is when you were there, too? I already been through all this—"

"Kai, Kai—*please.* You told the board that the child was skinny, and you told them why we left, and they said it wasn't our fault. *I need to know why it wasn't our fault.*" She looked afraid at what I might say next.

"I've had some bad days, Kai—seriously. With all this, I mean. I'm going a little nuts with it. I swear...'cause I'm just—it's...I've been running from it and it's really...it's getting strange almost. I've never felt anything like it. I'm taking it hard. I think this is what...when you take it hard—when they say you're taking it hard? I've been getting into a pretty dark place and when I get there, I can see all the way down—*the bottom.* You know? Like I'm falling—*I mean the very bottom.* You don't come back—you hit that and you don't come back. It happens. I gotta make some sense out of it, out of this—the whole thing. Ever since it happened I been running from it one way or another, trying to move on, but it's no use. I'm running, but this thing is faster. I'm gonna get creamed if I keep it up, you know? I gotta do something different—I gotta turn around, I think. Just face it—face the truth. It's the only way. I've tried everything else...

"So they say it wasn't our fault. It wasn't our fault the boy died—it was okay that we left. We left, and it was fine that we left because the baby was okay, but after we left, he died, and that wasn't our fault...I have a hard time with that, Kai." She bristled as I revealed the knife in my chest. "You're right—I was there, I know the truth. The way I see it? I'll tell you—I think it's *incredible* that we left him there...I think it's *bizarre* almost..."

"That's your own trip, brother," she said slowly.

"I see his face, Kai. Every fucking day. It takes my breath away. I see every crease and wrinkle, the little grimace on his lips—he was trying to hang on, he was in a struggle. I see it now. Remember his forehead?"

"No, no, Marc—c'mon, don't do it. I'm not going there—"

"There were so many lines in it. Those creases...I remember thinking it at the time. I remember thinking *Jeez, that little forehead's wrinkled up.* I remember actually thinking that as I looked at him. I thought it as I walked away."

"I'm not gonna listen to this, Marc—"

"Why wasn't it our fault?" We looked at each other a long time.

"They didn't tell me why it wasn't our fault," she said plainly. "And that's not a question anybody can answer for you, so keep it to yourself. That one you gotta do alone. We were exonerated but what you're talking about is something on a whole different level and it's got nothing to do with this job. Do I wish we would've taken that child to the hospital that night? Of course I do. Do I wish he was alive right now?" Her voice tripped. "Of course I do. Don't forget, Marc—he died after our period of responsibility. We did the right thing. He didn't need the hospital the night we saw him—he needed it three days later. Now, I got my own thing to take care of— don't even try to tell me that you're the only one going through the shit on this. All right? I'm the one that signed off on that case, Marc. I was the one who was gonna have to take the fall. As far as the board was concerned, you had very little to do with it."

"Well that's fine for them."

"Listen—it's over now. For me, anyways—you can torture yourself if you think it's really necessary, but it's over. It wasn't our fault. They paid those people a lot of money to figure that out. They'd say we messed up if we did—"

"Would they?"

"Hey—do they owe you a favor? Do they? You think they owe me a favor? They don't. They don't care who sinks or swims. We don't sign their checks, brother—don't get any illusions. They would've put us in the tank if they could have— makes no difference to them. The field office blew their mandate. They missed the time frame and the child died. It was on their clock, not ours."

"Thank God for that—nice of him to wait, wasn't it?"

"Hey—I'm gonna let it go now and you should too. Beating yourself up isn't going to change what happened. It's not going to bring him back."

"Okay—fine, so the problem was with the field office. But listen, go outside of the parameters of this job for one second. Think about what happened without the comforts of this damn agency—the mandates and protocols. Think about what happened as a living breathing person—"

"What the hell is wrong with you? We did our job, Marc —something terrible happened, and you don't feel any worse about it than anyone else. We did our job—"

"Oh, c'mon, Kai—be real about this. That's all I'm asking. This is just you and me now—I mean, *think about it* . . . think about what happened and tell me . . . you seem like you're fine right now—how do you reconcile it?"

". . . I don't even know what you're talking about, Marc . . . really. I don't. It's done, brother. That's what you should be thinking about. Whether you like it or not—it's over."

Kai cut me off with a hand in front of her face before I could say another thing, and walked over to her desk—not a lack of compassion, but a good dose of self-preservation. They said we did nothing wrong, so we did nothing wrong. She believed it. She knew what I was getting at, but Kai also knew how thin her ice was. Only a fool like me would venture out as far. She was happy to stay where it was safe, all bundled up on the shore. We did 100% of our job—the baby survived our mandate. I had no argument with that. So why wasn't 100% enough for me? Why wasn't 100% enough for the baby boy? Agency mandates keep everyone a safe distance from having to look into those teeth. Everyone is fine with what the protocol calls 100%. I could have been fine with it, but I wasn't.

Everyone around me had smiles on their faces and "we're doing our job" bouncing on their molars whether children live or die. Sure we did our job, but that's all we did.

7

DURING THE NEXT TWO WEEKS, the dreams were still present—less frequent, but doing a number all the same, against any strong arguments for sanity. They ranged from cheap gore to elaborate fiction. Regardless of their production values, they always made for a night where the only proof of sleep was in the passing hands of the clock. Baby Doe had been dead just under a month and a half. I say "Baby Doe" because I don't remember the child's name—never learned his name as a matter of fact. Didn't make the effort. It kills me every time I have to call him that. Doe. He had a name, of course, but he's just Doe to me.

At work, I continued handling in-house cases that amounted to little more than office paperwork. And I did a lot of walking. Sitting at the desk with nothing to do and everyone else up to their necks was enough to send me outside even on the coldest nights. As soon as I caught myself staring at the phone or a pen or my hand—as soon as I felt my eyes going dark and beady—I'd head out the door. On a typical night during those weeks, I'd check in and wait around anywhere from five to ten minutes. If there were no cases on my desk, I was back outside—walking and waiting—walking the grief and waiting the doubt. I called in sick a few times but it was becoming difficult to determine the lesser evil—a night spent staring at an empty desk or the same night at home knowing I should be at work but couldn't make it in. I wanted desperately to move on as Kai had done and as Sam and the rest of the bosses encouraged me to do—I was dying to get myself right and get back to work, but by the end of those two weeks I wasn't sure I'd ever be able to trust myself in the field.

It became clear at some point that simply facing the truth wasn't enough. The truth was obvious—I'd stared down its ugly throat from the first minutes it became clear: *The baby was very sick. It was not within the realm of the mother's ability to take note of this and act appropriately. Recognizing this, someone initiated a report and we were sent out to look things over and secure the safety of any children we might encounter. We didn't do this. The child died because we didn't do this.* That was the truth. But simply repeating *We let the child die* was getting me nowhere. I needed an answer—*Why did we let the child die?* I began the job at Emergency Children's Services with the highest hopes and the best intentions. I did it for love. I did it because I got off on helping children, pure and simple. I started each investigation with wide eyes and keen vision. "One of the best in the office," the bosses said. A few thousand cases and three years later and I walk out on a child that's dying. If it happened with me, might it happen with anyone? Might it happen with *everyone?* Do we all go bad after a while? Is it only a matter of time? And if that's true, why is it true? I'd looked under bottles of beer and bad whiskey, along miles of walking, and in front of twelve sunrises, on Coney Island boardwalks, under groaning bathwater, through screaming guitars, and in the endless turns of my own trumpeting head. The answers, if there were any, remained out of reach. So I continued to stay inside, doing work that didn't really matter and trying with my last nerve to keep from just losing it altogether.

But only for one more week.

8

ON THE PLATFORM at Canal Street waiting for the uptown C local. Gazing down the empty station. Twelve-thirty A.M.

Heading home after five more days as the reigning deadweight of the office. The third day of a depression like I've never known. I decided to quit ECS. Not my style to leave something with my head in my armpit—I hated it but there was nothing left to do. I was fried. It was no longer about pride or anything as lofty as finding answers to unanswerable questions. There was only survival. I had the weekend to think things through, but it didn't matter. I knew it as soon as it breezed through my head. I was quitting. I was out of there.

The train scraped into the station and pulled me in. I fell into the nearest seat, leaned my head back against the car, and closed my eyes to listen to the squeal of metal and the snap of electricity whisking me home. I felt like a boxer on his back who's lost, but who has stopped fighting, and the comfort of not being plowed in the face rises alone and above everything else. People got on and off at each stop. I cracked my eyelids to watch the exchange of bodies, then let them fall shut as the train moved on. A thick quiet overtook me. The back of my head rocked gently against the humming wall of the car as the train accelerated and slowed.

What a funny place for it to hit me. A recollection, a story planted in me so long ago. Ten years later with a soaking head of fire on a screaming train through the midnight bowels of the city, a recollection of a nun, and a desert, and a whole lot of stones.

8

Turning Stones

IT IS HOT WHERE SHE STANDS. She is old and her body feels
weak. She looks out, the creases on her face, determined. A dry
wind ruffles through her robes. They are black and the material
is heavy. The sun heats her body beneath them. As she surveys
the expanse before her, a bead of sweat threatens to drip into
her eye. It is just before one o'clock in the afternoon, the sun
is on the brink of its most unforgiving position. The horizon
portrays a bleak wash of brown hues, a stark beauty that's not
lost on the woman as she searches carefully across the immense
stretch of land. There's not a green leaf as far as her eyes can
see, quite a contrast to the rolling farms that decorate the wide-
open spaces of Central Wisconsin. The year is 1976. The place
is Death Valley National Monument, two hundred and eighty-

two feet below sea level, the lowest point in the nation. The lowest place she's ever been. The woman is a nun; her name is Sister Clara. It's her summer vacation and as a gift to commemorate the hundredth anniversary of the church back home, the parishioners scraped together enough money to send the whole convent on a monthlong tour across the Great Southwest.

They head south straight out of Wisconsin with one of the better-known tour operators from Milwaukee. The bus whisks them through Decatur and across the Missouri River at St. Louis—on through Springfield, Joplin, and Tulsa, past Oklahoma City, and straight into Amarillo with little more than an occasional snack and stretch. They begin to slow down and take in the scenery by the time they reach northern New Mexico. In Arizona, they hit the Painted Desert and the Grand Canyon, Lake Powell and Mount Trumbull before making a quick pass into Nevada to see the Hoover Dam. From there, they head farther south along the Colorado River, back into Arizona for a moment to breathe the sweet juniper air of the Sonoran Desert and after that, farther west into California where they cross the Chocolate Mountains and make their way up through the Mojave Desert. The gals have been on the road just over two weeks by the time the bus rolls into Death Valley.

The stop is brief. Many of the sisters, complaining about the heat, decide to stay in the air-conditioned comfort of the bus while the braver ones step out to enjoy the views and read bronze plaques describing the area's highlights and historical significance. They step lively, reading and looking out, reading again, bustling off to the next spot, gathering for a quick picture, smiling, saying cheese. Sister Clara isn't interested in plaques or pictures. She takes her time, wandering off into the landscape even as the rest of the sisters have started to board the bus. A few look back and are not surprised when they see her out past the fence that marks the trail, walking on her own with only a thin cane to steady her as she ventures along a slope and then down into a gully. She hasn't skipped a single stop across the entire country. They know what she plans to do. They don't know why, but they know what.

In the gully, Sister Clara takes a little breather and flaps her robe to cool her legs. She searches again, slowly and with care, all the way out to where the sun's heat distorts the distance. The bottom of the ravine holds a wide river of stones. She smiles a little, planting the cane carefully as she steps around the bigger ones. She knows she's in the right spot.

Back at the bus, the sisters are looking at the place in the distance where Clara slipped from view. Their concern rises, predictably, and several of them trudge out to see that she's okay. They see Sister Clara as they approach the edge of the slope where she disappeared. She is crouched over and tapping against a half-buried stone. The cane lies on the ground to her right. Clara feels the presence of the sisters and stops for a moment to look up at them. She flashes a small grin. She puts her hand up to shield the sun and get a better look at the group. She dabs beads of sweat from the top of her lip with the cuff of her robe. The sisters at the top of the slope peer down without expression. They know what she's doing.

Sister Clara turns her attention back to the stone, dropping to her knees and working the soil to loosen its grip. Dry yellow dirt scoots under her nails and fills the cracks in her hands. She heaves against the stone and it rocks ever so slightly from its hold. She works the sand again and heaves another time. She grunts. The sisters on the slope look tolerantly on. She pushes and pulls again. A black outline begins to smile around the stone. Sister Clara draws in a breath and holds it as she pulls back on the stone with all her strength. It rises reluctantly, dramatically, from the earth's hold and settles in a dusty mess on her lap where its momentum tumbles the both of them sideways across the ground. The sisters on the slope gasp and make their way quickly down into the ravine to help her. Before they reach her, Sister Clara rolls the stone from her legs and stands up on her own with a wide smile pressed across her red cheeks. She swats at the dirt on her robes, sending up dusty clouds that swirl around the sisters gingerly making their way to her. They stop where they are when they see that she is not hurt. They wait. They know what she's doing. They know she'll be done soon.

Clara finishes batting the dirt from her robes and turns to settle her eyes squarely on the stone. It lies near the broken earth that held it for—*centuries maybe,* she thinks. That makes her feel good, but she doesn't smile because she's feeling very serious. The routine has taken on a reverence since she began with the first stone outside of Milwaukee, fifty-six stops and almost three weeks ago. She leans in for a closer look. The stone is on its side. The bottom half that was held in the ground is dark and mottled. The top is flaky and parched. *Centuries maybe,* she thinks again. *Whole centuries.* She ponders this for a short time. Then she reaches down to do something *in that moment* that no other man or woman that ever lived or died, no matter how great or powerful—no president, no king or ruler, no order of government or unruly mob—something that no person and no thing on the entire planet could ever do at that exact point in time—

She grasps the stone in her hands and turns it over.

I sat at a small desk in seventh-grade History listening to Sister Mary tell us the story of her summer vacation. It was the beginning of class, kids were still streaming in from recess and putting their things away. Sister Mary sat on the front of her desk to tell the few of us who were already seated about Sister Clara turning stones in the Great Southwest. She spoke casually as she went on in the rambling tones of a sidetracked thought.

The nuns on the bus stare blankly out the windows at the place in the earth where Sister Clara and the others had slipped from view. The ground shivers with heat. The driver of the bus is standing by the front wheel with his hand at his forehead to shield his eyes from the sun. Their faces remain calm as the heads of their fellow nuns begin to emerge above the slope, but their mouths go slack when they see Sister Clara being helped along by the others and covered with dirt. They stare out in quiet disbelief as the group slowly makes their way to the bus. "Must've taken a fall," one of them finally says. "Lucky to still be walking," says another. "And that *heat.*" The sisters look down to the books in their laps as Clara boards the bus. Up to this point she had been politely tolerated. But here at the end of the third week, in Death Valley, California, and with the turn of the largest stone yet and the ensuing tumble across the dirt—well, she might get hurt, after all. She's the oldest one in the group. Somebody ought to say something.

Sister Clara takes her seat and the bus pulls off. Five minutes of near silence pass before one of the sisters asks loudly over the groan of the engine and for the benefit of the others on board, just what the purpose of all this might be. The sister expresses the concern of all those on board about the possibility that Sister Clara might be hurt somehow—bitten by a snake even. So why, exactly, does she do it, the sister asks. Why turn a stone at each stop?

Sister Clara looks back at the gathering of troubled faces. Their heads rock with the movements of the bus. Some have leaned into the aisle. She feels the warmth of their regard; the concern is not lost on her. She appreciates it and so she gives them an answer, "I turn a stone so that the place is different because I have been there." The look on their faces remains flat. She says again, louder, "I turn a stone . . . so that the place is different . . . because I have been there."

The nuns consider this for a moment. The only sound is the hum of the bus. The one who asked the question sinks back into her seat. The others slowly return their heads to their books. Sister Clara smiles gently and turns forward.

———

"Well, you know," Sister Mary said, as she leaned forward on her desk. Her nylons made a silvery sound under her dress. "I probably don't have to tell you that there were more than a few of us who were a little worried about her. Most of us didn't think too much of it when she began. We knew it right at the start of the trip, that she was running off and flipping stones. It was nothing to get upset about, she never went too far and the stones were all small. But this last episode was too much. Sister Clara in a gully with all those rocks—can you picture it? Our Sister Clara? And they were sharp, some of them. And it was hot—much hotter than it ever gets here, you can't imagine if you've never been to a place like that. It all seemed like a pretty risky thing to go through just to turn a stone over. So we told her, we told her she shouldn't do it, but the look on her face . . . we knew she wouldn't listen. So then we asked why she did it. Because if we couldn't stop her from breaking a leg, at least we could ask what it was all for."

Most of the kids were in from recess and seated. The rambling manner of Sister Mary's voice was replaced by a serious tone. "Well let me tell you, when she told us what she was doing, something in every one of us just clicked. Many of us already suspected the motivation for the whole thing—it was simple, really, the idea of it. I don't know what it was exactly, but to hear her say it out loud and the look on her face—the satisfaction. Something just swept through us. Something just got us."

It's a long ride to the next stop on the tour. The sisters are quiet for most of the way. They nap and read and play solitaire. Some pray. Some just knit. They don't say much between them. They are one body and the body is thinking. The bus heads north toward Yosemite National Park.

It's later in the day when they arrive and it's cooler so they all get out. The vast park is a Disneyland of nature—giant sequoias; inspiring gorges; and Yosemite Creek Falls, 1,430 feet of cascading water. The park has its fair share of stones as well. With her fellow nuns gazing at the planet's seventh-highest waterfall, Sister Clara wanders off and disappears over a hill. They turn to watch her as she goes. She turns back, smiling. "I'll be right back," she says before slipping from view. The sisters smile at her and wave.

Then they all do it. Secretly, but they do it—can't board the bus until it's done.

They try to return their attention to the falls—a spectacle that, a few hours ago, would've held them riveted—but it's only a matter of minutes before they sneak off on their own. Even the ones who think the whole idea is silly are compelled to do it—just a small one, flipped with the front of the shoe before getting on. Sister Miranda doesn't go far; she quietly flips one by her foot. Sister Pat and Sister Vera do the same. Sister Susan and Sister Katherine run off and do theirs together, laughing at each other but promising to keep it between them. Sister Kelly runs around the side of the bus and does hers quickly.

"We began by each just picking our own tiny stone to casually kick over," Sister Mary went on. "So as not to let on to each other about what we were doing. Now listen—I fought against it. Just to be stubborn, you know me. I tried to put it out of my mind but it was no use—I couldn't board to leave without kicking one over! When I saw Sister Lucille and Sister Elizabeth doing the same thing, I must say I was relieved to not be the only one. Well . . . a few stops later and the cat was out of the bag—we were all doing it. I asked Sister Pat if she was doing it, and she turned to ask Sister Katherine who in turn asked Sister Louisa and so on and so forth until we were all laughing at how funny the whole thing was. On the next stop we all jumped out laughing and running around, kicking over stones. At first most of us were just using the tips of our shoes to flip what we could, but a few stops later we'd moved on to more ambitious projects—working away, using whatever we could to tap and chip away at our chosen stones. Sister Clara began using her cane like a pry bar to turn the biggest ones she could. Pretty soon we were teaming up on larger and larger ones—all crowded around like dusty workmen with a 'heave ho!' until we'd succeed, sending the grander ones tumbling. We almost got flattened a few times with some of the hugies. It got so we didn't even care about the sites at each stop—as soon as the bus parked, we'd gallop into the open space to scout out the biggest, most impossible, most wonderful stone! We all felt a little silly at first, but by the last few days, we were serious. If Sister Clara was foolish, then we were all foolish—a whole bus full of fools by the end!"

There was a moment of quiet as the entire class rocked gently in the wake of the simple story. Sister Mary sat comfortably in the silence having been caught up in the story herself. Her eyes were far and away, stretched across thousands of miles through the Great Southwest—gushing with its sun-bleached glory, mysterious in its stark twilight, and beckoning with endless acres of unturned stones. Slowly, the eyes returned to her small Wisconsin classroom. She looked with purpose at each one of us, a gentle smile pressed to her lips. The look on her face was satisfaction. "And you know what I'm thinking?" she asked, "I'm thinking some of those stones are still turned over as I'm talking to you right now..."

She clapped her hands on the top of the desk with a "Well!" and hopped off the edge. She walked around to the podium with a *gris gris gris* sound, opened her history book, and began to read aloud.

The train pulled into 110th Street and I hauled myself out. I picked up a beer at the deli outside of the station and had it half gone by the time I reached my apartment door. The roommates were out for the night so the place was quiet. I headed straight for my room and flew into bed on the final sip. Waiting for sleep, my mind played with the memory of the nuns—scattered across a windswept landscape, some hunched over a stone, some trudging along looking for the right one. I hadn't thought about them for a long while, though the memory had come to me many times over the past fifteen years. From seventh grade until the train ride home, the thing my mind drifted to in daydreams, sometimes for no reason at all—an endless horizon of stones with an occasional nun.

Sometimes it was clear and sunny, other times there were huge white clouds or rain—the stones were up to their ankles, sometimes past their heads. The scene would change, but what stayed the same were the satisfied faces—the smile pressed across their cheeks, each one of them. Rain or shine.

It always struck me as strange that I remembered the story at all. There were adults in my childhood who took great care to give me nuggets of truth they hoped I would take to the grave; plain facts and common sense poured across generations, flowing gently into my ear with somber tones and piercing stares. I remember the times and the quietness of space when the wisdom was passed; at the death of my grandmother, when my dog was shot, camping trips with Dad. The times are clear, but the words have been lost. And then there's Sister Mary—not an important figure in my life. The story she told, nothing more than killing time—a teacher rambling on while her students trailed in from recess. She would've never imagined that I'd remember her casual words so clearly and for so long. I wouldn't have imagined it, either, but there it was—one of those things your brain holds on to like some trinket you can never get rid of. We aren't always able to choose the memories that persevere.

2

I WOKE UP THE NEXT MORNING after sleeping like a dead man. I kicked out of bed and grabbed a pair of jeans that were lying on the floor. The pale light in the room read about six-thirty, I figured. James was still asleep. The street, four stories below, was silent. I fell back to the futon and rolled on my jeans. Then for a moment I just lay there. Something inside of me was different. Deep in my chest, I felt a quiet excitement. It fluttered just behind my lungs and made my breath waver. My stomach clenched with the twinkle of anticipation, like rounding a curve before the first view of the ocean—the feeling you get when you're on the brink of a huge beautiful thing. As I looked around slowly, the room began to change, and right there on the floor, half in and half out of my jeans, I saw it all for what it was. The huge beautiful thing stretched out before me was acuity and realization. Suddenly I knew why. I knew why I had walked away and for the first time since it all happened, I began to cry. Not from a single emotion, but from the incongruence of two—joy and sadness conspiring like hot and cold in a storm cloud, but in my head producing tears instead of thunder. The joy came from finally knowing why. That the answer was so simple and that I'd missed it and lost Baby Doe—that was the sadness. It was crystal clear but I couldn't put it into words. I can barely put it into words now. Like trying to grasp the complexity of the ocean in a single glass of seawater, the plainness undercuts a deeper complexity: I'd lost perspective on the power of the moment. I'd lost perspective on the power to effect change.

I rolled to my feet, snapped up the jeans, and floated over to the dresser mirror. I looked at my face in the mirror as if it were a stranger's. The cheeks shone with wetness, the eyes looked sleepy. The expression was startled exhaustion—the look of a runner who's crossed the finish line of a marathon that almost put him down. Everyone was asleep and I wasn't in a mood to talk anyway, so I tossed on a dead guy jacket and headed for the Hungarian to polish off a few cheese blintzes and a hot pot of coffee. I began to wake up on the walk over and started feeling something I hadn't felt for weeks—rested. When I got to the shop, the women were still preparing to open. Through the locked door, I asked if I could come in. They said I was welcome to sit down but that the coffee wouldn't be ready for another five minutes. I said fine, and rambled over to a table and chair in the back. The sun was bright now. The new-day glow spilled across the women as they busied themselves around tables, pulling chairs to the floor and laying place settings. Then I began to feel good. Really good. Even before the coffee. By my first sip I was well on my way to putting the whole thing together.

For all the years I'd thought about the nuns, I could never decide if they were brilliant or pathetic. For a long time, the whole story struck me as pitiful—they felt so insignificant in the grand scheme of things that in order to grasp some proof of existence, some scrap of affirmation, they celebrate the turning of a stone as their unique mark on the tumult of the cosmos. I mean, the turning of a stone—*please*. Right?

Wrong. The nuns were right all along because at the very core of it, there's no difference between turning a stone and splitting the earth in half. At the very core of it, there's no such thing as a small change, there is only *change*. It is an event that either happens or doesn't and therefore can't be measured as a size but only as an occurrence. I'd been quantifying my actions with the families I visited. The lives I encountered were so thoroughly stained with hopelessness and despair that I saw nothing I could do in a single evening to turn things around—and if I couldn't make it all right, if I couldn't split the earth in half, then what was the use? What could I possibly do in one night to make the lives of the children I saw better? Their existence was appalling before my visit, and it would be just as bad after I left, regardless of what I did. So why bother? I wasn't doing the job for the money. I was in the fray to change people's lives. Anything less just wasn't worth it. It was a dangerous mixture of naïveté and arrogance, they so often go hand in hand. None of this was on a conscious level. I wasn't saying any of it out loud, but I was operating out of it—the hands on my steering wheel.

So while I was standing around waiting to throw my knockout punch at the despair and decay of the city, while my head was high with my eyes trained out across the overwhelming expanse of "children in peril," a little boy died right at my feet. More had died while I wallowed, for the last month and a half, in alcohol-soaked self-pity and loathing. Somewhere a child was in trouble as I sat there, and the thing that struck me as suddenly amazing was that I could do something about it. In two days I could be sitting at a desk covered with reports on children whom I could actually pull from harm's way. Suddenly, I couldn't wait to make up for lost time. The sun's yellow light began a creep up my leg. The warmth fell into me hard, and in that instant, I couldn't wait to get back to work—the real work, the hard work.

The weekend passed by in a gust of wind. By the time it was over, I saw this life for what it is—a chance to cause a change for the better—an opportunity that's so real and true it's staggering to fully comprehend at once. The truth of it sounded through me like an alarm: Changing the world is about talk—making the world a better place is about action, and on this ride, the action takes place on the backs of child protective workers, one broken kid at a time. Where despair and abuse spread back across generations, there are no such things as knockout punches. Baby Doe cried out for my regard while I stood around like a sucker, waiting to put in the big one. But a reformed sucker is the strongest soldier.

When I returned to the office, I told Sam and the rest that

I was ready to get back to doing real work, including field visits. They greeted the news with grins and handshakes. I was sent out immediately. When I made it to the streets, I wore an armor that read: *Rescuing one child from the harm of one night is glorious success. The evening is an opportunity to touch a life at a critical moment and make it better—not for a lifetime, not even for tomorrow, but for one moment. One moment— not to talk, but to act—not to change the world, but to make it better. It's all that can be done and not only is that enough —that's brilliant.*

When I got home from work that night, my mother called. I hadn't let her in on the crisis of the last weeks although the fact that I hadn't phoned in some time must've tipped her off to something wrong. It was late when I got in, way after midnight. The phone rang just after I'd peeled off the old police jacket. I raced over and picked up the receiver before the roommates woke. It was her. I said that it was late and asked if there was anything wrong. She was fine, she said. Was there anything wrong with me? I told her I was fine also.

"I've just been thinking about you an awful lot lately," she said. "We haven't heard from you in a while so I thought I'd call. I figured you'd just be getting home from work."

"I just took off my jacket," I said.

"How did it go tonight?"

"It's funny you ask."

"Oh yeah?"

"Yeah. For the first time in a long while, it went really well..."

She paused, waiting for me to clarify. "Sounds like there's more to that than you're telling me."

I told her she was right but that I couldn't put it into words just yet.

"Well, I called because I read something this evening that made me think about you and the people in your office and what you go up against every night. It just really struck me as something you might need to hear so I wanted to tell you about it. It's from a reporter who was interviewing Mother Teresa. The article's long—they talked about all sorts of things. At the very end of the conversation, he asked her why she continues her work when the numbers of starving children are so over-whelming—why she pours such care into the one child she's holding when hundreds are dying around her. After thinking for a moment, she looks up with a smile pressed to her cheeks and says, 'I do it not to change the world, but so that the world doesn't change me.'...Isn't that terrific? It made me think about you...it made me think about all of you out there. *I do it not to change the world, but so that the world doesn't change me.*"

I couldn't say a thing. The message and the timing were too perfect for words.

"I know why you started that job, Marc," she said after a moment. "Don't let the world change you."

"I know...," I said, finally. "It did though. I think...for a moment, it did...I'm back though."

"...well, I guess a moment isn't that long."

"It's long, Mom. That kind of a moment is long."

"Well as long as you're back then..."

"I am," I said, and actually felt it for the first time. "I'm really back..."

We hung up shortly after that and I went to sleep on the first new day in a long time with words ringing out of the same bones that so recently put forth the venomous declarations of the voice.

So that the place is different because I've been there—not to change the world, but so the world doesn't change me.

3

THE FOLLOWING FEW WEEKS AT THE JOB were like breathing again. The realities of the field were as I'd left them—too many cases and too little time, too many children from too many mothers, not enough food, kids left alone, suspicious bruises— all of it. Overwhelming, insurmountable, relentless, crushing— but not my job to go there. There was absolutely nothing overwhelming about one child in one home on one night. I walked through each door relishing the opportunity to exert an influence. My investigations had all the fresh vigor of a rookie without any of the green. I was amazed at how quickly things returned to normal. It was as if my body had been wait- ing all along for my head to pick up the rhythm, and when it did, I hit the ground running. A month later, I began to trust the transformation. I was good again and I would stay that way.

I did the job that fourth year, really did the job. I did every inch of it. No number of nights out till 4:00 A.M., no tumult of cases, no petty sniping or outworn advice from those above me—nothing could touch my investigations. It was brilliant, but brilliant at ECS was no big deal. At midnight with misery falling down like rain, brilliant was all there was. Anything less was begging a disaster. Where brilliance is required, good enough will never cut it. I'd lived through good enough, but a little boy died through it. The lesson was too expensive to ever forget. I saw hundreds of children in harm's way and reached out to clear a path of protection for each one of them—five days a week, from four o'clock to whenever, whatever it took and at any price: the children I encountered were safe on my watch. The paths I cleared were short but they were secure. When the ax is about to fall and you're dealing in the moment, the short road to safety is all that's needed. It was a privilege to open that road for the kids I encountered. I saw it, by the end of that fourth year, for what it was. I saw it as a privilege.

I'll not pretend to describe the feelings with which I decided, one week before I would do it, to walk out the doors of Emergency Children's Services and never return. The moment of decision came unexpectedly. I was sitting alone in the back of the office after a late night in the field, about a month and a half after my fourth year with the agency. All was quiet except for the murmur of a conversation up at the hot line. I'd just finished a long case write-up and was leaning back in my chair, feeling the bump on the knuckle of my middle finger where the pen sits, and thinking how much it had grown in four years. I'd felt that bump more than a few times in the past couple months. In the course of a long gaze down the empty office, I began to think about how many pages of material I'd written at ECS—around fifteen pages or more a night, I figured, comes to seventy-five a week, thirty-three hundred pages in eleven months, over thirteen thousand since I began, probably more. One hell of a ledger. I tried to imagine a stack of thirteen thousand papers and in the course of doing so suddenly found myself at a crossroads. The signpost on the right said, *Leave now,* the one to the left read, *Stay 'til you retire.* There was nothing going up the middle. If I didn't take one, I'd be taking the other. I didn't feel ready to make the decision, but it's not about feeling ready when the fork is coming at you. You have to make a move whether you like it or not because the ride doesn't slow down so you can think about it. The thought came as if on its own volition: I think I gotta quit this place. I took a deep breath, turned right, and was as gone, in one moment, as I am today. Just a speck of a thought in a fleeting moment, but when I rose from the desk I was permanently, and for all intents and purposes, gone from Emergency Children's Services forever.

A week later I was standing in front of the time clock waiting to punch out for the final time. The bosses were the only ones who knew I was leaving. I had asked them not to tell the rest of the office about it. I didn't want the party and the long good-byes, didn't want to have to look at the philodendron and the BEST-WISHES balloon. In front of the clock for the last time, I paused. My ears buzzed as I stood there, waiting for some spark of emotion or some thought to come like a well-spoken toast to mark the occasion—a brief speech, the smallest sadness, a limerick even. Nothing came.

Thunk-whump.

I pulled the card from the clock and placed it in its slot. On my way to the door, I stopped to look through the scratched-up Plexiglas partition into the nursery. Two little girls sat on either side of a red plastic cube eating sandwiches like they were having a picnic. They weren't related. A nursery worker braided the younger girl's hair, tickling her neck occasionally. Another child, a boy maybe six, sat on a chair alone with a new shirt and pair of pants folded on his lap. The nursery boss came out of the infant room with a newborn in one arm and The Purse hanging from the other. "You ain't put them clothes on yet?" she asked the boy in the chair. "They ain't doin' you any good sittin' on your lap like that. You go on an' put 'em on now—the ones you got on is stinky." The boy nodded. "We'll throw 'em in the trash and keep you in them good ones." The boy nodded again as she shooed him into the bathroom to change. When he came out he was beaming like he'd never felt a set of new clothes in his life. "Well there you go!" the aide said, reacting to the boy's delight. He returned to his seat on legs stiff with the thrill of it all; alone as he was, and in the middle of the night, there's always room for joy. The new clothes looked wonderful on him. He sat down as if they might break, grinning all the way back to his molars. The aide laughed as she spread a dollop of jam across a piece of bread for him. "Now all we gotta do is find you some shoes and you'll be ready to hit the big time!"

Every night in lower Manhattan.

Amazing feats aren't always about scaling Everest or sledding Antarctica. Not all heroes are putting out fires or chasing down criminals. Some are just tying pigtails and making jelly sandwiches. But all of them, if they're lucky enough to see what they're doing while they're doing it, *really see it*—if they grasp even the smallest implications of turning the stone before them—pride isn't what they feel. If they see it all for what it is, even for just a moment—that what we do in the moment matters, that no effort has an insignificant outcome—what they feel is satisfaction.

I turned away and rode the boy's gush of joy straight into the street. Hitting the sidewalk with the faces of four years' worth of children flooding my head, a smile pressed to my face, and I knew that I was one of the lucky ones because for just a moment, I had seen it all for what it was.

Epilogue

THERE ARE PEOPLE WHO'VE TOLD ME the things I've written about in this book could only happen to children in the big bad city of New York. I don't think it's true. New York is an urban microcosm for America. Nobody does anything on these streets that hasn't already been tried across the rest of the country. I'm writing this just after reading a story in the paper about two brothers in Tennessee, one and two years old, locked in a car and strapped in their seats from 3:30 A.M. to 1:00 P.M. the next day, while their mother drank beer in a nearby hotel room. The car was parked in the sun with its windows rolled up. Local weather reports said the high that day was 89 degrees. The boys watched each other slowly die of dehydration and asphyxiation. It hasn't even been a year since the nation mourned the deaths of two boys in North Carolina whose mother strapped them to their car seats and drove them into a quiet lake. A few months later, a man hacked off his son's head on the shoulder of the New Mexico interstate. Police pursued the man on a chase that took them into the desert. When the man was apprehended, he was still holding his boy's head. Just last week, a woman in Arizona jumped off a high-rise with her baby clutched to her breast. Sounds familiar. The mother died instantly. The baby died at the hospital.

These few stories are the ones that made it to the national news for their day in the sun. There's gotta be plenty more that never see the light of day—all points leading to one direction: if it happens in New York, it happens in your town, too—less frequently perhaps, but no less brutal. The things that work and the things that fail to work in the city go the same way for the rest of the country. The issues raised in these pages affect all of us and every one of America's children.

I don't know what ever happened to any of the children I've written about. I don't know what ended up happening to any of the families after I saw them. I wish I did.

Alexandra still works at ECS—still a caseworker, only now she has a second job during the day at a shelter for teenage girls. We talk on the phone once in a great while, but I haven't actually seen her for years. She recently gave me the lowdown on the old crew. Yvette is back at ECS as a supervisor. Jesse Knight works for Parole and has two children. He's not married. Jerry went back to Haiti. Sam retired and is probably smoking a pipe and listening to old jazz records as I write this. Many of my old supervisors are still on the job. I talk with Dana on occasion. She lives on the West Coast now and is working on a master's degree. She plans to be a therapist. Laura got married to a great guy and lives in Brooklyn. She works as a casting director for major films and just gave birth to her first child. A little girl. Kai isn't at ECS these days. I don't know what happened to her. We haven't talked.

I bumped into Willie Samuels recently at a park and we spoke for the first time in years. He looked quite a bit older than when I knew him, though he could probably say the same about me. His teeth were missing and he had a jagged scar across his neck. He was selling newspapers for the homeless and told me he was living in a shelter. He still sings doo-wop but now he does lead. "Can't do tenor anymore," he said. "Too high—lost my falsetto when I got stabbed with the bottle." I asked him about his teeth. "A fight," he said, "I got a bridge and the motherfucker cost me...," he trailed off, shaking his head. "I only wear it for job interviews. People tell me, 'Willie—why don't you wear them teeth all the time? Look better with 'em in.' But I don't like anything fake. You remember me, Marc—I always been a what-you-see-is-what-you-get kinda guy. Right? I don't go for nothing' that ain't real... Got 'em in my bag though. I slip 'em in if I got an interview." We talked a little longer. I bought one of his papers with a ten-dollar bill and told him to keep the change. He bumped my fist just like he used to and told me to "have a happy" as I turned to leave.

The story of what happened to me over the four years of battling child abuse isn't really important on its own. What is important is the fact that there are others like me, working this very moment and on whose shoulders the entire welfare of our children's safety depends. Let mayors and commissioners discuss policy and procedure, the conclusions they arrive at are meaningful, but they're only words; after all is said and done, the true work is done in the field, in people's homes—it's here that children are saved or lost. The caseworkers at the front lines are the ones who make or break investigations. If we examine the toll taken on these people, maybe we come to a relevant discussion of how to keep them empowered—how to keep them from losing track of the vital importance of their work.

When the country takes an active interest in the affairs of child welfare agencies, it will be a significant first step. The outside pressure of public scrutiny has an enormous impact on the way things work and is imperative to ensuring the integrity of investigative policy and practice. I saw numerous examples of this at ECS. When I began, there was no nursery at the office. There was no food, there were no beds, no nurses, and barely a spare chair to set a child in. When you removed children from their home, you took them to your desk until you could secure a placement. Many nights I held a phone in one hand and a child in the other, as I made calls to beg foster parents for a place to stay. When no place could be found, children slept on chairs, on my desk, and on the floor. It was a deplorable situation that made every caseworker in the office sick to their stomach. We tried to do something about it, speaking individually and collectively about the situation to every boss and director that would listen. We wrote memos and drafted proposals. Nothing was done for almost a year. And then something happened. One of the newspapers in the city snuck into the office and photographed the haphazard gathering of chairs and furniture that was our makeshift nursery. The picture ran on the front page. There was an outrage. The following day— *the very next day*—Emergency Children's Services had a nursery. That one photograph and the public outrage that followed accomplished what all of us combined couldn't get done in almost a year. Today at ECS, there's an entire floor and a full staff dedicated to the care of children removed from their homes. Things *do* change for the better.

The whole idea of child protection is still evolving. When I joined ECS, I was told the office was an experiment that was five years old. In the beginning, it was the only one of its kind in the nation—the only nighttime agency in the business of investigating abuse and removing imperiled children from their homes. Prior to its inception, child protection was just one more of the many tasks we required of our police departments.

Now, there are nighttime child protective offices in every major city across the country as well as in many outlying areas. A child in trouble has it better today than when I was a kid, and it's getting better all the time. I believe it. We're a long throw from perfect, but as we keep trying, improvement is inevitable.

It's important to understand, as we aspire to this perfection, that the abuse of children will never be eradicated. If someone wishes to inflict harm on their child, they will succeed in doing so much of the time. So, why fight a battle that can never be won? If putting an end to child abuse is the only measure of victory, then we're really missing the point. When it comes to kids, we have to do better than that. There's a modicum of success in every episode where a child is removed from harm's way—every broken bone prevented, every life spared. It's not a win-lose operation. The battle to protect children from the parents who would hurt them is a process. It's a process that calls for our fullest attention and most persistent efforts. Getting overwhelmed just isn't good enough. Maybe it's obvious, but I'll say it just the same—There are little ones in danger at this very moment who are crying out for help. I've seen them. We owe the best we can give to every precious one.

Acknowledgments

Thanks now and always to my parents, Kevin and Maxine Parent, as well as to my sisters and brothers, Denise, Aimeé, Ted, and Brodie.

Enormous thanks to champion agent and dear friend, David Black.

Endless river of heartfelt thanks to Anna Quindlen.

A serious debt of gratitude to my editor, Walter Bode, whose time and effort have made this a better book than it would've been without him.

Thanks to my copy editor, Rachel Myers. Thanks also to Theo Lieber and Dori Weintraub.

For support and essential doses of enthusiasm in the early stages of the manuscript, thank you friends and family, especially: James MacDonald, Joseph Murphy, Paul Skemp, Steve Alden, and Karen Rizzo.

Thanks to Ken Davis and Joanne Davis for early support and guidance.

For help in remembering some of the details of "The Hex," thanks to my friend Laura Rosenthal.

Thanks to Samuel Henriques and Rebecca Lax.

A debt of gratitude to The Writer's Room in New York City, where the majority of this book was written.

For more than I could ever put into words, deepest gratitude to my dear wife, Susan. This book would never have been written without her.